W9-BKC-587

Organizing
Plain & Simple

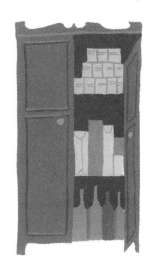

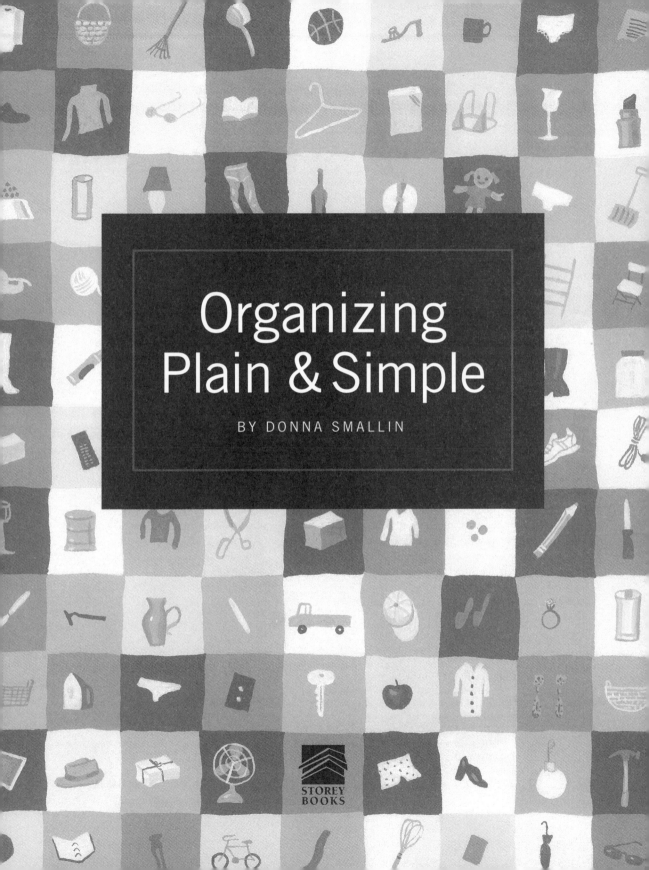

Organizing
Plain & Simple

BY DONNA SMALLIN

STOREY
BOOKS

The mission of Storey Publishing is to serve our customers
by publishing practical information that encourages personal independence
in harmony with the environment.

Edited by Dianne M. Cutillo and Marie A. Salter
Copyedited by Shannon Donovan
Cover and text design by Wendy Palitz
Text layout and production by Susan Bernier
Production assistance by Jennifer Jepson Smith
Cover art and illustrations by Juliette Borda
Indexed by Nan Badgett/Word•a•bil•i•ty

Copyright © 2002 by Donna Marie Smallin

All rights reserved. No part of this book may be reproduced without written permission from the publisher, except by a reviewer who may quote brief passages or reproduce illustrations in a review with appropriate credits; nor may any part of this book be reproduced, stored in a retrieval system, or transmitted in any form or by any means — electronic, mechanical, photocopying, recording, or other — without written permission from the publisher.

The information in this book is true and complete to the best of our knowledge. All recommendations are made without guarantee on the part of the author or Storey Publishing. The author and publisher disclaim any liability in connection with the use of this information. For additional information please contact Storey Books, 210 MASS MoCA Way, North Adams, MA 01247.

Storey books are available for special premium and promotional uses and for customized editions. For further information, please call Storey's Custom Publishing Department at 1-800-793-9396.

Printed in the United States by Banta Book Group
10 9 8 7 6 5 4 3

Library of Congress Cataloging-in-Publication Data

Smallin, Donna, 1960-
    Organizing plain & simple / Donna Smallin.
       p. cm.
    Includes index.
    ISBN 1-58017-448-5 (alk. paper)
    1. Home economics.   2. Time management.   3. Storage in the home.
  4. Organization.   I. Title: Organizing plain and simple. II. Title.
TX147.S6224 2002
640—dc21   2002001586

For my mother-in-law, Audrey Smallin,
organizer extraordinaire

CONTENTS

INTRODUCTION

Life is short. What's that got to do with getting organized? Everything. I believe that the whole point of getting organized is to create more time, space, and energy in your life for the people and things that matter most to you.

You can spend precious minutes and hours every day looking for things you know are "around here somewhere," or you can find a place for everything so you always know exactly where to look. You can go through life in "catch-up" mode, with high levels of frustration and stress, or you can learn how to simplify daily living with the organizational systems and tools described in this book.

When I tell people that I have written several books about uncluttering and organizing one's home and life, they invariably ask whether I am super-organized. Well, I may be super-organized by some standards, but I like to think of myself as *simply* organized. By that I mean that I am as organized as I need to be. I could spend all day organizing, but instead I choose to spend only as much time as necessary to keep my life running smoothly.

Here's my secret: Don't make organizing difficult; keep it plain and simple. Find simple strategies, systems, and tools that work for you, and then use them regularly.

This may come as a surprise, but there is no one right way to get organized. That's why, in this book, I have presented many different solutions to the most common organizational challenges, so you can choose the one that appeals most to you; you might even try a variation of an idea. If a technique works for you, it's the perfect solution. If it doesn't work for you, try something different.

One of the aspects I find most rewarding about the process of organizing is that it helps you figure out what's most important to you. And knowing this can help to simplify your life. Organizing also brings with it a certain freedom. With less clutter to weigh you down, you have more time to pursue the things that bring you the greatest happiness and satisfaction. I wish you well!

Note: The Internet is a wonderful source of information on organizing. For this reason, I have referenced a number of Web sites throughout this book. Wherever possible, I have tried to include non-Web alternatives as well.

ACKNOWLEDGMENTS

In writing this book, I have had the honor and privilege of meeting dozens of organizing experts who readily contributed proven tips, strategies, and solutions. I am very grateful for their support, encouragement, and inspiration. I thank my research assistant, Danielle Francois, who helped me to get started on this huge organization project by setting up interviews, doing research, and handling lots of little details. I owe my husband, Terry, many hugs and kisses for helping me finish this book by running errands, doing grocery shopping, putting dinner on the table, and even decorating the house for the holidays (beautifully, I might add!). Lastly, I would be remiss if I did not acknowledge the patience and guidance of my editor, Dianne Cutillo, who really knows how to work with writers.

PART I

Getting Started

So, you want to get organized. Well, there's no better time than today to get started. After all, the sooner you start, the sooner you'll achieve your goal. But simply *wanting* to get organized won't make it happen. You have to make it happen by *choosing* to begin and then taking that all-important first step.

Getting started is often the most difficult part of getting organized. You may not know where or how to begin, but you can learn these things. More important is belief in yourself. Believe that with patience, perseverance, and a little know-how, you can accomplish anything. Choose to get organized and soon you'll enjoy the benefits of a simpler life. Organizing requires you to think about what's most important to you — what you really love and want — and to make decisions based on that knowledge. It can change your life for the better. So go ahead and take that first step.

CHAPTER 1

FIRST THINGS FIRST

Ask yourself why you want to get organized. What's in it for you? How did you come to your current disorganized state? Scrutinizing your relationship to clutter and disorganization is the first step toward getting organized. The more you understand about that relationship — and your role in it — the more successful you will be at bringing about lasting change. So don't skip this step!

The Rewards of Organization

The benefits of being organized go far beyond having an uncluttered home or being able to find things. Being organized can add hours to your day and days to your month because being organized saves time. The more organized you get, the more time you have to spend on the things in life that give you the greatest joy. And you'll reap physical, emotional, and financial rewards, too.

Disorganization creates unnecessary stress, and too much stress over a prolonged period can lead to serious health problems. And just think of the energy you waste each day searching for things. Getting organized can help increase your energy level and decrease your stress level.

If you have an abundance of clutter in your home, frequently miss appointments, or pay bills late, your self-esteem can really take a beating. Even low levels of disorganization can make you feel out of control and create feelings of dissatisfaction with yourself and your life. Good organizational systems, in contrast, instill confidence in yourself and your abilities.

Have you ever bought a replacement for something only to find the original item later? Do you often have to pay late fees on bills? Do you shop on credit and carry balances? Do you eat out frequently because you don't have the time to cook or don't have the makings of a meal in your cupboards or refrigerator? In the process of getting organized, you may discover that greater financial security and success is within your grasp. You might even be able to make money by selling belongings that are just taking up space in your home or office.

The Challenge

Perhaps you have tried to get organized in the past but only ended up with a bigger mess. Or maybe you succeeded, but your success was only temporary and now you're faced with the challenge of getting organized all over again.

Organizing *is* a challenge, not so much because of the time and commitment it takes, but because it requires us to change our behavior — and that's not easy. It takes time, patience, and awareness to change the way we do things. It also requires the proper motivation, planning, preparation, commitment, and action. Organization is not something that just happens; you have to make it happen. The way to do that is to **ACT**:

> **A**ssess your situation
>
> **C**ommit to a plan
>
> **T**ake action

Getting organized is really about taking control of your life, sorting through everything that demands your time and space, determining what's really important to you, and letting go of what's not. To get the wheels of this process in motion, start by assessing your situation.

What's Your Situation?

There are as many reasons why disorganization prevails as there are people. But if you really want to get organized, there's hope, even if you believe yourself to be the most disor-

ganized person who ever lived. The following questions are designed to get you thinking about your unique situation, your relationship with clutter, and your specific challenges. (Taking the quiz on page 8 will provide you with further insights.)

- **Have you always been disorganized?** If so, think about this: Were you ever taught organization skills? Probably not. But you can learn organization skills at any age and, by applying these skills, you can turn chaos into order and regain control of your life.

- **Are you just temporarily disorganized?** Think back to a time when you were more organized. What has been the most dramatic change in your life since that time? Can you find a relationship between that change and your current disorganized state? What advice would you give to someone in your situation?

the cost of disorganization

Think about how much time you spend every day looking for your car keys, unpaid bills, checkbook, the belt that goes with your blue suit, or whatever. For the purposes of this exercise, let's say you spend fifteen minutes each day searching for things. How much do you earn at your job? If you earn $20 per hour, disorganization is costing you $5 per day. That works out to $35 per week, $140 per month, and $1,680 per year — a hefty price to pay.

● **Do you spend a great deal of time shopping?** It's America's number one pastime, and it helps explain the proliferation of clutter in our lives. We don't just buy an item to replace one that is broken or worn out. We buy because we can't pass up a sale or because we think we have to have the latest gadget or clothing style. It seems like the more we earn, the more we spend — and the more we own. We keep bringing stuff into our already cluttered homes and, in some cases, digging ourselves deeper in debt.

● **Are you secretly afraid of getting organized?** Because organization is a process of change, it is inherently an emotional process. We all have thoughts and feelings attached to the concept of organization, some of which can prevent us from reaching our goals. Many people, for example, fear that getting organized means having to get rid of things they are not ready to part with. Others envision "uncluttered" as "sterile" and fear that living and working in an uncluttered space will thwart their creativity. And some of us believe that we just can't do it because we've tried once, twice, or many times before and failed; we feel defeated before we even start. What are your thoughts and feelings about getting organized? What do you fear might happen in the process or as a result of getting more organized?

● **Are you a perfectionist?** You might think that a perfectionist would have a perfectly ordered home, but more often than not, the opposite is true. That's because perfectionists want to do everything just right, or not at all. So they keep putting off getting organized until they can do it perfectly. Judith Kolberg, director of the National Study Group on Chronic Disorganization, says, "Often, our best intentions are left in stacks." She calls this tendency *deferred decision-making*.

What's Your Plan?

If you want to be successful at getting organized, you've got to have a plan. A plan is the map that will get you where you want to go. A good plan includes what you want and why, when you want it by, and what you are willing to do to achieve it. To create your plan for success, write down your answers to the following questions:

- What made you choose to read this book?
- What do you hope to accomplish?
- How might getting organized improve your life?
- In what ways has being disorganized detracted from your life?
- What are you willing to do to get organized?
- Why is it important for you to do this now?

PUT IT IN WRITING

If you want to achieve something, whatever it is, write it down. Be as clear and specific as possible. You are more likely to realize your goals if you put them in writing. Maybe it makes them more concrete, I don't know. I only know that it works.

—*Harriet Schechter, The Miracle Worker Organizing Service*

Knowing why you want to get organized is vital to your success. This is your motivation to get started and to stick with it until you are satisfied with the result. Your plan should also include a deadline to keep you focused on your goal. It's difficult to predict how long it will take to undo weeks, months, even years of disorganization, however.

Rather than guessing or setting an unrealistic deadline, create a one-month plan. Choose five things you most want to accomplish during the month. List these items from highest to lowest priority. Be as specific as you can. At the end of the month, if you have not yet accomplished all five tasks, create a new one-month plan that outlines what you hope to achieve this month — and what you are willing to do to make it happen.

Taking Action

Once you have a plan, you're ready to implement it. Harness the power of your mind, and let it lead you toward your goals.

Remember, getting organized requires us to change our behavior, and that's not easy. Be patient with yourself. If you believe that you are an organized person, you'll have a much greater chance of becoming one. If you catch yourself saying or thinking negative things like "I can't do this" or "I'm so disorganized," counter with, "That's not true. I am a very capable person, and I can do whatever I set my mind to do."

It helps to envision order. If you can visualize your space as you would like to see it, you are more likely to achieve your goal. See yourself walking from one uncluttered room to the

sample plan

What I Want
- I want to organize my closets and drawers so I can get dressed more quickly in the morning.
- I want to learn how to keep track of important dates, appointments, and things to do so I don't forget them.
- I want to develop a system for paying my bills so that I don't owe late fees.
- I want to figure out how to make more time for myself so that I can exercise.
- I want to clean out my garage so that I can park my car in it.

When I Want It
By [insert date one month from today]

What I Am Willing to Do
Turn off the television from 7 to 8 P.M. every Tuesday and Thursday night and spend that hour working on organizing activities.

Do you need to get motivated? Consider enlisting the help of a friend. Tell this person what you want to accomplish by what date, and ask him or her to check in on your progress.

next. Picture a friend walking with you and complimenting you on your achievement. Feel the pride that comes from a job well done.

Affirmations are another way to take mental action toward your goal. An affirmation is a positive statement with personal meaning that you repeat often. Example: "I am organized out of respect for myself and others." Or "I am getting my life in order so I can more fully enjoy living."

Now, let's get started!

what's your organizing IQ?

Choose the number (1–4) that best describes your response to each of the following statements.

1 = Rarely or never
2 = Sometimes
3 = Quite often
4 = Almost always

☐ I get tired just thinking about what it will take for me to get organized.

☐ My co-workers or housemates think I am disorganized.

☐ Lack of time or space keeps me from getting more organized.

☐ I find myself wishing I could be more organized.

☐ I spend a significant amount of time looking for things every day.

☐ I am disorganized.

☐ I let mail pile up until I have time to deal with it.

☐ I save things that I think I might need someday.

☐ I feel guilty about throwing away things.

☐ I leave things out as a reminder to myself to do something.

☐ I have no time for myself.

☐ When it comes to clutter, I think, "Why bother? It will just get cluttered again."

☐ I can't bear the thought of parting with anything I own.

☐ I dread opening one or more closets in my home or office.

☐ When the profusion of clutter in my home gets to me, I go out.

☐ If someone stops by unexpectedly, I try to avoid letting them in.

☐ I miss scheduled appointments or forget important things to do.

☐ I have trouble keeping up with birthdays, holidays, and season changes.

☐ I feel like I accomplish very little in any given day.

☐ I equate busy-ness with success.

☐ I am pulled in three different directions at once.

☐ I use late notices as reminders to pay bills.

☐ I carry credit card debt from month to month.

☐ I live from paycheck to paycheck.

☐ I find it difficult to maintain a balance in my savings account.

_____ **TOTAL**

rating your score

81–100: You have so much to gain from organizing your home and life! Taking the time to get and stay organized will dramatically decrease your high level of stress and frustration, free up time and energy to pursue whatever brings you joy, and remove obstacles to achieving your definition of success. Make the commitment to get started today, and stick with it!

61–80: You are probably suffering because of the cumulative effects of disorganization. Clutter has been building for some time, and it seems like with each passing month and year, you get more and more disorganized. But there is no reason why you can't turn things around with the right combination of organizing systems and strategies. Just don't expect it to happen overnight!

41–60: You probably don't consider yourself a disorganized person, but for whatever reason, you may be feeling more disorganized than usual. Chances are, you are adjusting to a major change in your life — a new job, home, or relationship, or loss of one of these things. Taking the time to get organized will add the structure you need right now during this time of transition. If the disorganization in your home and life has always been at this level, learning some new organization skills will help.

25–40: Your organizational skills are very well honed, and you derive pleasure from being organized because you see the benefits. Because you stay on top of things, you accomplish most of what you set out to do each day. If you are looking for a new career in a helping profession, you might consider becoming a professional organizer.

CHAPTER 2

UNCLUTTERING YOUR HOME

You've got a plan. You're motivated and you're ready to get organized once and for all. Start by freeing yourself from clutter — all the excess stuff in your life that you could live without. Make it your goal to surround yourself with only things you love and use, and let go of everything else that's just taking up valuable space.

Where to Start

It really doesn't matter where you start. But starting in the room where you spend the most time is going to give you the greatest satisfaction, and motivate you to unclutter the rest of your home. An alternative place to start is in the room that contains the most frustrating amount of clutter or disarray. Once you decide on a room, make it your goal to start with the most visible clutter first, then work on uncluttering the stuff that's out of sight.

If just the *thought* of "weeding out" or "paring down" your belongings is scary or uncomfortable for you, relax. In theory, you could keep everything and still create a beautifully organized home. It will just take a little longer to find a place for everything so that you can find what you want when you want it.

However, if you're like most people, some (maybe even many) things in your home have outlived their usefulness or appeal. You could easily live without these things and never even miss them. Really! If you aren't using something or don't like it anymore, it's just taking up valuable space in your home. If you can bring yourself to let go of such things, you will create more space for what you really love and use.

When to Unclutter

Any time is a fine time to unclutter, but if you find it difficult to throw things out, you might want to plan your start date to coincide with trash day. That way, your throwaways won't be hanging around and tempting you to come and take them back. You might also plan your uncluttering around an upcoming church tag sale, neighborhood garage sale, or community trash day, but only if these events are taking place in the very near future. You want to get started now!

Uncluttering is best accomplished by focusing your time and attention on one clearly defined area. If you try to unclutter a whole room all at once, you'll probably make a bigger mess. The uncluttering process is also far less daunting and more manageable if you determine in advance how much "uncluttering time" you will spend in any given day.

Keep in mind that your home didn't get cluttered overnight, and it's probably going to take some time to get it organized. If you can spare a whole day here and there, great. But you don't have to put your life on hold to get organized. Just setting aside fifteen minutes to one hour each day can quickly add up to a job well done.

What's important is not how much time you spend on any given day, but that you get started. If you've allocated one hour for uncluttering, set a kitchen timer or alarm clock for one hour, or put on your favorite CD. When the timer sounds or the music stops, it's quitting time. There may be days when you want to continue on for another hour. But if you've had enough for one day, just walk away. The clutter has been there for awhile, right? It'll be there when you come back to it tomorrow.

How to Unclutter

Uncluttering is a great project for a rainy day. Wear comfortable clothes, put on your favorite music, and focus all of your attention on your

goal. Uncluttering takes time, but it's not complicated. It's a sorting process.

Charge in, but don't take on too much at once. Start with a defined space, such as a counter, table or desktop, or shelf. Empty that space of its contents. Then sort items into five categories. Use labeled boxes or bags to collect items that belong in categories two through five:

1. Things you love and/or use; you'll keep these
2. Things you could give to someone else
3. Things that belong in the trash
4. Things you could sell
5. Things that belong elsewhere

In the process of uncluttering room by room, you will come across things that belong in another room or somewhere else altogether, such as books and videos that need to be returned or something you borrowed from a friend.

What You Need

- ❑ Four boxes or bags labeled "Give Away," "Throw Away," "Sell," and "Store Elsewhere"
- ❑ Small spiral notebook
- ❑ Pen or pencil
- ❑ Alarm clock or kitchen timer

An uncluttered house looks cleaner than a clean house that's cluttered.

—Judy Warmington,
Woman Time Management

Use the spiral notebook and pen or pencil to jot yourself a reminder to return these things, and make notes about other things you need to do that come to mind while you are uncluttering. Deposit these items in a box or bag labeled "Store Elsewhere." When you are finished organizing for the day, take these items where they belong. If items belong in the room you are organizing, but not where you found them (on the kitchen counter, for example), give them a temporary home somewhere in a space that you have not yet uncluttered.

Obviously, things you love are things you want to keep, even if you never use them. You'll also want to keep things you *do* use, even if it's only once a year. If you have more than one of something, however, ask yourself how many of these items you really need. If you're uncluttering a junk drawer, for example, and you find that you have an exorbitant number of pens or rubberbands, ask yourself how many is enough. Keep what you can use and give away the rest.

What about parts and pieces that you find? Or things that are missing parts and pieces? Set up a "lost and found" box somewhere, and put these items into it as you find them. You might also put in this box things that don't have a home yet and things you can't identify. When you finish uncluttering your entire home, go through the box to see if you found any matches for these items or if you now have a home for them. Discard the junk.

If you're undecided about an item, take the "Keep or Toss" quiz. If you're still undecided, ask yourself, "What's the worst possible thing that could happen if I got rid of this?" Still undecided? Then keep it for now, along with the things you love and use. Or put that item in a box labeled "Undecided." When you finish uncluttering your home, seal the box, write the current month, day, and year on it, and store it away. If you haven't had a need to open that box one year from now, then you know that you don't *need* what's inside and you can let it go.

Don't worry about cleaning during the uncluttering process. That's something you can do later, when the room is organized to your satisfaction. Cleaning as you go might slow you down, and you don't want that. You want to work as quickly as you can so that you can see the end result that much sooner. Also, it's easier to clean an uncluttered room — one of the benefits of organizing that you're sure to appreciate.

MAKE A DATE

Consider making a daily or biweekly uncluttering appointment with yourself. Write it in your planner like you would any other appointment.

—*Mitzi Weinman, TimeFinder*

Letting Go

Uncluttering requires letting go and that can be difficult — even painful. Sandra Felton, founder of Messies Anonymous, says, "Be willing to take a risk that you may want later what you discarded. Also realize that it may cause temporary pain to throw something out. However, it also causes definite pain to keep it. Throwing it out is mild pain compared with the pain which comes from having to live helplessly with all the clutter that finds its way into the house."

Following are some tips to help you let go of material possessions you no longer love or use.

- **If you are afraid to let go of something, do it scared.** Once you get over the initial shock, you'll be amazed at how much lighter and freer you feel. You may find that letting go of material possessions helps you to let go of emotional clutter, because the physical act of letting go can trigger a release of frustration, anger, guilt, and other emotional baggage.

- **Imagine that you're moving.** Ask yourself: Is this item worth the effort and expense of packing it up, carrying it out to the moving van, and unpacking it at the new place? If not, give it a new home.

- **Get someone else to help you go through your things.** Have that person hold each object. Holding it yourself emphasizes your attachment to it. This is precisely why a good salesperson will encourage you to touch something or try it on.

keep or toss?

What if you're undecided about what to do with a particular item? It's probably something you could give away, throw away or sell, but for whatever reason, you're not quite ready to part with it. Ask yourself:

- Have I used this item in the past year? **Yes/No**
- Has anyone else in my home used it in the past year? **Yes/No**
- Do I have a definite use for this in the foreseeable future? **Yes/No**
- If it's broken, is it worth fixing? **Yes/No**
- Does this item serve a worthwhile purpose in my life? **Yes/No**
- Do I need to keep it for legal or tax purposes? **Yes/No**
- Is it more important to me to keep this item than to have the space it occupies? **Yes/No**
- Do I love it? **Yes/No**
- Does someone in my household love it? **Yes/No**
- Would it be difficult or expensive for me to get another one? **Yes/No**

Scoring: There are no right or wrong answers, but a "Yes" answer to any one of the above questions provides a sound reason to keep that item. A "No" answer, on the other hand, gives you good reason to toss it.

TAMING PAPER MONSTERS

What You Need:
A package of 10 x 13
manila envelopes and a black magic
marker. As you unclutter your home
(especially your kitchen), you're bound
to find an assortment of loose papers:
phone numbers, recipes, notes from
school, flyers, coupons, warranty book-
lets, and more. Ask yourself:

- **Do I** *need* **it or do I** *want* **it? (There's a big difference.)**
- **Is it too late to do this? Is this out of date?**
- **Does anybody care if I do this?**
- **Do I have time to read this?**
- **Will I possibly receive this again?**
- **Is there another resource for this if I decide I need it later?**

Whatever you do, do not take time to
read — just skim the information and
decide whether to keep it or toss it.
Place the papers in your de-cluttering
process in an appropriately marked
envelope. This will make the organizing
process easier when you reach the next
stage. For instance, if you find a loose
recipe that you want to keep, put it in
a manila envelope and write "Recipes"
on it. Put all the recipes you find in this
envelope so that when you get around
to organizing your recipes, they are all
together. If you come across a bill that
needs to be paid, put it in an envelope
labeled "Current Bills" to be delivered
later that day to your bill paying center.

— Julie Signore, 1,2,3 SORT IT

- **Think about your abundance.** If you have more than one of something, be honest with yourself. How many do you really need? Be grateful for the abundance in your life. Then make a decision from the heart to share your wealth with others who may be less fortunate.

- **Play Judith's game.** Judith Kolberg, Director of the National Study Group on Chronic Disorganization, developed an uncluttering game called Friends, Acquaintances, and Strangers which you can play with your belongings. As you look at each item, ask yourself if it is a friend, an acquaintance, or a stranger. An outfit you wear often is a friend. Something you bought but never wore is an acquaintance. Clothes that don't fit or that you haven't worn in a year or more are strangers. Find a new home for acquaintances that have overstayed their welcome. Kick out the strangers.

- **Give up the caretaker job.** The more stuff you have, the more stuff you have to take care of and the more space you need to store it. Make a conscious decision to let someone else take over the caretaking.

- **Come back to it.** If you've been doing pretty well with letting go but get stuck trying to decide between keeping a particular item or not, set it aside for a day. You may simply be too tired to decide. Or maybe there are other things going on in your life that are interfering with your decision-making ability.

The Great Giveaway

Uncluttering your home gives you the perfect excuse to get rid of all those things you really don't want or use anymore — everything from hair accessories to books to furniture. Just because you bought it or someone bought it for you doesn't mean you have to keep it forever. Wouldn't you prefer to surround yourself with things you love and use? Give yourself permission to give away the things that no longer suit your taste or lifestyle.

Think of someone you know who might enjoy having what you no longer want. Ask if that person would be willing to come and get whatever you are giving away. One thing you don't want is a box full of stuff that you have to deliver to every corner of the world, because you know what will happen: The box will just sit there and become a source of frustration.

It may be more convenient to donate your whole box of giveaways to one charitable organization and be done with it. Think first of the one place that accepts everything from toys to clothing to household furnishings. Or separate your giveaways into several bags for delivery to several donation stations. The chart below is a partial list of what you can take where.

You may be able to deduct your donation from your income taxes. Be sure to keep a list of the items you donated and the value of each item, and ask for a tax receipt from the charitable organization.

It Pays to Unclutter

For some people, selling unwanted belongings makes it easier to part with them. You won't get rich uncluttering your house, but you may end up with enough for a little splurge. The primary outlets for selling secondhand items are consignment shops, classified advertising, Internet auction sites and, of course, yard and garage sales.

Donation Stations

Item	Where to Donate
Clothing	Goodwill, religious organization, domestic violence shelter (women's and children's clothing), Dress for Success affiliate (women's suits and work apparel), thrift store, theater (for costumes)
Kitchen and housewares	Goodwill, religious organization, domestic violence shelter, thrift store
Toys	Police station (for holiday drives), religious organization, domestic violence shelter, thrift store, hospital
Books (except textbooks)	Library, thrift store, secondhand bookstore
Textbooks	Prisons
Fabric, sewing and craft materials	Senior citizen's center, grade school, theater (for costumes)

If you have clothes, furnishings, and other items in excellent or even like-new condition, consider selling them on consignment. Consignment shops will accept secondhand belongings and give you a percentage of the selling price, generally 40 to 50 percent. Items will remain for sale until the end of a specified contract period (usually 60 to 90 days), after which you can collect your earnings. Most shops offer to donate unsold items to charity. Take them up on it! There's no sense in bringing things back home. To find a shop near you, look in the Yellow Pages under "Consignment Shops" or "Secondhand Shops."

WHEN TO BRING CLOTHING TO A CONSIGNMENT SHOP

Clothing Season	Drop off In
Spring/summer	Mid-February
Fall	Mid-August
Winter	End of September/ early October

To maximize your earnings, check out a few stores before choosing one and compare their stock and policies. Also, take location into account. Don't choose a store that is off the beaten path unless you are sure that it does lots of business.

Consignment shops accept all kinds of things, including:

- Clothing and accessories
- Furniture
- Kitchenware
- Decorative household items
- Sporting equipment
- Toys
- Infant furniture and items
- Videos and books

Some stores specialize in specific items, such as used sporting equipment, books, or children's clothing. Clothes must be in excellent condition with no loose or missing buttons, no falling hems or tears in the material, and no stains. Newer clothes, designer labels, and classic styles sell best. Bring them to the store cleaned, pressed, and on hangers. Bear in mind that consignment shops want seasonal clothing that is coming into season.

If it's too late in the season to bring in your clothes, put them in storage and make a note to yourself to get them out before the beginning of the next season. (See page 157 to learn about an effective reminder system known as a tickler file.)

Perhaps best of all, selling on consignment lets you earn back at least some of your original purchase price, which may make it easier to let go of things that are just taking up space. And it's simple to do.

Selling Direct. You can sell larger items directly to buyers by placing a classified advertisement in one of your local newspapers or weekly shopping papers. Items to consider advertising include furniture sets, large appliances or power equipment, and computer equipment. Direct selling generally brings the best price, but you do have to pay a fee for the advertisement. Also you'll have to spend time on the telephone and in person with prospective buyers.

To sell valuable items, such as jewelry, antiques, coin collections, and musical instruments, look for stores that specialize in buying and selling these items. The Yellow Pages of the telephone book is a good place to start. You may wish to get more than one estimate to ensure that you're getting a fair price.

Selling On-line. You can sell just about anything on the Internet. The world's largest on-line marketplace is eBay. People use eBay to buy and sell all sorts of things, including:

- Antiques and art
- Books, movies, and music
- Business, office, and industrial items
- Clothing and accessories
- Collectibles
- Computers and peripherals
- Dolls and teddy bears
- Home and garden items

For Simplicity's Sake

If you're new to the process of uncluttering, start with the easy stuff. Walk through your home with a large trash bag. Throw out anything that is clearly garbage:

- Candy and gum wrappers
- Expired coupons
- Outdated flyers and calendars
- Spoiled food
- Expired medicines
- Rusty tools and utensils
- Socks with no mate
- Broken items that aren't worth fixing

- Jewelry, gemstones, and watches
- Photo and electronic equipment
- Pottery and glass
- Sports equipment and memorabilia
- Tickets for events and travel
- Toys and hobbies

eBay assesses two selling fees: a nominal insertion fee to list each item (or quantity of same items) and a final value fee, which ranges from 1.25 to 5 percent of your final sale price. Additional fees apply for optional services, such as an on-line payment service that allows eBay to collect payment from buyers and deposit it directly into your bank account.

Selling at a Garage Sale. A time-proven way to get rid of unwanted stuff and make a few bucks in the process is to hold a garage or yard sale. Planning ahead will minimize time and effort while maximizing sales. The seven simple steps outlined here will help make any sale a success.

SALE-DAY MUSTS

• Try to be ready at least an hour earlier than your advertised start time, unless you indicated "no early birds" in your ad.

• Plan for a busy day. Dress comfortably (in particular, wear appropriate shoes) and eat a hearty breakfast. Make your lunch before the sale starts. Have a chair and beverage handy.

• For safety's sake, lock your house and do not allow strangers inside for any reason.

• Leash your dog or confine him to the house for the duration of the sale, especially if he is likely to bark, jump on people, or otherwise scare away potential buyers.

• When the sale is over, load unsold items in your car to donate to a pre-selected charity organization, such as The Salvation Army, or arrange ahead of time for a pick-up.

—Helen Volk, Beyond Clutter

1. Set a date. Check first to find out whether your municipality requires a permit to hold a garage sale or puts any restrictions on garage sales. Then pick a date for your garage sale, preferably a Saturday. One day should be sufficient, but if you have a lot of stuff to sell and time to spare, make it a two-day sale. Most buyers arrive in the morning; you may want to end your sale by 2 P.M. rather than waiting around for stragglers.

2. Write and place an advertisement for your sale. List your big-ticket items and some of the more desirable things. Unless you are willing to start selling at the crack of dawn, include the phrase "no early birds." List the hours of your sale. Run the ad three days before and on the day of the sale.

3. Designate a collection spot. Set up one area of your garage or home for collecting, sorting, and pricing items to be sold. Keep similar items together: for example, furniture, sporting equipment, books and videos, infant clothing and toys, kitchenware, and linens.

4. Put a price on everything. Use stickers or signs. It's easier on you when prospective customers don't have to ask, "How much is this?" If you are unfamiliar with garage sale pricing, go to some garage sales and look for items similar to those you will be selling. As you collect items for your garage sale, price them.

5. Make and post location signs. Check with your municipality or development association to make sure it's OK to hang signs advertising your sale and to find out whether there are restrictions concerning sign placement, when signs can be posted, and so forth. Post signs at strategic locations, including the nearest intersection with a main road, the end of your street, and your driveway. Write in large capital letters with black marker on a brightly colored card stock. Keep it simple:

GARAGE SALE
Sat., May 5, 8 A.M.–2 P.M.
125 Main Street

Draw an arrow pointing the way. Hang up the signs up to one week before your sale. Make a note of every location and be sure to take down every sign immediately after your sale.

6. Arrange your wares attractively. To display smaller items, use tables or lay a sheet of plywood over two sawhorses and drape with a tablecloth. Put all clothes on hangers, hang on a length of clothesline, and clip with clothespins. Or, if you have two stepladders, insert a long pole or broom between the two

PRICE TO SELL

Simplify pricing by group; for example, all ladies shirts $1 or all paperbacks 25 cents. Then you only have to create a few signs instead of many price stickers.

• Price cheap. Don't get hung up on value. Remember, your goal is to get rid of stuff.

• Use whole values such as $5, $1, 50 cents, and 25 cents to simplify addition and make it easy to make change.

—*Treva Berends, The Organizing Specialists*

for a clothes rod. Separate men's, women's, and children's clothing and accessories. Put out at least one long mirror so that shoppers can see if the style, color, and size is right. Run heavy-duty extension cords for testing electrical appliances. The more you can set up your sale along the lines of a retail store, the easier it is for customers to browse and find things. Remove from the garage sale vicinity any items that are not for sale, or attach a sign to them that reads "Not for Sale." Put a box of stuff out by the road with a "Free" sign to attract passersby.

7. Be prepared. Think about how you will handle money. Will you wear a fanny pack or apron, or use a cash box? Will you need a helper? Be sure that you have enough coins and bills to make change for two twenty-dollar

One Challenge . . .

I have certain items that I don't use or even like for that matter, but because these things were given to me as gifts, I feel compelled to hang on to them.

Three Solutions

1 FROM JULIE SIGNORE, *1, 2, 3 SORT IT*: If you feel that the person who gave you the gift will expect to see it in your home, ask your kids if one of them would like the item for when they leave for college or have a place of their own. The next time you see the person who gave you the gift you can say, "Gee, Susan, that gift was so special that Sally decided she wants to keep it in a safe place until she leaves for college." If you doubt you will ever be asked about the gift in the future and no one in the family wants the item, donate it to a charitable agency in your community. Remember, the worst part of receiving a gift or item that is not your style is not being questioned about its whereabouts in the future by the giver; it's holding on to something that is perfectly good and not using it, when there are others who need it!

2 FROM TREVA BERENDS, *THE ORGANIZING SPECIALISTS*: When you receive a gift you don't particularly like or need, make a choice to display or use it for a period of time. Then pass it along to someone who will appreciate it — maybe to someone who admires it in your home. If you choose to honor the giver, use or display gifts, but limit your own acquisition of similar items, for example, a picture frame. When giving gifts, keep in mind that consumable gifts are always a good choice, especially for people who have everything. Give a gift certificate to a spa, favorite restaurant, or store, or a basket of store-bought or homemade edibles.

3 FROM DOROTHY MADDEN, *ORGANIZE IT!*: If the giver is a person who plays a major role in your life, such as a mother-in-law, hold on to it for the sake of the relationship. People are more important than things. If, on the other hand, the giver is not someone who is likely to look for the gift in your home, give yourself permission to give it away. A gift is a gift. It's meant for you to do with it what you will.

bills — five fives, thirteen ones, and two dollars in loose change that fits your pricing system (for example, you may only need quarters). Have a calculator or paper and pencil handy for quick addition. You'll also want shopping bags and a few boxes, as well as newspaper for wrapping breakables. Set up as much as possible the night before your sale. Be sure you have enough light in your garage, or if you are having a yard sale, that you are prepared for rain. Consider selecting and listing a rain date in your advertisements, just in case. And to help move items in the last hour of your sale, consider reducing everything to half-price as the crowds begin to wane.

To encourage your children to unclutter their rooms, offer to let them keep whatever money they make from selling their stuff. If you don't have lot of stuff or can't stand the thought of going it alone, invite friends and family members to join you in your garage sale effort, with the understanding that they do all their own pricing and set-up, they help you on the day of the sale, and they take all unsold items with them when they leave. You'll need a system to track who sells what to keep proceeds straight. If you're working with just one other person, you can simply direct buyers to the appropriate money-taker. Or you might use color-coded price stickers.

One way to draw a larger crowd to your garage sale is to make it a neighborhood or block sale. Let your neighbors know that you are planning a garage sale on such-and-such a date, and ask if they are interested in having a sale of their own on that day. A benefit of

recycling stuff

Rather than add to the landfill, recycle. For example, take plastic grocery bags back to the supermarket and return wire hangers to the dry cleaner. You can also recycle used inkjet printer and laser printer cartridges through the manufacturer or school fundraising programs.

Dare to be creative. Turn an old golf bag with wheels into a garden-tool caddy or umbrella stand. Or "plant" your old mailbox in your garden for storing hand tools.

Whatever you decide to do, do it within a specified time frame to keep this stuff from continuing to take up space in your home.

joining forces is that you can advertise the block sale together and split the cost of advertising. You may even be able to buy a larger ad, which is more likely to get noticed. Be sure to give your neighbors plenty of advance warning (at least one month) so they have time to go through their homes and set aside items they want to sell. A neighborhood or block sale also generates a strong sense of community, so get out there and have fun.

CHAPTER 3

ORGANIZING BASICS

Uncluttering is half the battle. Organizing is the other half. Without organizing, you'll find that you have to unclutter over and over again. Getting organized shouldn't be complicated; the more complicated your organizational system, the less likely it is that you'll be able to maintain it. So keep it simple. And remember that the only "right" way to get organized is the way that works best for you.

A Home for Everything

More often than not, things don't get put away because they don't have a home. How can you put everything in its place if you don't have a place for everything? The key to getting organized is to find the best possible home for all of your belongings, everything from measuring cups to memorabilia.

When choosing a home for an item, don't think, "Where shall I put this?" Instead, think, "Where am I most likely to look for this?" Ideally, the home you create will be close to where the item gets used and where others might be apt to look for it. As you look at where things are stored in a particular room, ask yourself the following questions to help you determine where each item belongs:

- How often do I use it?
- Where do I use it?
- How accessible is it?
  How accessible should it be?
- Does it belong in this room?

Things you use often should be visible or easily accessible. Store the things you use most often between neck and knee height and toward the front of a closet or cabinet. Store things you rarely use on higher or lower shelves or in your long-term storage area. You may find that the best place for some items, such as a broken lamp, is in the trash. Other items might belong in other rooms. Still other items, such as a suit you no longer wear, might belong better in someone else's home.

If you have a place for storing a particular item, but that place isn't being used, figure out why. Perhaps it is not conveniently located. A good example is the hamper. If your kids get undressed in the bedroom but the hamper is in the bathroom or the laundry room, it's no wonder their dirty clothes always wind up on the floor. Put a hamper in each bedroom.

Work with Clutter

Organizing your home and possessions to fit your lifestyle can go a long way toward minimizing clutter. Where do you tend to drop your keys when you come in the door? Where do you put things you need to take with you when you leave for work? Where do you pay bills?

Walk through your home and look at what's lying around. Consider how you use each room. Work *with* clutter by organizing these logical storage places. Ask these questions:

- What causes clutter in this room?
- What items end up here that should be somewhere else? Why?
- What things should be in this room that are not here now?
- What organizing products could I use here? (See page 26 for ideas.)

Is your dining room table or kitchen counter, for example, a dumping ground for anything and everything that comes in the door? Can you find or create a better place nearby to store these things, perhaps on a shelf or in a cabinet? You may not be able to eliminate clutter, but you *can* control it.

An effective way to minimize clutter is to set up work centers for specific activities, such as handling mail and bills, sewing, hobbies, and laundry. A workstation that includes all the tools you need close at hand saves you time. You also may find that it is most efficient to have certain things, such as scissors, in more than one location. You might want to keep a pair with your office supplies and another pair with your gift-wrapping supplies, for instance.

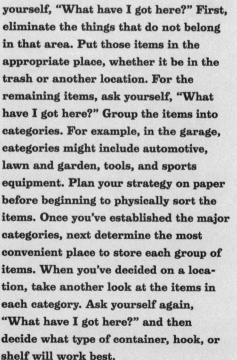

WHAT HAVE YOU GOT?

Look at an area of your home and ask yourself, "What have I got here?" First, eliminate the things that do not belong in that area. Put those items in the appropriate place, whether it be in the trash or another location. For the remaining items, ask yourself, "What have I got here?" Group the items into categories. For example, in the garage, categories might include automotive, lawn and garden, tools, and sports equipment. Plan your strategy on paper before beginning to physically sort the items. Once you've established the major categories, next determine the most convenient place to store each group of items. When you've decided on a location, take another look at the items in each category. Ask yourself again, "What have I got here?" and then decide what type of container, hook, or shelf will work best.

—Judy Stern, Organize NOW

Consider establishing clutter-free zones. Make the dining room a no-toy zone, or lay down ground rules for using the living room: for example, "If you carry it in, carry it out when you leave." You might also consider creating your own personal sanctuary — a space you can call your own, where you can read or write or think in privacy. If you live with others and cannot claim an entire room for yourself, claim a portion of a room and declare it off limits to everyone but yourself. As you begin to assert control over clutter, space by space, room by room, you will begin to regain control of your environment — and your life.

One Challenge . . .

I often leave notes and things out as a reminder to do something. If I put everything away, I'm afraid that I will forget something important that I was supposed to do or where I put something that I need.

Three Solutions

1 FROM DONNA D. McMILLAN, McMILLAN & COMPANY PROFESSIONAL ORGANIZING: Is that really the reason why you leave things out? Or do you leave things out because you don't know what else to do with them? Give everything a home or a place to live. Then, when you're finished with it, get in the habit of taking it back home. It could be cotton swabs that belong on the second shelf of the medicine cabinet to the right. When you give things a home, you can always find whatever you're looking for, even in the dark!

2 FROM JUDY STERN, ORGANIZE NOW: When you leave things out where you can see them, generally you don't see them again. They become part of the wallpaper. A more effective reminder system is to keep notepads available in locations where they'll come in handy for jotting down reminders. Once you've written something down on a list, you no longer need the item itself as a reminder, and you can feel comfortable putting it away.

3 FROM LORRAINE CHALICKI, YOUNEEDME.COM: Some visual cues are okay if you're disciplined. For example, near the door, you might allow only things that you will take with you on your next trip out the door. In your office, you might write "To Do Today" reminders on colorful sticky notes that you affix to a stand-up acrylic holder placed on your desk. As you address each item, pull the reminder off, throw it away, and congratulate yourself for getting it done.

Contain Yourself

Use containers to organize your belongings. Think of drawers, shelves, and clothes rods as containers, in addition to boxes, crates, baskets, and bags. Keep like items together in separate containers. This makes it easy to find what you're looking for, even if you never get around to organizing the contents of the container.

Group items together in whatever way makes sense to you. In your closet, clothes can be sorted and hung by shirts, pants, skirts, dresses, and suits, or by color. Small items, such as cookie cutters, can be put in resealable plastic bags to keep them separate from other small kitchen gadgets in a drawer. Familiarize yourself with organizing products designed to help you contain all kinds of things. You may be surprised at the variety of producers available.

To maximize existing storage space, think vertical. Think about what you might be able to hang on walls, from the ceiling, and behind closed doors. A shoe rack hung over the back of a door, for example, takes up less space than a standing shoe rack. Use same-size storage boxes that stack easily on shelves to make use of space at the top of closets. In cabinets, you might be able to mount an organizing product to the inside of a door to store spices or pot lids.

If you have a lot of wasted space at the top of your cabinets, try raising or lowering shelves to create more usable space. Or use freestanding shelving or hanging wire baskets under shelves to create additional storage. Consider replacing fixed shelves with adjustable shelving that rolls out, so that even

items in the back are accessible. You can buy a do-it-yourself kit for this purpose at hardware and home stores.

Designate temporary storage areas for garage sale items, gifts purchased in advance of the occasion, clothing to go to the dry cleaner, library books, and rented videos to be returned. Store a marker and stickers with your garage sale items so that you can price them as you put them into storage.

Don't just toss things into storage. Take the time to put them where they belong, or create a home for them, so that you don't have to spend hours or days reorganizing your storage at a future date. But do keep an open, "catch-all" box in your storage area to gather all the things you find throughout the year that belong in one of the packed boxes. Rather than pull out all the boxes just to put away one item, you can put away everything in the "catch-all" box periodically.

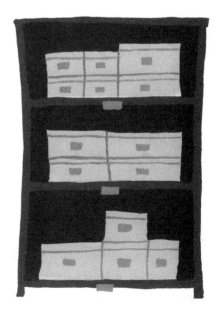

LABEL EVERYTHING

It's easier to stay organized when things are labeled. Consider buying a battery-powered electronic label maker that prints on a white or transparent label. Use it to label where things go on shelves and in cabinets and drawers. You can also use this handy organizing gadget to create neatly lettered labels for file folders, storage cartons, computer disks, videotapes, spice racks, plant stakes, and more. It makes a great gift, too!

—*Jackie Tiani, Organizing Systems, Inc.*

Organizing Products

There are some terrific products available to help organize your possessions. But remember: For every one thing you buy, something must go, and that goes for organizing products, too! Be careful that you're not just organizing clutter; you want to pare down as well. Resist the temptation to buy organizing products until you know what you need to contain. And be sure to measure your space so that you buy the right-size product.

Organized and disorganized people alike swear by clear plastic storage bins with lids. Disorganized people throw stuff in them and hide them just to get it out of sight — which is a start. Organized people use them to store everything from puzzle pieces to scuba diving equipment, craft supplies, and holiday decorations. Why are these bins so popular?

- They're clear, so you can see at a glance what's inside.
- They come in lots of different sizes.
- They're stackable.
- They're airtight and watertight, so you can store things in the basement or garage without worrying about them getting wet.
- They keep out dust, dirt, and insects.
- They're fairly inexpensive and go on sale several times a year.
- They're readily available at mass merchandise stores.

Sometimes, the best organizing product is something you have in your home that you acquired but are not using. A magnetic knife holder, for example, can be mounted inside a cabinet door to hold nail clippers, tweezers, and scissors. Hat boxes, decorative tins, and woven baskets can contain clutter on shelves while enhancing the decor of any room.

A filing cabinet or bookcase is probably a worthwhile investment, but in general, you don't have to spend a lot of money on organizing products. Check out your local dollar store for inexpensive jewelry organizers and shoe bags. Following are some ideas for recycling everyday items into free organizers.

- In a bathroom cabinet or drawer, use empty baby-wipe containers to separate and store first-aid supplies, make-up, pain relievers, and vitamins.
- Stack plastic milk crates or wooden produce boxes against a wall or in a closet, open side out. Use them to store books or games.

- Use cardboard copier paper boxes or produce boxes with lids for long-term storage.
- To store odds and ends in the kitchen junk drawer, workshop, or office drawer, use recycled microwave food trays, check boxes, margarine tubs, or aerosol can tops.
- Use a liquor carton with cardboard partitions to store rolled-up artwork. Or use one in your coat closet to store dry umbrellas.
- Empty egg cartons can be useful for storing small items. Remove the lid and place it in a desk drawer to hold paper clips and other small items. Or keep the lid on and store small crafts supplies in it.
- Use shoeboxes to store photos or as dresser drawer organizers.
- Film canisters are very useful for storing small items, such as buttons, safety pins, screws, nails, even quarters and tokens. Use masking tape to label each container, or use a piece of clear tape to attach a sample item to the outside of the container.

Achieving Your Goals

If you find the challenge of getting organized too overwhelming, break it down. Take it one step at a time. Strive for excellence, not perfection. There's a concept called the *law of diminishing returns,* which states that perfectionism rarely pays out. Be the best imperfect person you can be, and get started on achieving your goal. Also, on completion of each step, reward yourself with something you enjoy that you don't often get to do, such as meeting a friend for lunch or getting a manicure or pedicure. That will help keep you motivated.

- **If you have the desire and determination, all you need is a plan.** Make a list of the rooms that you want to organize. Take a walk through each room and jot down the things that need to be uncluttered or organized. Be specific: for example, organize books or clean out refrigerator. Then prioritize your list. Write the number one next to the thing, area, or room that bugs you most. Focus on that challenge. When you're done, check it off your list, give yourself the reward you promised yourself, and decide what is your next priority. Focus only on that challenge.
- **Set a start date and an end date for your home organization project.** If you're not done by then, you can always adjust the end date, but it helps to have one. The end date might be a holiday or party, or a date that you set for a garage sale. Just be sure to allow yourself enough time. How much time is enough? That varies widely from person to person, and it depends on how large your home is and whether you have help. It wouldn't hurt to allow yourself three months or more to do the job right. If you finish earlier, you can enjoy the rewards of organization that much sooner.
- **Focus on the big picture.** For example, if you have papers strewn all over your home, gather them in one place and put them in a cardboard box or other container, maybe even an empty filing cabinet drawer. You can make individual files later. In the meantime, you've

reduced clutter, and you know where all your papers are. Use this same strategy to organize drawers, shelves, and any container. The important thing is to get started by sorting and containing things.

- **Commit to your goal.** Decide how much time you are willing to spend each day on organizing and then schedule it. Even if you commit only five to fifteen minutes a day, you will eventually reach your goals. It's better to get there slowly and surely than to try to do it all at once and get so overwhelmed that you come to a complete standstill.

Help Is on the Way

Don't be afraid to ask for help if you need it. For example, when you get ready to sort through your clothes, invite a friend to help you determine what does and does not look good on you. Minimize distractions during the time you've set aside for uncluttering. Let the answering machine take your calls, and let housemates know that you don't want to be disturbed.

What if you are so overwhelmed that you can't even get started, or you get overwhelmed in the middle of organizing your closet? Professional organizers can help you get and stay organized. These organizing experts can provide ideas, information, structure, solutions, and systems to help you regain control over your time and space. There are thousands of professional organizers in cities around the world. Professional organizers offer the following services:

- Behavior modification
- Closet design and organizing
- Computer consulting
- Errands and personal shopping
- Events and meeting planning
- Filing systems
- Financial/bookkeeping
- Office organizing
- Packing, moving, and relocating
- Paper management
- Project management
- Records management
- Residential organizing
- Seminars, workshops, and training
- Space planning
- Time management

Hourly rates range from $20 to $300, depending on the organizer's level of experience and areas of specialty. To find a professional organizer near you, look in the Yellow Pages under "Organizing Services," or request a free referral through the National Association of Professional Organizers. This group will provide a list of member organizers in your area. Members have pledged to follow a strict professional code of conduct, which includes complete confidentiality.

When choosing a professional organizer, ask about experience with situations similar to yours. Don't hesitate to ask for referrals. Be sure to choose someone you feel comfortable with, since you will be working together closely.

There are at least two support group programs for people who are chronically disorganized. One is Clutterless Recovery Groups, Inc., a nonprofit self-help organization run by clutterers for clutterers. In addition to providing on-line information and support, this group offers workshops and meetings in cities throughout the United States.

Another support group is offered through Messies Anonymous, an organization founded in 1981 to provide educational and motivational aid to chronically disorganized people. Messies Anonymous sponsors twelve-step support groups in which participants set goals, discuss problems, and celebrate victories.

The Internet is a wonderful resource for organizing. Use any search engine to conduct a search for "organizing," and you will find many excellent Web sites, including sites where you can post questions about organizing. (You'll find some of these sites listed in the Resources, which begin on page 278.)

Some people thrive on organizational challenges. If you're one of them, consider giving "the gift of organization" to less organized friends and family members. You might even consider becoming a professional organizer.

Typically, professional organizers are compassionate people who genuinely enjoy helping others discover the benefits of getting organized. Successful organizers are also the type who enjoy running their own businesses. For more information about how to become a professional organizer, contact the National Association of Professional Organizers (see page 278).

If you can't find something in thirty seconds, it's in the wrong place.

—Donna D. McMillan,
McMillan & Company Professional Organizing

CHAPTER 4

STAYING ORGANIZED

Staying organized is even more challenging than getting organized, because you have to train yourself to do things differently. It takes twenty-one consecutive days to establish a new habit, by making a conscious effort every day *not* to do the same old thing. Once you've uncluttered your home, staying organized involves picking up, putting away, and discarding excess stuff on a regular basis.

Simple Everyday Strategies

The best way to stay organized is to take care of today's things today. It's easier to keep up than it is to catch up. Procrastinating usually makes more work later, which can take more time. It can also create more stress and sometimes even more expense. Following are some simple everyday strategies for staying organized by taking care of the little things.

• **Don't put it down, put it away.** Before you put something down, ask yourself, "Is this where it belongs?" In the beginning, it will feel like work, but if you keep after yourself, it will soon become second nature to put things away. Take dressing and undressing, for example. Even when you're in a hurry, remind yourself

that it takes just a minute or two to put away clothes after undressing — far less time than it takes to pick up and put away several weeks' worth of clothing. And it's not just *that* time and work you save when you put away clothes immediately. How often have you had to launder or iron an article of clothing because it was left on the floor overnight or for a week?

• **Lay down the law with household members.** Whoever makes a mess is responsible for cleaning it up — now, not later. That means everyone cleans up their own bathroom mess, their own kitchen mess, and their own bedroom mess. Set minimum standards at first, especially for younger family members, then raise the bar. (For ideas on ways to motivate family participation, see page 35.)

- **Unclutter as you go.** Every morning or evening, walk through your home for five minutes with a basket or tote bag in hand, collecting stray items and returning them to their rightful homes. When you go to the basement, attic, garage, or upstairs or downstairs, take something with you to put away. When you file something in a folder, flip through the folder to see if you can toss anything. A few minutes here and there every day can add up to uncluttering in no time.

- **Leave your "campground" cleaner than you found it.** Make it your policy never to leave a room without improving its appearance. Toss the newspaper in the recycling bin. Straighten pictures and lampshades. Close cabinet doors and drawers. Put dishes in the dishwasher. Make your bed after your morning shower or breakfast — it not only makes the room look nicer, it feels nicer to get into a made bed. If you share a bed, make it a rule that the last one up makes the bed. If you get up earlier every day, you may never have to make the bed again!

For Simplicity's Sake

House Rules

- If you take it out, put it back.
- If you carry it in, carry it out.
- If you borrow it, return it.
- If you open it, close it.
- If you throw it down, pick it up.
- If you take if off, hang it up.
- If you break it, fix it.

Organizing is a process. It's not a one-day project.

—Donna D. McMillan,
McMillan & Company Professional Organizing

- **Make it easy to stay organized.** Designate a "drop off" box for library books and videos that need to be returned. Keep a "put away" basket in a central location, or one in every room, to collect things that belong elsewhere. Make putting away a daily family chore. (And if you get unexpected visitors, you can use these receptacles to pick up and stash clutter in a hurry.) If you find yourself picking up the same areas over and over again, see if you can come up with a simple, practical solution for preventing or reducing future messes. For example, if your kitchen counter is littered with empty beverage bottles and cans, move the recycling bin closer to that area.

- **Make standard "to do" or "to remember" lists.** Make lists for anything you do on a regular basis, such as closing up your summer home or packing to go to the beach. File all of these lists in the same folder in your filing cabinet. Or, if you prefer, keep individual lists with related items so that you'll be sure to find them when you start looking for your stuff. This technique works for the smaller things in life, too. For instance, in your gym bag, keep a list of what you need to take with you. That way, you won't waste energy thinking about what you need every time, and you'll never end up at the gym without your sneakers or a towel.

- **Set limits on recyclable items.** How many plastic shopping bags do you need to save? How many empty margarine tubs and yogurt containers are enough? Being frugal is fine, but if you have more than you need, you're wasting valuable space rather than money. Keep just a few and recycle the others. Do the same with cardboard boxes, rubber bands, twist ties, and similar items you've been collecting.

- **Buy less.** Do you really need more stuff? Think twice about buying things that require extra upkeep, such as knickknacks that have to be dusted regularly and clothing with special washing instructions. Think three times before buying souvenirs; take photographs or keep a journal instead.

- **Simplify your life with the 80/20 rule.** Most people use only about 20 percent of what they own. The other 80 percent is just taking up valuable space, getting in the way, and causing more work than is necessary. In other words, it's clutter. Keep your home clutter-free by making a conscious decision to surround yourself with only the things you love and use.

TAKE ACTION

If something needs to be done, do something about it in the first two minutes you think about it.

—*Judy Warmington, Woman Time Management*

Minimizing Paper Pile-up

If there's one thing that clutters up a home fast, it's paper in its many forms. The best strategy for avoiding paper pile-up has three parts.

1. Limit the amount of incoming paper.
2. Develop a system for storing paper items.
3. Recycle regularly. Keep trash cans handy wherever unwanted paper tends to accumulate.

Junk mail and catalogs are like door-to-door salespeople. Occasionally, you're interested in what they're selling, but more often, you're annoyed at the intrusion. The difference is that you can be as rude as you like to junk mail and catalogs. If you have piles of unopened mail offers, solicitations and catalogs, dump them. Don't even give it a second thought, because you know you'll get more.

Open and sort mail daily into five categories: not for me, action items, to read, to file, and trash. Immediately discard junk mail. (This is easiest to do if you sort your mail near a trash can or recycling bin.) Don't even open it; you know it's junk. Place items to be filed in a folder labeled "To File." Place items to read in a folder labeled just that, then take it to your reading place. If a piece of mail requires action, you don't have to respond immediately, but try to minimize the number of times you handle it. For example, put mail you need to take care of today in a folder labeled "To Do." Place mail for other household members into labeled stacking trays or a vertical file. This is also a good place to keep your filing, reading, and "To Do Today" folders.

When you receive bills, save only the bill and payment envelope. Recycle or throw away the outer envelope and advertising inserts. If you can't bring yourself to just toss them, scan quickly for information that may be interesting or relevant, then toss them. Be sure to read any important notices. Take bills to the place in your home where you write out the checks for them. Create a simple system for storing bills, such as a folder labeled "Bills to Be Paid" or a large, labeled envelope that you keep in a drawer. For tips on paying bills, see page 123.

File regularly to avoid build-up of paper clutter. Do it daily, weekly, monthly, or quarterly, depending on the volume of paper. If you don't file regularly, at least put all items to be filed in a "To File" folder or basket. As you file something, flip through the folder to see if something else can be thrown out. Once a

For Safety's Sake

Protect your credit. Open credit card and other financial offers to make sure that they do not contain live checks connected to one of your credit card accounts. If you aren't going to use these checks, destroy them immediately to prevent them from ending up in the wrong hands. It's also a good idea to destroy preapproved credit card offers in your name. Consider buying an inexpensive paper shredder to destroy these items, or burn the paper the next time you use your fireplace.

Every piece of paper has a decision attached to it.

—LaNita Filer, LFJ Organizing Concepts Plus

year, purge old folders and papers from your filing cabinet. Put only what you really need to keep in long-term storage.

Beware of the paper clutter you create. Think twice before duplicating documents on the copier or printing out e-mails. Use the copier only when absolutely necessary. Store e-mail messages in folders on your computer, or simply make a note of the information you need and delete them. Also, think twice before bringing home free brochures and pamphlets. Read them on the spot if you can and then put them back. Bring home just the information you need by jotting down a note in your daily planner or in a spiral-bound notebook that you carry with you. Finally, recycle or throw away cardboard boxes unless you have a definite or immediate use for them.

Just Say No. To reduce the amount of unsolicited mail you receive, send a postcard or letter to the Direct Marketing Association (see Resources, page 287) asking to have your name removed from all mailing lists. Be sure to include your name and address exactly as it appears on the mail you receive. Allow several months for the deluge to subside. Meanwhile, make a commitment to throw out every catalog and direct-mail offer without even looking at it. Likewise, if you want telemarketers to stop calling, send a note to the Direct Marketing Association Telephone Preference Service (see Resources, page 287) and ask to be removed from national solicitation lists.

Periodic Purges

The easiest way to maintain a clutter-free home is this: For every one item you bring in the front door, send one packing out the back door. Apply the one-in/one-out rule to everything from household items to clothing to paper. Decide before you go shopping what you intend to let go of to make room for your purchase. When you receive a gift, do the same. Keep in mind that what goes out does not have to be equal in value or size to what comes in.

When your child receives a new toy, donate an old one to charity. A good time to ask kids for a donation is just before or just after Christmas, a birthday, or another occasion on which they typically receive gifts. Keep a cardboard box in each child's room for collecting outgrown toys and clothes. When the box is full, take it to your favorite charity, a consignment shop, or to your designated garage/yard sale collection area.

Set aside a specific time each day for picking up. For example, do it while your morning coffee or tea is brewing or just before you go to bed. If it takes longer than fifteen minutes, consider it an early warning that you may be falling back into old habits. When you catch yourself thinking "I'll do it later," stop and do it *now*. Take the extra thirty seconds or five steps it takes to put things where they belong.

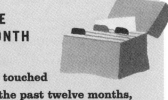

FOLLOW THE TWELVE-MONTH RULE

If you haven't touched something in the past twelve months, chances are that you're not going to use it in the next twelve. Clothes and sporting goods seem to be some of the worst offenders. It's natural for people to have a hard time letting go of the past. If an old outfit or a bowling ball really means that much to you, then put it away with your keepsakes. If you feel like you need to hang on to ancient financial paperwork, put it in a remote storage area of your home. Just don't take up valuable space in your active storage areas with items you don't use.

—*Ramona Creel, OnlineOrganizing.com*

Take an inventory of clothing and accessories at the end of each season. Seriously consider donating items that were not worn or used during the past season or that no longer fit. Or set them aside for a garage sale (but only if you are definitely going to have a garage sale!). Wash or dry clean all seasonal clothing before storing it; that way, they'll be ready if you wish to sell items on consignment. Place a reminder in your tickler file to take items to the consignment shop at the appropriate time of year. (See page 16 for more information on consignment shops.)

At least once a year, host a party. Getting ready for the party is fun and gives you extra incentive to do a thorough uncluttering. This is also a good time to rearrange your knick-knacks and framed photographs and get rid of any that are no longer meaningful.

In January each year, clean out your filing cabinet to make room for the new year's files. Save only what you need and discard the rest. Chapter 11, The Office, offers tips on filing and retaining records.

Kid Clutter Patrol

You have opportunities to teach your children organizational skills that will last a lifetime. Don't waste those moments by picking up after them. Help them find a place for everything, and train them to put everything in its place.

Establish a morning pick-up routine that might include making beds, hanging up towels in the bathroom, and putting away pajamas. The evening pick-up routine might include putting toys away and clothes in the hamper. Kids want some privacy. Let them know that if they keep their rooms picked up, you will not have to enter except for periodic, preannounced inspections.

Picking up is even more boring for children than it is for adults. Make it fun for children to help. Following are a few ways to make picking up after themselves more like a game than work.

- **Play clutter tag.** To make other family members more aware of their clutter trails, get a roll of peel-off stickers (the easily removable kind) and tag each item that's left out. Just making them aware may make them think twice about leaving things out. Children may enjoy helping you tag items, and the act of tag-ging will make them more likely to put away their own belongings.

- **Establish a "penalty box."** If Mom or Dad has to pick up something one of the kids left out, it will be forfeited until Saturday morning. To reclaim the item, its owner must pay a penalty of one extra chore. If anyone chooses not to do the chore, you know that the item isn't important to him or her. Give it away or throw it away without guilt.

- **Beat the clock!** This is a good way to make cleaning up a messy bedroom or playroom more fun. Assign a "put away" basket or pillowcase to each child. Set a timer for thirty seconds and see who can pick up the most stuff. Repeat as necessary and keep score. Reward the winner with a couple of quarters, or allow him or her to stay up a little later that night.

- **"You be the boss."** Let your children take turns being boss for ten minutes. Their job is to supervise the other children as they pick up their belongings and straighten up their rooms. In learning to be a good supervisor, children also learn to pay more attention to details.

One Challenge . . .

I've always been very neat and organized, but my husband is the exact opposite and it's driving me crazy. Can you give me some practical ways to cope with a messy partner?

Three Solutions

1 FROM LORRAINE CHALICKI, YOUNEEDME.COM PERSONAL SYSTEMS: Don't make the mistake of labeling your partner "wrong." For years, I would get on my husband's case about his messy desk, but after researching the differences between left and right brain thinkers, I realized that for him, a drawer is a black hole. He needs organizational systems that are very visual and hands-on. Once I understood this, we were able to organize his desktop with upright cascading files for storing folders out in the open, stacking wooden boxes for notebooks and CDs, and a big, white, erasable marker board for managing project deadlines. His desktop isn't "neat and tidy" by some standards, but it's organized for him and that's what matters.

2 FROM PAULA ROYALTY, WORKSMART PRODUCTIVITY CONSULTING: Set aside time to discuss the issue with your husband. Try to reach agreement on how you can live together more harmoniously. Ideally, you want the house to be clean, neat, and tidy, but in reality, what's your minimum standard? You might be happy, for example, if he would agree to leave nothing on the floor and put recyclables in a designated area.

3 FROM DONNA D. MCMILLAN, MCMILLAN & COMPANY PROFESSIONAL ORGANIZING: You shouldn't have to feel like you're nagging. Agree to bring in a professional organizer so that you don't have to be the "bad guy." I can't make anyone do what I suggest, but your spouse may be more likely to take advice from a professional who is not a family member or friend.

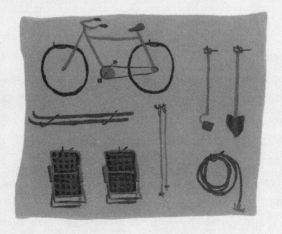

- **Blow the whistle on clutter.** Plan a fifteen-minute family pick-up time with a special reward at the end, such as a bowl of popcorn and a movie. Have everyone start in the same room. Blow a whistle as the signal for family members to start putting things away. When that room looks good, blow the whistle again and yell out a room name. "Players" run to the next room and start picking up in that room. Wrap up the game with praise for a job well done.

Sometimes you have to get tough. If family members leave their belongings where they don't belong, gather them up in a large garbage bag and take it out to the garage. When they ask if you've seen a particular item you picked up, tell them it's out in the garage. When they ask why, tell them you found it lying around and thought it was garbage. They should get the idea pretty fast.

Another "tough love" idea is to let your kids know that whatever you find lying on the floor at such-and-such a time will go into the garbage. Then carry through. Throw out or donate the first thing that gets left out. A variation that works well with younger children who can't yet tell time is to tell them that

For Simplicity's Sake

If you find it difficult to get rid of junk, think before bringing anything into your home. Learn to say "no thanks" to things you don't want or need.

whatever the vacuum cleaner touches gets vacuumed up or goes in the garbage. Once they see that you mean business, they'll scramble to pick up their things when you get out the vacuum cleaner.

Establish playtime rules. Teach very young children to take out only a few toys at a time. If they've already got two or three toys out, they must put one away. Consider restricting toys to one room of the house.

Reminder Systems

Have you ever wondered how some people always manage to remember your birthday? It probably doesn't have anything to do with memory at all. Much of being organized has to do with developing routines and reminder systems. You might, for example, get in the habit of doing laundry every Monday, cleaning out your refrigerator on trash night, or sweeping away cobwebs on the first of every month. After awhile, it just becomes habit. But many of us also need reminder systems for routine as well as nonroutine activities.

The tickler file described on page 157 is a simple reminder system that works great, as long as you use it. To remind yourself to check smoke detector batteries once a month, write a note to yourself and file it in next month's folder. When the first of the month rolls around, you'll find the note so you can act on the reminder and then refile the note in the following month's folder. To remember birthdays and anniversaries, type a list of special dates in calendar order and then file the list in your tickler file according to the first date on the list. It's best to file the reminder one week before the actual date to give yourself time to buy and mail the card. Refile the list according to the next date on your list.

If you like visual cues and you refer daily to a wall calendar, the best reminder system for you might be to note all important events and reminders on the appropriate dates throughout the year when you get your new calendar. If you learn of a new birthday or anniversary as the year progresses, write it on your calendar. At the end of the year, transcribe all of the birthdays and anniversaries onto your new calendar.

Another way to remember birthdays and anniversaries is by using a "Days to Remember" book. This is a perennial calendar of months and days that allows you to record birthdays, anniversaries, and other special days. You can also include the year of the birth or wedding for future reference. As new birthdays and weddings take place, write them in your book. You'll never have to transcribe these dates, but you will need to remember to check the book occasionally. This method works best if you get in the habit of buying cards in advance and filing them in your tickler file.

If you prefer a more high-tech approach to organizing, have your computer remind you of special days and things to do. Free Internet reminder services allow you to set up e-mail reminders for important dates and events. Several such services are listed in the Resources beginning on page 278.

If you have scheduling software installed on your computer, you can enter tasks, such as "Buy birthday card for Mom," and then specify the date and time you want to be reminded about that task. And, if you have a personal digital assistant (PDA), simply download your calendar from your computer, and you can be reminded of what you need to do even when you're away from home.

ORGANIZING GREETING CARDS

Buy greeting cards at random when you see ones you like. Store them in a file caddy or other sturdy container that accommodates 9 X 12-inch manila envelopes upended on their sides. Label envelopes by category:

- Adult Birthday/Children's Birthday/Belated Birthday
- Anniversary/Wedding
- Friendship/Thank You
- Get Well/Feel Better/Sympathy
- Congratulations/Baby/New Home
- Special Occasion/Holiday
- Blank

Using envelopes instead of file folders keeps the greeting cards in like-new condition. Labeling the envelopes along the top edge (upended side) makes it easy to flip through your collection to find the appropriate category. Having an assortment of greeting cards on hand saves you from having to run out and buy them when you may not have the time to do so.

—Bette Martin, Necessary Indulgence Professional Organizing

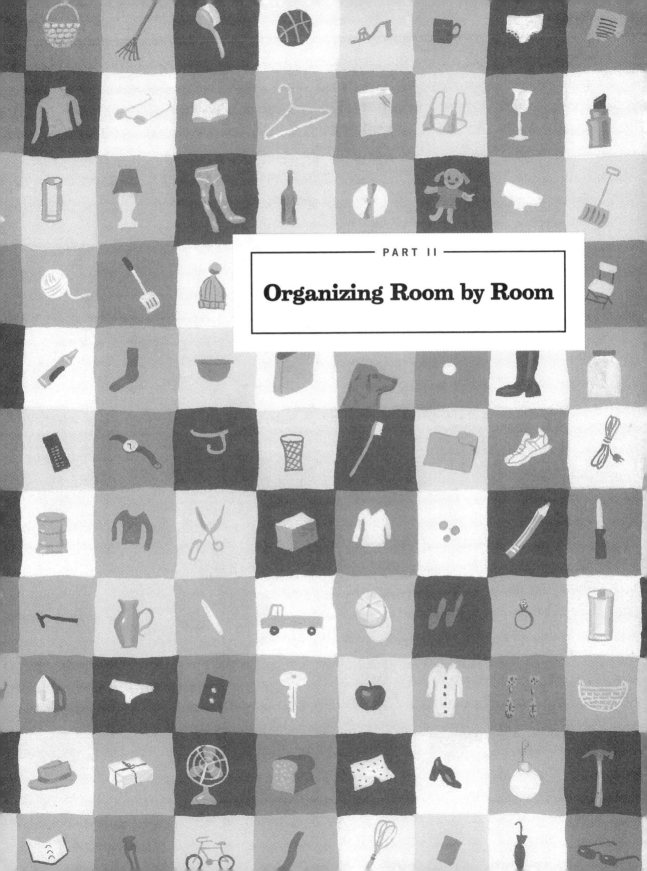

PART II

Organizing Room by Room

Any large organizing project is best accomplished by breaking it down into smaller, more manageable tasks. This is particularly true when organizing a home. The simplest way to divide this enormous project is to work one room at a time. Envision the rooms in your home as containers of related items. Organizing a single container is far easier than trying to organize many containers simultaneously. Simply choose the room that you want to organize first and begin. Within the room that you've chosen, organize one drawer, shelf, or defined space at a time.

The chapters in this section focus on a particular part of the home for quick and easy reference. Because there are so many different types and sizes of homes, some rooms, such as storage rooms, are grouped into chapters by utility.

CHAPTER 5

ENTRYWAYS

When you think of the entrances to your home, think of first impressions. An uncluttered entrance is open and inviting. Think of the feeling you get when you receive a warm handshake or greeting. Now picture a large, muscular man with arms crossed against his chest, blocking your doorway. That's the impression a cluttered entrance makes. What impression do your entryways make?

Uncluttering Entrances

The problem with clutter is that after awhile, you tend not to see it, unless you trip over it — and in that case, you see it after the fact. If you want to know what your entryways *really* look like, step outside for a moment and close the door behind you. Pretend you are a neighbor or friend who has never been to your house. Invite yourself in. Now, look around as if you are seeing your home for the first time. What's your first impression? On a scale of 1 to 10, with 10 being the most favorable, how would you rate your first impression of your home? How far off is your impression from the impression you would like to make?

Take a look at the things that are cluttering your entryways. Where do they belong? Is it easy or difficult to put these things where they belong? For example, if coats belong in the coat closet, but there are no hangers or the closet is already too crowded, putting away coats becomes impossible.

As you begin to unclutter your entryways one by one, use a box or bag labeled "Store Elsewhere" to collect items that belong elsewhere in your home. In another box, collect items that should go in your car so that you can take them where they belong. Such items include library books to return, clothes to drop off at the dry cleaner, and merchandise to be returned to the store. To avoid putting them in the trunk and then forgetting about them, post a sticky note on your dashboard as a reminder to deliver them or make a note in your calendar.

Homes for the Homeless

Now, look at what's left in your entryway. Put away things that have a home. Look at what's left. Is there anything you could throw away or give away? Do it. All that should be left now are those items that you need to create homes for, which might include the following:

- **Shoes.** Place a shoe rack, large wicker basket, or other receptacle near the front door to collect shoes. If you always take off your shoes at the door, you won't have to go searching for them later and your carpets and floors will stay cleaner.
- **Wet shoes and boots.** In winter or wet weather, set out enough rubber or plastic boot trays, bath mats, or towels, to accommodate wet shoes and boots for residents and visitors. If you use a shoe or boot rack for this purpose, be sure to cover the floor beneath it.
- **Mittens and gloves.** Use a hanging shoe bag with clear plastic pockets to keep pairs of mittens and gloves together. Hang it behind the closet door or from the rod. Reserve lower pockets for shorter household members. Or hang a nylon mesh bag from a hook or peg in the coat closet. At the end of the season, simply take the bag down, launder the contents, return them to the bag, and store with your out-of-season coats and clothing. To dry wet mittens and gloves, glue clothespins to a strip of

wood that you can nail into the wall above a heater. Varnish or paint the wood and clothespins to make them more attractive.

- **Hats and scarves.** Store brimmed hats flat on a shelf or in hatboxes. Hang caps and other hats on coat pegs, or store them with scarves in a hall storage bench or on a shelf in your coat closet. If you always wear the same scarf with the same coat, hang them together. Otherwise, fold and hang scarves on hangers in your coat closet. Keep these hangers together off to one side of the closet.

- **Umbrellas.** Store wet and dry umbrellas in an umbrella stand just inside the door or just outside the door (if that area is sheltered). Dry umbrellas can be hung on a standing coat rack, wall hook, or peg.
- **Backpacks and book bags.** Install a double coat hook that will accommodate one backpack and one jacket. Install one hook per child at the appropriate heights.
- **Other school paraphernalia.** Create a "launch pad" in a hall closet or along one wall of the hallway. Stack however many plastic crates you need — one for each child — for collecting lunchboxes, graded homework and tests, announcements, and paperwork to be signed.

Assign crates by color, or label with names. Encourage your children to put everything in their crate when they come home and to take everything out when they leave in the morning. That way, their stuff won't clutter up your hallway or kitchen, and they will know where to find it. You and your partner may want crates, too, for storing pocketbooks, briefcases, and anything else that will head out the door with you (for example, library books or dry cleaning). If you don't like the look of crates, try a bookcase with cubbyholes or a standard bookcase. Place same-size baskets or wire bins on the shelves for each family member.

- **Keys.** Hang your keys on a nail near the door, and get into the habit of putting them there as soon as you come in. If you don't like the look of a bare nail, buy a decorative key hanger. Or hang a door-knob basket and drop your keys into it when you come home. If the basket is big enough, you'll also have a handy holding station for outgoing mail.

Everybody thinks that their mess is the worst mess I've ever seen. Relax, I say. You're working with a natural disaster here. Life is naturally messy.

— Sheila Delson, FREEDomain Concepts

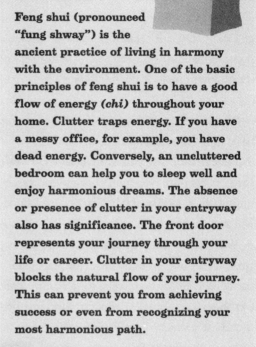

CLEARING OBSTACLES

Feng shui (pronounced "fung shway") is the ancient practice of living in harmony with the environment. One of the basic principles of feng shui is to have a good flow of energy (*chi*) throughout your home. Clutter traps energy. If you have a messy office, for example, you have dead energy. Conversely, an uncluttered bedroom can help you to sleep well and enjoy harmonious dreams. The absence or presence of clutter in your entryway also has significance. The front door represents your journey through your life or career. Clutter in your entryway blocks the natural flow of your journey. This can prevent you from achieving success or even from recognizing your most harmonious path.

— *Lorraine M. Duvall, feng shui consultant*

Organizing Coats

Sort through coats and separate into two categories: in season and out of season. Then sort the out-of-season coats into two categories: coats you will most likely wear next season and coats you are not likely to wear because of fit, style, color, or age. Set aside the coats you won't wear again for someone who will. Give them to a family member or friend, donate to a charitable organization, or take them to a consignment shop before the start of the season. Now look at the out-of-season coats that you will wear again next season. If any coats need to be cleaned, bring them to your laundry room or put them in your car to take to the dry cleaner.

Next, sort through in-season coats. Are there any you didn't wear last season? Any you probably won't wear again ever? Put them with the coats you plan to give to someone else. Consider yourself fortunate that you are in a position to share. Hang all the coats you're keeping on sturdy hangers and arrange by type of coat (sporting, casual, and dress, or short and long) or by family member. Add a few extra sturdy hangers for hanging guests' coats. Replace wire hangers with sturdy coat hangers.

What else is in your coat closet? Hats, gloves, umbrellas, boots? Discard items that are worn or broken beyond repair. Put anything you don't use or wear in your "Give Away" box. Clean and put away all out-of-season items. If there's nowhere to put them except the coat closet, put them on the upper shelves, on the floor in back, or in a corner. Remove items that don't belong in the coat closet and put in your "Store Elsewhere" box.

If you don't have a shelf above the clothes rod or you have only one shelf, consider installing shelving that goes up to the ceiling to make use of all that wasted space. Upper shelves are great for storing out-of-season clothing and sporting gear, old photograph albums and memorabilia, or anything requiring long-term storage. Use clear plastic bins so you can see what's inside, or clearly label boxes. On the shelf just above the clothes rod, use wire bins to separate and contain accessories, such as gloves and mittens.

Most coat closets have only one long rod hung at about the shoulder height of an adult. If you want children to hang up their coats, make it possible for them by installing a rod at their shoulder height or Shaker-style pegs along the back wall, at one end of the closet, or in the hallway.

Neatness Counts

Many homes have a "formal" entrance and a "family" entrance. It's generally easier to keep the formal entrance clutter-free, simply because it isn't used as often as the family entrance. And it goes without saying that the more use a room or space gets, the more clutter it attracts; this is especially true of entrances.

The best way to combat this natural tendency to clutter is to find a place for everything that *belongs* in the entryway and to return those items to their homes when you are finished using them. But what about things that you leave in the entryway temporarily, such as books and videos to be returned? It's simple: Give them a home, too. Try a decorative basket by the door, or put these items in a tote bag that can be hung on a hook or peg inside the coat closet.

TIME-SAVER

60

Do you like to know how you look before you leave home? Avoid backtracking to another room by hanging a mirror in your entryway or behind the door of your coat closet.

CHAPTER 6

KITCHEN AND DINING AREA

In *Cooking as Therapy*, Louis Parrish wrote, "If you can organize your kitchen, you can organize your life." The kitchen is home to an incredible number of items, from gadgets, appliances, and tools to foodstuffs. It's also where we spend a great deal of time — not just preparing and eating food, but also managing the household and hanging out. It's no wonder this room attracts so much clutter.

Getting Started

Organizing the kitchen can easily be a full-day job. If you can't spare an entire day, break the task down into smaller jobs. Unclutter the counter today, tackle the refrigerator and freezer tomorrow, and unclutter everything else one day at a time until you are satisfied with the results.

The countertop is a good place to start. Just uncluttering your countertop can make your whole kitchen look neat and organized. Simply remove everything from the counter, and then put back only those things you use at least twice a week. Find a new home for everything else — possibly in another room or in the "Give Away" or "Sell" box. The next step is to organize for efficiency.

Where to Store What

Think about the types of activities that take place in your kitchen. They might include food preparation, cooking, washing dishes, eating, opening mail, and paying bills. Then think about where in the kitchen you do these things and what tools you need to do them. Now look at nearby storage areas in each of these activity areas. Tools should be stored as close as possible to where you use them. For example, keep the toaster near the breadbox, pots and pans near the stove, and the coffeemaker near the sink.

Before you start lamenting your lack of cabinet or counter space, look at your walls and ceiling as potential storage spaces. In a restaurant kitchen, the chef's main tools are hung up rather than stored away because it's more efficient. If you have a handsome set of pots and pans, consider hanging them on a wall or from a ceiling-mounted rack. Hang knives on a magnetic bar attached to the wall, and hang cooking utensils on a pegboard or rail system with hooks mounted near your stove.

When replacing small appliances, consider ones that mount under cabinets (coffeemaker, microwave, toaster, and can opener are good examples). Another way to gain counter space is to put your microwave on a rolling cart that has shelves and drawers, where you can store cookbooks and measuring cups and spoons.

Organizing Cabinets

Take everything out of your cabinets, one cabinet at a time. Throw away plastic containers without lids, and give away those in odd sizes

make your own

Hanging Rack

What You Need:
- Old ladder 3 to 4 feet in length
- Sturdy chain
- S-hooks
- Ceiling hooks

Cut an old ladder to the desired size. Refinish to match your kitchen decor. Use chains to suspend the ladder from hooks screwed into the ceiling joists. Hang pots and pans on S-hooks dangling from the ladder.

that you never use. If you have more than enough coffee mugs or glasses, get rid of some. Discard or hold aside for donation anything else in your cabinets that's just taking up space.

The most efficient place to store dishes, glassware, and silverware is close to your dishwasher or sink, so that it's fast and easy to put them away after being washed. You also might store them near the table, so a helper can get to the table without getting in the way of the cook in the food-preparation zone. A great way to optimize storage space for dishes is to install a wire shelf unit that attaches to the underside of your existing shelving. Also, consider using cup hooks underneath shelving for hanging coffee cups and mugs. Glassware should be stored upside down to keep the inside dust-free. Stemware can be hung by using an organizing product that clips to the underside of a shelf.

kitchen essentials

Following is a list of basic kitchen tools you'll need if you're setting up a new kitchen. If you already have more than the specified number of these items, ask yourself, "How many of these do I really need?" Only you know the answer. If you have an item that is not on this list, ask yourself, "Am I using this item?" If not, you could unclutter your kitchen by paring down your kitchen tools to those that you do use and need.

For food preparation
- Cutting board
- Bread knife with serrated edge
- 8- or 10-inch chef's knife, for chopping
- Paring knife
- Vegetable peeler
- Vegetable scrubbing brush
- Egg beater
- Grater
- Kitchen shears
- Can opener
- Set of nested mixing bowls
- Rubber spatula
- Dry and liquid measuring cups (2 sets)
- Measuring spoons (2 sets)

For cooking
- Small, medium, and large pots with lids
- Extra-large pot with lid
- Small, medium, and large skillets
- Whisk
- Tongs
- Metal spatula
- Wooden spoons (2 sizes)
- Slotted spoon

For baking
- Roaster pan with rack and cover
- Two oven-to-table casserole dishes (one 1-quart and one 2-quart)
- Oblong 13 x 9 baking pan
- Two baking sheets with edges
- 9-inch pie plate
- Muffin tin with 12 cups
- Two round layer-cake pans
- 9-inch by 5-inch loaf pan
- Large cooling rack or two small racks
- Rolling pin
- Flour sifter
- Pastry blender

For serving and cleanup
- Ladle
- Colander
- Carving knife and fork
- Potato masher
- Assorted plastic containers for leftovers

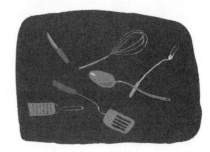

The Organized Pantry

Canned and packaged foods should be stored in a cool (below 70°F), dry area, away from light. Don't store these foods in cabinets near the oven or on shelves near the ceiling. In your food cabinets or pantry, designate specific shelves or sections of shelves for certain categories of foods; eventually, you won't even have to think about what goes where. Categories might include the following:

- Baking supplies
- Cereals and breakfast items
- Crackers and snack foods
- Canned meat and fish
- Canned soup and broth
- Canned vegetables
- Canned fruit
- Baby food
- Dry goods, such as pasta, rice, and beans
- Spices and seasoning packets
- Oils and vinegars

Start organizing by removing all foodstuffs from your cabinets. Throw away all outdated food items, and give away any others that you will never use. Line your shelves with easy-to-wipe shelf paper to keep them clean. Store opened bags of chips, cookies, rice, dry beans, and other dry goods in stackable plastic bins that let you see what's inside. One staple that should *not* be stored in your pantry is whole-wheat flour, which needs to be refrigerated to keep from going rancid. If you find spoiled or infested foods, throw out the food and clean the area with a weak solution of vinegar and water.

make your own

Pot Lid Holder

What You Need:
- Small towel rack
- Screws
- Screwdriver

Before mounting the rack, check that it will hold your lids and that it does not interfere with closing the door. Screw a small towel rack to the inside of your cabinet door. Slide the pot lid behind the rack until the handle rests on top.

To keep food items visible and accessible in your cabinets, use freestanding wire shelves, stepped organizers, or single- or double-decker turntables. Arrange cans, bottles, and boxes on shelves with the labels facing out. If you use a turntable, put tall items or extra supplies in the center of the turntable. On shelves, move older items to the front when adding newer purchases. Keep like items, such as baking supplies, easily accessible by storing them in a stack-and-slide basket.

Canned goods can pose problems in your cabinets. Because of the depth of the shelves, stacking the cans one in front of the other is just not practical. You will forget what you've got stored in the back because you can't see it. The staff at The Container Store recommend storing canned goods on a three-tiered shelf that resembles a staircase. This product is expandable to fit the width of your cabinet and provides you with a full view of your canned goods. A gravity-feed can rack is another popular choice. This rack serves as a dispenser for your canned food while allowing you to see your entire collection of cans.

Label shelves with what goes where so that other household members can put away groceries. Do this after your shelves are arranged to your satisfaction. Sometimes, in the process of organizing, you discover a better arrangement than the one you started with.

If your shelves are deep, store less frequently used items or extra staples behind those you use more frequently. Sliding drawer racks make good use of space in deep cabinets and make food items more accessible. You could also use the space in back to store infrequently used appliances. If you have a pantry with a door, use the inside of the door for additional storage by installing over-the-door wire rack shelving.

make your own

Under-Cabinet Storage

What You Need:

- Recycled food jars
- Two screws for each jar
- Power screwdriver

If you have sufficient clearance underneath your upper cabinets, you may be able to use that space for decorative and functional row storage using recycled food jars. Use two screws to fasten the lids securely to the underside of your cabinets. Fill the jars with rice, beans, peas, pasta, popcorn, tea bags, nuts, raisins, and spices. Then screw the jars to the lids.

Go through your spices. Open each jar and sniff the contents. If you don't smell anything, you won't taste anything. Discard jars and tins of outdated spices. You can buy spice organizers that attach to the wall or inside the cabinet door, or you can use a double-decker turntable or expanding, stepped shelf organizer. A "pull-down" spice organizer is available that attaches to the underside of a shelf. Store spice jars and tins with the labels facing out. Group spices that are often used together, such as nutmeg, cinnamon, and cloves, or alphabetize your spice collection. Keep taller jars together

TIME-SAVER

If you have bottles that tend to drip, wipe them well and place a plastic lid from a coffee can underneath them to prevent dripping on clean shelves.

or behind smaller jars. "File" seasoning packets face forward in a narrow box that lets you flip through them easily.

Organizing Your Refrigerator

To organize your refrigerator, start by uncluttering it. The best time to do this is the night you put out your trash or just before going to the dump. Start with the top shelf and work your way down. Open and unwrap everything, and check expiration dates. Throw out anything that is clearly bad or questionable. Discard useless bits of food and consolidate small but edible amounts of food in small containers. Also consolidate any "twos" or "threes" of things in jars or bottles.

Take note of how many foods went bad because they were buried or forgotten. Organizing your refrigerator can help to reduce the amount of spoilage and save money. Planning your food purchases can also help. See "Smart Food Shopping" on page 211 for suggestions.

Another way to reduce spoilage is to hang a magnetic erasable dry-marker board on the front of your refrigerator that lists the leftovers, cold cuts, vegetables, and other perishables inside. This list also minimizes the amount of time the refrigerator door is open, which will save energy and help keep food fresher longer.

The outside of your refrigerator may also be in need of uncluttering. Remove items that are outdated or that don't serve a purpose for you any longer. If you like to display photographs, consider purchasing inexpensive, magnetic-backed plastic frames to keep photographs flat, clean, and neatly arranged. For a really uncluttered look, consider keeping the front of your refrigerator clear of all magnets and hanging items.

For Safety's Sake

Have you ever wondered how long food stays fresh in the refrigerator? Play it safe by disposing of foods according to this recommended schedule.

Food	Dispose of If Not Used Within
Fresh fish	1–2 days
Ground meat	1–2 days
Fresh chicken or turkey	1–2 days
Fresh pork, beef, veal, lamb	3–5 days
Hot dogs, bacon	7 days if opened
Smoked breakfast links, sausage patties	7 days
Lunch meats	3–5 days if opened
Raw eggs	4–5 weeks
Boiled eggs	7 days
Egg, chicken, tuna, ham, and macaroni salads	3–5 days
Soups and stews, cooked poultry, cooked meat and meat dishes	3–4 days
Ham, fully cooked	7 days
Store-cooked convenience foods	3–4 days
Commercial mayonnaise	2 months after opening

Source: U.S. Food and Drug Administration Center for Food Safety and Applied Nutrition (www.cfsan.fda.gov/~dms/fttstore.html)

upgrade shelving

If your refrigerator has wire shelves, ask your local hardware store if they have sheets of acrylic or plastic that can be cut to fit the width and depth of your shelves. This will help to keep smaller items from tipping over and make cleaning up spills much easier. Don't forget to bring measurements with you.

Now that your refrigerator is uncluttered, organize it. The first thing to decide is what to store where. The meat/deli tray is the coldest spot in your refrigerator — do use it to store all deli meats and frozen meats that you want to thaw in the refrigerator.

The crisper drawer is designed to seal tightly to keep in humidity. Storing vegetables in the crisper will help them to retain moisture. Lettuce will stay fresher if you wash it, shake off the leaves, wrap them in a paper towel, and store them in a heavy-duty, resealable plastic bag; squeeze out air as you close the bag. Other vegetables best stored in plastic bags are broccoli, carrots, cauliflower, celery, green beans, and scallions.

Washing and storing these vegetables in a sealed plastic bag will not only help them last longer but also keep your crisper cleaner. As long as the food inside remains fresh until used, the plastic bags can be washed and reused.

To store peppers, eggplant, summer squash, beets, cabbage, and mushrooms, use a loose plastic covering and place them in the crisper.

Store fresh herbs unwashed and loosely wrapped in the crisper.

Some vegetables should *not* be stored in the refrigerator. Cold air destroys the flavor of cucumbers; instead, dip them in cold water and store in a cool, dry place. If you want to serve them cold, chill just before serving. Potatoes should not be stored in the refrigerator because the starch breaks down quickly. If you bake a potato that has been refrigerated, it will be mushy. Potatoes, winter squash, dry garlic, gingerroot, and mature onions are best stored in a cool, dry place.

Most fruits are best stored at room temperature until they ripen. This includes apples, melons, pears, plums, avocados, peaches, and pineapples. You can hasten ripening by putting fruit in a paper bag. Do not wash grapes and berries until you are ready to eat them; the dusty stuff on them is a preservative. Refrigerate grapes and berries in a plastic bag with perforated holes or covered loosely with plastic wrap. Never refrigerate tomatoes; store in a cool, dry place and eat when ripened. Bananas should be hung to encourage proper ripening. Ripened fruits (except bananas) and cut fruit should be refrigerated to extend their life. Citrus fruits are best stored at room temperature because they have a waxy coating that seals in moisture.

Load up the door of your refrigerator with bottled and jarred foods. Group like items together. You might, for example, use one door shelf for jams, jellies and syrups, and another shelf for condiments. Eggs should not be stored in the door. Every time the door is opened, the eggs are exposed to oxygen, which causes them to deteriorate faster. To keep eggs fresh longer, keep them in their cartons on a shelf, away from the door.

Many helpful refrigerator organization products are available. A turntable on one or more shelves helps prevent perishables from being forgotten and makes food items more accessible. You can also use a tray that pulls out.

Another way to make items more accessible is to store similar foods, such as cheeses, in a clear plastic bin (with or without lid) that you can pull out of the refrigerator. This is also a great way to contain jarred and bottled foods that don't fit on the door shelves.

For neat and uncluttered storage of leftovers, invest in a supply of stackable glass or plastic food storage containers. Square containers make more efficient use of space than round containers, and clear plastic allows you to take a quick visual inventory. It's also a good idea to label and date containers — simply write with a marker on a piece of masking tape. Always store leftovers in the same place in your refrigerator, and see what you have there every day to reduce the amount of food that goes to waste. Do not refrigerate opened cans of foods; transfer the leftover contents to a plastic or glass container.

If you have lots of hungry mouths in your house, consider keeping one large container labeled "Snacks" on a lower shelf. Use it to store hard-boiled eggs, string cheese, leftover chicken or pizza, and other perishable snacks.

You can also buy a container that neatly stores and dispenses up to twelve cans of soda and a two-liter bottle holder that clips to the underside of a shelf.

Be sure not to overpack your refrigerator. Cool air must circulate to keep food from spoiling prematurely.

Organizing Your Freezer

Although frozen foods will keep indefinitely at 0°F, their quality will deteriorate over time. Take a look at everything in your freezer. Throw out meats that are covered with a thick layer of frost, anything you cannot identify, and anything that's been in there for longer than one year.

Many freezer units have little or no shelving, which makes it difficult to organize frozen foods. You can create your own shelving by using coated wire racks or stackable wire baskets. Store together similar items, such as vegetables, meats, poultry, fish and shellfish, breads, and desserts, to make retrieval and inventory easier.

When you buy meat, store the newest purchases behind or under previous purchases so that you use the food that's been there longest first. Label and date leftovers and repackaged meats. Store in the freezer door items that require frequent access, including frozen juice concentrates, frozen breakfast items, frozen confections, and coffee beans.

Organizing is a matter of making better use of the space you have.

— Melinda Louise, Organize It

Organizing Kitchen Drawers

In your kitchen, you probably have one or two drawers containing silverware and other cutlery and at least one junk drawer. You may be fortunate enough to have additional drawers for dish towels, potholders, and other items. Go through the drawers one at a time.

When organizing, start with your silverware drawer. Take out the cutlery tray (you do have one, right?) and everything else in there. Take everything out of the cutlery tray, then put back only the knives, forks and spoons. Put the cutlery tray back in the drawer. Look at how much room you have left in the drawer, and look at the remaining items to go back into it. Which of them are essential in your kitchen? Put those items in the front of the drawer for easy access. What's left? Is there anything that was just taking up space in the drawer? Give yourself permission to get rid of it. Put it in a box labeled "Donate."

There's nothing wrong with having a junk drawer. Where else can you store those odds and ends you need from time to time? But some of what ends up in the junk drawer really *is* junk, such as unfixable items, pens that don't work, expired coupons, and a piece to a game you sold at a garage sale five years ago. Take everything out of your junk drawer and sort it into two piles: what you definitely need and use, and what's just taking up space. If you can't decide which pile an item belongs in, be honest with yourself. Is it really worth keeping?

Before you put items back into your junk drawer, think about how you can organize the contents by keeping similar items together. An

For Simplicity's Sake

Store all outdoor table necessities together in one cabinet or in a plastic storage container that you can keep on or carry out to the porch. Include paper plates, napkins, plastic cups and flatware, tablecloth, citronella candles, and bug repellent.

old cutlery tray might work well for organizing melon ballers, olive forks, cheese knives, and serving spoons or for containing pens and pencils in your junk drawer. Adjustable drawer dividers are another option.

You may have organizing "products" right at your fingertips. Checkbook boxes are great for containing small items, such as matches or batteries. Use resealable plastic storage bags to store all kinds of small things that you need only occasionally, such as cookie cutters or birthday candles. Use rubber bands or twist ties to keep together sets of things like fondue forks, basting pins, chopsticks, and kebab skewers.

Throw out worn potholders and stained dishtowels or convert to dust rags, but *only* if you need more dust rags. Keep only as many of these items as you need. If you like to put out a clean towel each day and you do laundry once a week, seven to ten towels should be plenty.

Organizing Under the Kitchen Sink

Install sliding wire bins or a turntable under the kitchen sink to provide easier access to kitchen cleaning items, such as dishwashing detergent, scouring powder, steel wool pads, and sponges. If you keep your kitchen trashcan under the sink or close by, this is the perfect place to store trash bags.

If you have small children, be cautious about storing cleaning agents under the sink, even if you use child safety locks on the doors. Eventually, children learn how to get around these safety measures, and the results could be disastrous.

Organizing Wraps and Bags

There's probably a place in your kitchen — one section of your counter, perhaps — where you tend to use foil, plastic wrap, freezer bags, and other food wraps. Store these food wraps close to where you use them, ideally at or close to counter height. Wall-mount dispensers for various kitchen wraps are available; however, they don't hold all types of food wraps. The same goes for dispensers that mount inside cabinet doors. You'll still have to find a place for sandwich and freezer bags, for example.

A great product for organizing food wraps is a set of sliding wire baskets that you can place in a cabinet above or below your counter. Each basket generally holds up to four boxes of food wraps. Try to store food wraps and plastic containers for leftovers close together, since these products are often used for the same purpose.

A nifty place to store trash bags is at the bottom of the trash can or recycling bin. That way, you always have a new bag handy. And the unused bags don't take up room in your cabinets.

Get out of the habit of saving every plastic bag that you bring home from the grocery store. Think about how many you really need, and for what. See if you can survive with about ten. Store them where you are most likely to use them. Special dispensers that mount on the wall are available, or you can make your own storage container from an empty oatmeal or coffee can with lid, empty tissue box, or plastic milk or water jug. (See the simple instructions below.) Take any unneeded grocery bags back to the store for recycling.

make your own

Plastic Bag Dispenser

What You Need:
- One-gallon plastic milk jug, large oatmeal container, coffee can with lid, *or* empty tissue box
- Hook (optional)
- Scissors

Cut a 3-inch hole in the side of the container. Stuff plastic shopping bags into it one at a time; if you do this, you can almost always pull them out one at a time. Set the container on a shelf or hang it from a hook.

Organizing Cookbooks and Recipes

Ideally, your cookbooks should not take up space on your counter. If you don't have shelves in your kitchen, consider using the top of your refrigerator for storing cookbooks between two bookends or in your pantry.

While you're organizing your kitchen, go through your cookbooks. Are there any you never use or don't like? If you've been cooking for a long time, your style of cooking and level of expertise may have changed over the years. Get rid of any cookbooks that don't fit your new style of cooking or degree of know-how. You may be able to sell them at a secondhand bookstore and get store credit or cash in exchange.

If you have a lot of cookbooks, group them by category or alphabetize them by title or author. If you have just a few cookbooks, perhaps arrange them by height, from tallest to shortest.

Whereas organizing cookbooks is pretty simple, organizing loose recipes can be a challenge. The traditional method of organizing recipes is a recipe card box with alphabetical or cookbook-style dividers. This works well if you don't mind transcribing new recipes onto cards. The number of recipes you can save, however, is limited by the size of the box.

A less limiting and less labor-intensive method of storing loose recipes is to keep them in a three-ring binder with plastic photograph album sleeves. Simply insert recipes from various sources and in various formats. You may have to tape index cards in to keep them from slipping.

The three-ring binder allows you to create sections by adding divider tabs similar to those in store-bought cookbooks. You might even consider keeping all untested recipes together in one section. Start by creating one book of your favorite recipes. Eventually, you may wish to create several binders for different types of recipes, such as quick and easy dinners, holidays, or family recipes. If you use a computer to type and print out your recipes, you could easily create copies of your cookbooks to give as gifts for weddings, housewarmings, or other special occasions.

Another way to store recipes is on your computer. You can create an electronic folder for recipes and then create subfolders for different types of recipes, such as appetizers or desserts. You can easily print them on demand when someone asks you for a copy, and your paperless "cookbook" takes up no space in your kitchen!

Compact discs are another paperless source of searchable recipes. You can even subscribe to one of many general and special interest e-mail newsletters available for free from numerous Web sites such as FabulousFoods.com, Cooking.com, and 30DayGourmet.com.

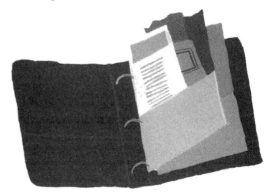

Don't forget to go through your self-assembled cookbooks, whether three-ring binders or computer file folders, from time to time and discard recipes that you didn't enjoy.

The Internet is a great source for recipes. You can cut and paste them into your word-processing program and store them in electronic folders. One of the most popular food-related Web sites is Allrecipes.com, a worldwide community cookbook that contains twenty-three chapters covering appetizers to vegetarian recipes. At this site, you can search for recipes by ingredient or category, create a personal recipe box, and make a shopping list for your weekly meal plan.

The Dining Room

A hutch in the dining room is the best place to store formal china, crystal and silverware, tablecloths and other linens, placemats, infrequently used serving dishes, and special occasion accoutrements for your table, such as candlesticks. If you don't have a hutch or china closet, store these items in an out-of-the-way spot in your kitchen.

Keep good china free of dust by using special covers or dishtowels. But if your dining room storage is limited and you never use certain items, remove these things from your house or put them in long-term storage to free up some space.

To prevent sterling silver items from tarnishing, use them often. Tarnish-retarding storage chests and wraps for silver flatware are available. Less frequently used pieces may be tightly covered with plastic wrap or placed in a

resealable plastic bag to retard tarnishing. "Dip and shine" polishes are not recommended for finely engraved silver, as they tend to lighten the darker pattern areas that form part of the design. Polish silver periodically with good silver polish, and wash in hot soapy water before drying and putting away.

Discourage dumping of mail, books, and backpacks on the kitchen or dining room table by keeping it set with a tablecloth and place settings. This trick also reduces the amount of storage space you need for dishes and glassware. If you have children, have them reset the table each night.

For Simplicity's Sake

To organize and store holiday tablecloths, hang an over-the-door towel rod on the inside of your linen closet. Keep table linens from creasing by padding the rods with paper towel tubes; slice the tubes lengthwise and roll them over the rod.

CHAPTER 7

FAMILY ROOM

Whether you call it a family room or the living room, this is where you relax with your family and entertain guests. It may also double as a playroom or office. You might not mind the living room looking "lived-in," but it's frustrating to clear the coffee table for the umpteenth time in a week or to trip over things on the floor. The key to organizing the family room can be summed up in one word: contain.

General Room Organization

When decorating, keep it simple. The less you have out, the less you have to keep tidy. Unclutter your walls. Take down everything and put back only what you love in locations where you can enjoy looking at them. Do the same with knickknacks and collections on shelves.

Make clutter "invisible." No, this isn't a magic trick, but the right kind of storage does seem to make clutter disappear. Wire baskets tend to "disappear" into the background, and wicker baskets blend nicely with almost any decor. Store small, loose items, such as playing cards and pens, in a pretty bowl or woven basket set high enough on a shelf that you can't see the contents. Hide a corner office or playroom area behind decorative screens.

When buying furniture for your family room, look for pieces that are functional as well as comfortable and attractive. A chest-style coffee table, for example, doubles as a storage unit.

A Place for Everything

The biggest reasons why things don't get put away are that there's no place to put them or it's difficult to put them in their place. Look around your family room. Do the things on your coffee table belong there? Or did they get left there because they have no home?

Clear everything off your coffee table and put back only what belongs there. This may be coasters, or nothing at all. Find a convenient storage place for everything else, and get in the habit of returning these things to their homes. Keep remote controls in a basket on your coffee table, along with the television listings guide. Or attach them to their respective appliances with adhesive material (hook-and-loop fastener works well) and store the guide on top of the television set. Put a wastebasket in the family room to reduce littering. Create a home for pet toys and teach your pets where to find them. You might even want to teach them to put their toys away!

You might not need to find a place for *everything* in your family room. Stray items, such as coats, backpacks, toys, and school papers, may belong in another room. At the end of each day, or when visitors show up unexpectedly, pick up what needs to go somewhere else and put it in a "go to" box or basket near the door. Make it a weekly task to empty the "go to" box. You might also want to designate a holding place for rented movies and library books that need to be returned.

Think about all the activities that take place in your living area. Ideally, everything you need to perform these activities should be close at hand. For example, if you always clip coupons in the family room, store a pair of

TIME-SAVER

Storing books so that the spines are flush with the edge of the shelf prevents dust from collecting on the shelf edges, which means you'll need to dust less frequently.

60

scissors in the drawer of an end table or in a lidded box that fits under the sofa. You could also keep paper and pencil handy for jotting down notes or ideas.

The space under your sofa is great for hiding all kinds of things: games, puzzles, telephone books, photo albums, linens for the pull-out sofa mattress, or extra leaves for your dining room table. You might also use this space to store a collapsible tray for snacks or entertaining. If you store lots of small items under your sofa, place them on the lid of an old copy paper box for easy access.

Books, Books, Books

Are your bookshelves overflowing? You might think that the solution is to buy more bookcases or put up more shelves, and you might be right. But before you do that, go through your books shelf by shelf to see if you could free up space by giving some away or selling them.

Have you ever questioned why you hold on to every book that comes into your possession? Perhaps you love books and take pleasure in your growing library. But maybe you just got in the habit of shelving books, and now that you think about it, you'd be happy to sell some books to the used bookstore in exchange for cash or credit. Remember, if you donate or sell a book and miss it later, it's generally pretty easy to get another copy, even if it means borrowing it from the library.

Organize your books into categories, such as fiction, nonfiction, reference, and children's. In libraries and bookstores, fiction is arranged alphabetically by author. You could also organize by genre, such as historical fiction, romance, or mystery. Nonfiction books are typically organ-

ized by subject: for example, gardening, parenting, or travel. If you have an extensive collection of nonfiction books, alphabetize by author within subject. Creating categories makes it easy to find books and even easier to return them to their proper spot. Keep children's books on the lower shelves or in bookcases in their rooms. If your bookshelves are overflowing but you have no room to add shelves, consider storing books horizontally rather than vertically. You may be able to fit more books on a shelf this way. The down side is that it's harder to find books and take them off the shelves.

Audio and Video Storage

Numerous products are available for organizing your videotapes, DVDs, CDs, and cassettes. It's worth doing a little research to find a system that's best suited to your space. Start by counting up your videotapes, DVDs, CDs, and cassettes so that you can select a system that will accommodate your existing collection and give you room to expand. Then look at your space and think about what storage system will work best.

You may find that it's simplest to store videotapes and CDs on shelves. Organize videotapes alphabetically by title or by genre, such as action, children's, comedy, drama, and suspense.

UNCLUTTER YOUR DECOR

Use the largest coffee table possible and eliminate end tables. Replace end-table lamps with swing-away wall lamps, which will eliminate clutter. They are available in all price ranges. For maximum versatility, choose lamps with a three-way switch. Simplify "the box" (the top, bottom, and sides of the room) by painting ceiling and walls the same color. Note that to achieve the illusion of the same color and to compensate for the effects of lighting, you'll need to paint the ceiling two shades lighter than the walls if the wall color is medium to dark. Group together collections of similar items, such as candlesticks and figurines, on shelves or on pretty trays. Paintings, framed photographs, and other wall hangings that are too small to stand alone look more stylish and impressive in groups.

—*Barbara Landsman, Dial-a-Decorator*

Organize CDs by such categories as jazz, classical, rock, and '70s, and then alphabetically by artist. Use separate shelves or sections of shelves for different genres or categories. Store videotapes and CDs like books — vertically, with the spines facing out — and use bookends to keep sections upright. Professional organizer Sheila Delson recommends storing VHS videotapes in 11 x 8 x 4½-inch photo boxes, which hold up to ten videos per box. Then simply assign each box a number, and make an index list of the contents by title. This makes access easier and saves time when looking for that one special title. You can also purchase shelving units that are specially designed for multimedia storage.

If you have space in a cabinet near your television or stereo, create a flip file for DVDs or compact discs by using narrow boxes or wire baskets. Stack-and-slide baskets are especially convenient. Store DVDs and CDs in their original cases. Organize alphabetically by title, or use separate boxes or baskets for different types of music or movies. If you like to take your music with you when you travel, you might prefer to remove CDs from their jewel cases and store them in a zippered carrying case with see-through pockets. Store audiocassettes in specially designed holders.

If your storage space is limited, consider CD and DVD organizers that mount to the wall, or mount shelves for this purpose. You can also buy over-the-door video racks that work well if you have a closet in your family room.

When buying a freestanding storage unit, match the color of the unit to the color of your

make your own

CD Storage

What You Need:
- Old dresser
- Plexiglas *or* fiberboard

Ever wonder what to do with that old dresser? Transform it into a unique CD library. Simply remove the drawers, then make shelves using Plexiglas or fiberboard. Store frequently used CDs in front and less frequently used CDs on the back of the shelves.

stereo components for a uniform, uncluttered look. Avoid CD towers with individual, preset slots; they can be difficult to reorganize when you buy new CDs. If your collection is alphabetized by artist, for example, you'll have to rearrange the entire collection to make space for a new CD in the appropriate slot.

Magazines, Newspapers, and Catalogs

Don't feel that you must catch up on back issues of magazines. Keep the latest issue only, and recycle or donate the rest. In fact, getting rid of back issues may make you feel good because you feel "all caught up" on your reading. Donate magazines to your local gym, a nearby hospital, doctor's office, nursing home, hospice, or wherever people are looking for something to help them pass the time. Before doing this, however, protect your privacy by clipping out the mailing label with your name and address.

Following are some tips for keeping magazines from piling up in the future.

• **Cancel subscriptions to publications you aren't reading.** If you haven't read the last three issues of a magazine, consider canceling your subscription. Maybe you're not as interested in the subject as you were when you subscribed, or maybe you don't have the time

to read it right now. Did you know that you can usually get a refund for the unused portion of magazine subscriptions? If you want to subscribe again in the future, you can respond to one of the offers you are sure to receive.

• **Save only the articles, not the whole magazine.** If you tend to do a lot of reading all at once, scan the table of contents and highlight the article you wish to read. Better yet, tear out those articles, put them in a "To Read" folder or a binder with magnetic photo album sleeves, and place the folder in a basket or rack near your favorite chair, at your bedside, or wherever you most often do your reading. If you tend to read in the bathroom, put a magazine rack in there. Or place reading material in a folder in your briefcase for something to do when you're waiting at the doctor's office, commuting via public transportation, or traveling. By saving only selected articles, you can reduce your reading pile by half or more.

• **Set aside a regular reading time.** If you're having trouble keeping up with your reading, but you don't want to cancel a subscription, set aside some time every day for

old news

Is your coffee table littered with old newspapers? Maybe you have a place to put them (a recycling bin in your garage, perhaps, or a basket near your woodstove), but it's not convenient to take them there every day. Create a temporary home for old newspapers where they can be stored after reading — a basket with a handle or a large tote bag might work well. When the basket or bag gets full, carry it where it needs to go.

reading. Do some recreational reading during your lunch break, try turning off the television at 9 P.M. or not turning it on until then, or read while riding your stationary bicycle.

• **Think twice before saving articles.** Can you look up the information elsewhere if you need it in the future? If you do save articles, file them where you are most likely to look for them. For more tips on creating filing systems, see page 97.

• **Toss the old with the new.** Get in the habit of tossing out the old issue when the new issue arrives. Better yet, recycle it as soon as you're done reading it.

• **Don't sign up for a subscription because of a sweepstakes.** Ordering does not increase your chances of winning. By law, all entries received must be included in the sweepstakes. You are not required to purchase anything.

Set up one rack, basket, or box for catalogs and one for magazines. If you prefer to keep magazines and catalogs together, keep all catalogs in front and all magazines in back so that you don't have to rummage through every-

RACK 'EM UP

The biggest mistake you can make in storing magazines and catalogs is to store them lying flat. Stand them up so you can flip through them easily and have them at your fingertips. Alphabetize them or group them into categories. This system allows you to find and replace a magazine or catalog with the latest edition in only a few seconds.

—Nancy Black, Organization Plus

thing to find what you're looking for. If you refer often to your catalogs and magazines, arrange them alphabetically or by subject, such as children's items, women's clothing, and sportswear.

When catalogs arrive, decide which ones you want to keep and immediately put them in the catalog box or basket. If you didn't request a catalog or have no interest in it, put it in the recycling box right away. If you have favorite catalogs, limit yourself to saving one issue at a time. When the new one arrives, throw out the old one, even if you haven't yet looked at it; it's outdated. If you are browsing through a catalog and see something you might like to buy in the near future, tear out the page, along with the order form and back cover (the order-takers always ask for the source code on the back of your catalog). Put only these pages in your tickler file (see page 157). Recycle the rest of the catalog.

If you need to save specific catalogs as resources for work, create folders for them in your filing cabinet. If necessary, categorize them to make it easier to find them in the future. Save only the most current version of the catalog. If you prefer to keep catalogs in plain sight or if they are too bulky to store in a file folder, store them in labeled acrylic magazine holders, which are inexpensive and available at office supply stores.

Organizing Photographs

There are only two ways to avoid photograph clutter: Don't take any photographs, or organize photographs immediately after developing. Not taking photographs probably isn't an option though you might impose a moratorium on picture-taking until you at least *start* organizing the photographs you have.

When you have film developed, order doubles only if you have a definite need for them. If the second set of prints is offered for free and you don't need them, decline the offer. You don't have to take them just because they're free. If you're offered a choice between a free second set of prints and free film, take the film. It may not be the brand you usually buy, but the quality may be identical. If you requested double prints, separate the first and second sets when you get them. Put the first set of prints directly into your photo album or photo boxes, and do whatever you planned to do with the second set — mail it to a friend right away, for example.

Save only good photographs. Throw away the ones that didn't come out right or are very similar to other, better photographs. Take bad photos back to the developer for credit. Some developers give credit for any photographs you don't like; look for a developer with this policy if you want to save some money.

If you have a computer, take photo processing to the next level: Have your developer deliver your photographs by e-mail or on a disk. Getting your photographs electronically eliminates having to file anything and allows you to share photos easily with friends and family via your Web site or e-mail.

When you need to replace your camera, consider getting a digital camera that allows you to upload and store images on your computer. To organize photographs on your hard drive, create a master file for digital images and subfolders for each set of photographs you take: for example, "Summer Vacation 2002" or "Tommy's Kindergarten Graduation." If you want prints, you can print them on your own color printer using special photograph paper, or send them to the Web site of a company that will "develop" them.

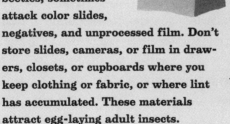

BEWARE OF BUGS

Insects, such as carpet beetles, sometimes attack color slides, negatives, and unprocessed film. Don't store slides, cameras, or film in drawers, closets, or cupboards where you keep clothing or fabric, or where lint has accumulated. These materials attract egg-laying adult insects.

—*Courtesy Eastman Kodak Company*

One Challenge . . .

I have years and years of loose photographs that I want to organize, but honestly, I get overwhelmed just thinking about where to start.

Three Solutions

1 FROM HELEN VOLK, BEYOND CLUTTER: Start by dividing photos into manageable segments. Think about your life and how you can divide it into three or four huge time periods or events, such as college days, wedding, or early married years. Sort photos, put them into separate boxes, and label them. If you do nothing else, at least you know what box to look in for a particular photo. The next step is to take one box and further sort the contents into smaller divisions until you get them down to shoe box size, so you can organize them. The nice thing about using shoe boxes as holding boxes is that you can just grab one and do your organizing anywhere.

2 FROM TREVA BERENDS, THE ORGANIZING SPECIALISTS: Start by organizing your most current photos and resolve to stay current from this point forward. Worry about the past later. When you have time, start with one particular event, time frame, or family member. Find all related photos and organize them. Choose the method of storage that works for you — photo boxes, albums, memory scrapbooks, or scanning into your computer.

3 FROM JUDY WARMINGTON, WOMAN TIME MANAGEMENT: Forget about trying to organize photographs chronologically. Organize instead by people or events, such as family vacations or holidays. Sort photographs by using labeled paper bags that have been cut down to about six inches high. Buy albums after sorting because you'll have a better idea of how many you need. Buy enough pages so that you can add to your albums if necessary. Make an appointment to start your photograph-organizing project. Decide how much time you can spend at any given session. When your time is up, put the project away and schedule another appointment.

The simplest way to organize and store recent photographs is chronologically, in a photo box with dividers to separate sections. You can also use shoeboxes and buy indexed dividers from an office supply store. It's best to store photographs on an open bookshelf, in a closet, or under your bed. Make sure the location is dark and does not get warmer than 75°F; otherwise the photos might be damaged.

Schedule some time each week to sort and organize photographs until you are caught up to date. Save only the best photographs; throw out the rest. Mail duplicates to a friend or family member, along with a quick greeting, or just throw them away. Do something fun with doubles of your favorite photos: Have them imprinted on a coffee mug, T-shirt, or computer mouse pad and give personalized gifts to your favorite people.

Whether you use albums or boxes to organize your photos, try to get them all in the same size for easy storage. Start a new album or box for each new child or grandchild. Consider putting formal portraits (baby, school, wedding, and family) in a family album.

When organizing older photographs, label each one with the name of the subject, date, location, and other details that you might not remember ten or twenty years from now. Use a soft-tipped, smudge-free marker to write on the back of the photo, or write on a piece of masking tape and affix to the back.

To preserve your most treasured memories, use archival photo boxes or archival pages. To keep negatives clean, use plastic sleeves or negative envelopes. Label them and store with your photographs. Or create an album for negative storage: Use three-hole punched negative sleeves, label with the month and year or event, and file them chronologically. Protect negatives from light, heat, and high humidity in storage.

Crafts Storage

Unless you have a room or area dedicated to sewing, quilting, or other crafts, you may gravitate to the family room to work on craft projects. If that's the case, the family room may be the ideal place to store your craft tools and supplies. Following are some tips for storing your craft supplies.

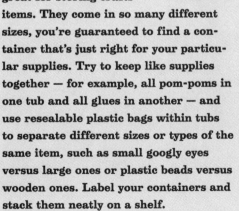

TUBS ARE TOPS

Stackable, clear plastic tubs with lids are great for storing crafts items. They come in so many different sizes, you're guaranteed to find a container that's just right for your particular supplies. Try to keep like supplies together — for example, all pom-poms in one tub and all glues in another — and use resealable plastic bags within tubs to separate different sizes or types of the same item, such as small googly eyes versus large ones or plastic beads versus wooden ones. Label your containers and stack them neatly on a shelf.

—*Ramona Creel, OnlineOrganizing.com*

- **Hang it.** If you have a closet in the family room, hang an over-the-door-style shoe bag with clear plastic pockets on the inside of the door. Use the pockets for storing scissors, paintbrushes, bottles or tubes of paint, spools of thread, and other tools and supplies.

- **Shelve it.** Store craft supplies with craft books on your bookshelves. Find a matching set of open tin boxes, hat boxes, or rectangular woven baskets with cloth liners. Use separate containers to hold different types of tools and supplies. Clear compartment boxes allow you to sort and organize small notions, such as buttons and beads, within each container, or you can use resealable plastic bags.

- **Stow it.** Can you make some storage room in a cabinet? Plastic multidrawer organizers are ideal for holding sewing and craft supplies. Many crafters use tackle boxes to store small, loose items such as beads. For larger items, clear plastic boxes that stack also work well, as do labeled shoeboxes. Old lunch boxes are stackable, sturdy enough to hold metal tools, and portable. Look for lunch boxes at garage sales and thrift stores.

- **Hide it.** You may be able to hide materials and supplies under the sofa in a flat, plastic storage box, or in a large storage trunk that doubles as your coffee table. Keep material on one side and supplies on the other.

- **Tote it.** If you can't create storage space for your crafts in your family room (or wherever you work on crafting projects), invest in a portable chest or rolling bin with drawers that you can keep elsewhere and bring out when you need it. A wheeled suitcase might also do

make your own

Crafts Center

Debbie Williams of Let's Get It Together says you can create a crafts center anywhere. Use a freestanding clothes closet to store craft or sewing supplies and works in progress. For a work surface, use a card table or metal banquet table that can be stored under the sofa or a bed when not in use. Disguise your workspace with a folding screen.

the trick. You could use plastic, lidded containers or even resealable plastic bags to keep like items together inside the suitcase. Large canvas tote bags are another option for separating, storing, and carrying things such as yarn and fabric scraps.

There are lots of ready-made solutions for organizing, storing, and carrying crafts tools and supplies. Look for these products at the back of crafts magazines, in mail-order catalogs dedicated to organization products, and through Internet retailers. You may even have the perfect organizing "product" right under your roof. Look around for unused boxes, bags, and other containers that may be perfectly suited to your needs.

CHAPTER 8

BEDROOM

If all you did in your bedroom was sleep, you could make your room look neat and organized just by making your bed. But you probably also use the bedroom to get dressed, watch television, read, play with your kids, or do craftwork. The solution is not to change the way you live but, rather, to implement organizing strategies that will create an uncluttered, restful environment that you enjoy.

Uncluttering Closets

Do you need more closet space for clothes? Create space by removing clothing items you don't wear because they don't fit, don't look good on you, need mending, or are out of season.

The best way to unclutter your closet is to pull *everything* out and put back only what you wear on a regular basis. Try on everything else. If the clothes make you look and feel good, keep them. If not, put them in a pile to give away, donate, or sell. Why keep clothes that don't make you feel good about yourself?

If you have clothes that no longer fit, you have two choices. You can donate or sell them, or store them elsewhere until they do fit again — or until you're ready to let go of them. Maybe once another season or year has passed

without wearing these clothes, you'll come to accept the fact that they no longer serve a purpose in your life.

What's the worst possible thing that could happen if you got rid of clothes you aren't wearing? Let's say, for example, that you have a whole wardrobe full of size eight clothing, but you've been a size twelve for the past five years. If you gave away all of your size eight clothing and then did get back into the smaller size, the worst that could happen is that you would have to buy a new wardrobe. But wouldn't that be a great way to reward yourself for losing weight? You might have to buy new clothes anyway, if your clothes are no longer stylish or your tastes have changed. If it seems wasteful to get rid of perfectly good suits and whatever, think of it this way: They're going to waste hanging in your closet. Give away, donate, or sell clothes now, while they can be worn and appreciated by someone else.

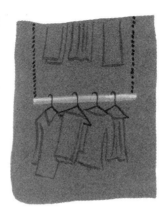

If you have clothes that need mending, look at each item and decide whether it's worth repairing. Do you still like it? Is it still in style? Put clothing you decide to repair in a bag or box to be delivered to your sewing place or to a tailor. Discard all other items, and make a note to yourself if you need to replace an item.

Simplify your wardrobe. How many outfits do you really need for dirty work like gardening or painting? Consider keeping only pieces that you can mix and match with other pieces. And pare down to only colors that really compliment your complexion. Most people look best in either brown and warm (yellow, red, orange, gold) tones or black and cool (pink, blue, green, silver) tones. If you don't know which category you fit into, notice what colors you are wearing when someone says, "You look very nice today." They may be reacting more strongly to the color than to the outfit itself.

Organizing Closets

Once you've uncluttered your closet and freed up some space, your next goal is to make everything visible and accessible. If a single clothes rod will suffice for hanging all of your clothes, great. But if your clothes are jammed together tightly, it's difficult to find things, let alone put them away.

A simple fix is to install a second rod a couple of feet below your existing rod to create hanging space for shorter items, such as shirts or blouses. You can buy a rod that mounts to the back wall, or you can hang a second rod from the first. To do this, you'll need a piece of PVC pipe, a sturdy chain, and two S-hooks. Cut the pipe to the desired length — perhaps half the length of the main rod. Thread the chain through the pipe, leaving enough length at either end for hanging. Attach the chain ends to the S-hooks and the S-hooks to the existing rod.

Installing a second rod maximizes existing space, which is the key to organizing your closet. Just be sure to allow room for longer hanging items, too.

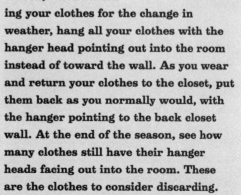

THE HANGER TRICK

At the start of each season, when switching your clothes for the change in weather, hang all your clothes with the hanger head pointing out into the room instead of toward the wall. As you wear and return your clothes to the closet, put them back as you normally would, with the hanger pointing to the back closet wall. At the end of the season, see how many clothes still have their hanger heads facing out into the room. These are the clothes to consider discarding.

—Kim Cosentino, The De-Clutter Box, Inc.

Sort and hang similar clothing together. For example, hang all of your jackets together, and do the same for pants, skirts, dresses, and blouses. Or you might prefer to create separate sections for hanging casual, work, and dressy clothes. If you really want to get organized, use prelabeled rod dividers to keep groups separate. You might even arrange clothes within groups by color, from light to dark.

Don't overthink the grouping decision. Choose categories that make sense to you; you can always rearrange them later. Do hang the clothes you wear most often where they are easy to see and reach when you open the door. Also, hang things so that the fronts are facing you. It keeps your closet neater when everything is hanging in the same direction and makes it easier to identify items at a glance.

Use only plastic, wooden, or padded hangers. Wire hangers do not properly support clothes and often bend or sag, causing creases in your clothes and a messy-looking closet. Use plastic hangers to color-code clothing groups. For example, you can use three colors to divide clothes into casual, work, and dressy. To keep jackets and shirts from twisting and sliding off hangers, always close the first few buttons.

Do you share a closet with one or more people? Since space is at a premium, weeding out what you don't wear is a critical first step. Then sort clothes into sections for each person. Store extra hangers between groupings. Or assign hangers of a different color to visually separate one person's section from another.

If your closet space is very limited, try using tiered hangers that allow you to hang multiple skirts and slacks together. Hanging swing-out trouser racks also save space.

Closet-organizing products provide affordable, do-it-yourself solutions that maximize existing space and make it easier to stay organized. You'll find closet organizer kits, individual organizing products, and custom-designed solutions in specialized mail-order catalogs, at most home centers, in the housewares section at large department stores, and at on-line organizing stores.

Some specialized organizing stores offer free closet and space planning service. Simply bring your closet measurements to the retail store, or request a consultation through an on-line store or by telephone. A closet organization expert will design a system of ventilated wire shelving and drawers to suit your space and needs. Another option is to hire a professional closet design company to come to your home. Look in the Yellow Pages under "Closets and Closet Accessories."

Clothes that you'll wear again before laundering, such as pajamas, don't have to be hung

TIME-SAVER

When you take an item out of your closet, remove it from its hanger and then place the empty hanger at one end of your clothes rod. Keeping empty hangers together makes it easy to find a hanger when you need one and keeps your closet looking neater.

For Simplicity's Sake

Store panty hose in a hanging shoe bag with clear plastic pouches. Organize by color and type, such as knee-highs, dress sheers, and tights. This system works beautifully for organizing socks too. You don't even have to fold them!

up or put in a drawer after wearing; they need to be aired. But instead of leaving them on your bed or over a chair, find a place in your bedroom where you can screw in a couple of hooks or pegs — maybe on the back of your bedroom door or inside a closet door. A free-standing coat rack works well too.

Hang a nylon bag on a hook in your closet or behind a door to hold items that need to go the dry cleaner. Hang another bag for panty-hose and other delicate items that require hand washing. This simple system will help to ensure that special-care items don't accidentally end up with the regular wash.

Accessories

Now it's time to do with your accessories what you did with your clothes: weed out the things that are only taking up closet space. If you can't bring yourself to let go of them, at least remove them from your closet. Box them up and store them with your out-of-season clothing.

If you have only one shelf or no shelves in your closet, you may be able to make use of the space above the clothes rod. Install one or more shelves for storing things like pocket-books, hats, and bulky sweaters. Inexpensive, clip-on shelf dividers help to keep items separated. You might also use same-size clear plastic bins or wire baskets to contain like items. Plain cardboard boxes work fine too, as long as you label the boxes with what's inside.

An alternative to shelving is an organizing product with drawers, such as a sturdy cardboard dresser, roll-away wire bin organizer, or hanging garment bag with shelves. These work well if you lack dresser space but your closet is big enough to accommodate them.

How you store accessories depends on your storage space and personal preferences. Following are some suggestions.

Hats and Caps. Caps can be stacked or hung from hooks or pegs on the back of your closet door or along one wall. An accordion-style rack allows you to hang several caps neatly. Hang brimmed hats on a peg, or place them directly on a shelf. If you don't wear them often, protect hats from dust by storing them in a box. Or insert a hat in a brown paper grocery bag, staple it shut, use a marker to label the bag, and place the bag on an upper shelf.

make your own

Accessory Organizer

What You Need:
- Shower curtain rings
- Sturdy hangers

Slide a shower curtain ring over the hook of a sturdy hanger and let it rest around the top of the hanger. Clip other shower rings to it to create a chain of rings. Hang the hanger on the clothes rod. To hang belts and pocketbooks, simply unclip a shower ring, thread the buckle or strap through the ring, and reclip. Scarves and ties can just be threaded through the individual rings.

Pocketbooks. To keep them clean and dust-free, store pocketbooks and handbags in a plastic bin or labeled box on a shelf, or in a drawer. Store those you use often in open wire bins on a shelf for easy access, or hang them from pegs. You can keep pocketbooks without straps in a hanging canvas or nylon bag.

Belts, Ties, and Scarves. A hanging belt or tie organizer makes it easier to find what you want, when you want it. All you need is some space on a wall of your closet or behind a door.

Count up your ties, belts, and scarves, and then choose an organizer with at least that many hooks. Or you can tap a row of nails or small hooks into the wall. If wall space is limited, consider using the back wall of your closet or the center support for your clothes rod. A hanging shoe bag with clear plastic pouches also works well for storing rolled belts, ties, and scarves. If you always wear certain accessories with a particular outfit, hang them together.

Shoes. Weed out shoes you aren't wearing, and then work on organizing. Put unwanted shoes into a box to be donated. If shoes are worn beyond repair, throw them away. Sort the shoes you do wear into categories such as work, dress, or casual, or group them by color. Count up your pairs of shoes and look for a shoe organizer that holds at least that many pairs. Multitiered, expandable shoe racks allow you to store many pairs in a small amount of space. Over-the-door shoe racks are also available.

If you want to keep shoes clean, especially seasonal or special-occasion shoes, save the original shoe box or store them in clear, plastic shoe boxes. If you use opaque boxes, take an instant photo and tape it to the front of the box to help you remember its contents. Store these boxes on shelves rather than floors, because keeping the floors clear makes it easier to vacuum.

Most shoe racks are not designed to hold men's shoes. Organizing experts at The Container Store recommend installing a series of short, closely spaced shelves from floor to ceiling to accommodate large shoes.

Organizing Drawers

The best way to organize drawers is to empty them completely, so you can see what you've got and then sort into categories. Use your bed as a sorting place. Categories might include the following:

- Undergarments
- Sleepwear
- T-shirts
- Active wear (gym clothes, bathing suits)
- Jeans and shorts
- Casual shirts
- Sweaters

Go through each category, one at a time. Sort each category into things you wear and things you don't wear, which might include socks with no matches, worn-out underwear, and jeans that are too tight. Take a look at quantities of each item. How many T-shirts do you really need? Try to reduce what you have to what you actually wear. Put things you don't wear in a box or bag labeled "Give Away" or "Throw Away."

Once you're done sorting, designate specific dresser drawers for specific items: socks and underwear, shirts, shorts, sweaters, and workout clothes, for example. You may have to combine similar categories, such as underwear and sleepwear or T-shirts and shorts. Now put everything back where it belongs.

Drawer organizers help keep things separate, especially the smaller items in your underwear drawer. If you have a lot of socks, you might separate them into dress, casual, and sport socks. Fold or roll socks; don't ball them up, because this causes them to lose their elasticity over time. If you really want to get organized, sort socks and undergarments by color within their sections.

To help keep shirts and sweaters neat and wrinkle free in your drawers, fold everything the way retailers fold them. Lay the item face down with arms spread out. Criss-cross the arms behind the shirt or sweater, keeping the shoulders even with the sides. Fold in one whole side to the halfway point, then the other side. Fold up the bottom so that the hem touches the neckline and turn over.

If your drawer space is limited, store bulkier items, such as sweaters or jeans, on shelves in your closet. You might even decide to hang some things you used to store in your dresser such as jeans. Just because you've always stored something in a particular place doesn't mean that's the best place to store it forever and ever.

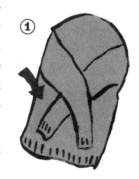

Organize the top of your dresser, too. Use a large canning jar or piggy bank to collect loose change. Corral everyday pocket items or jewelry in an attractive dish or tray. Give away perfumes and colognes you don't wear; throw away bottles that are virtually empty or make it a point to use them up.

Organizing Jewelry

Professional organizers agree that we wear about 20 percent of our clothing 80 percent of the time. The same applies to jewelry. You may even wear all of your *favorite* jewelry all of the time. The jewelry you don't wear doesn't take up much space, but it can be annoying to sort through it looking for the pieces you do wear. A jewelry box is useful for storing men's and women's jewelry, especially watches, bracelets, cuff links, tie clips, and rings. Other types of

For Simplicity's Sake

Provide every bedroom with a hamper of some sort for collecting dirty laundry. Put a mesh or nylon bag in the hamper to make it easy to carry dirty laundry to the laundry room or laundromat. The most efficient hamper is a basket that you can also use to carry clean laundry back to your room.

jewelry, such as necklaces and earrings, are better stored out of the box.

Hang necklaces to eliminate knotting and tangling and potential for breakage. You can buy a special jewelry organizer or use a tie rack. Cup hooks and nails also work fine. If you have just a few necklaces, you may be able to hang them over the top corners of a mirror. Another option is to hang only your fine-chain necklaces and keep pearl-type or costume jewelry in a glass bowl on your dresser top for easy access; this looks pretty, too. A baby-sized hanger with rubber bands stretched around it from top to bottom keeps necklaces from sliding into each other and getting tangled.

Earring trees reduce the amount of time you might spend looking for a set of earrings. If you store earrings in a jewelry box, clip hoop-type earrings together when you remove them to keep the set together. Another way to keep sets together is to store them in a clear plastic container with small compartments, such as a fishing tackle box. You can store bracelets, pins, and necklaces in the larger compartment below. It's not pretty, but it's functional. Earrings and fine-chain necklaces can also be stored in ice cube trays; place one set of earrings or chain in each "cube." The trays can be stacked in a dresser or vanity drawer.

Do you have every piece of jewelry you've ever purchased or received as a gift? If you love it all or wear it all, great. If not, lay out all of your jewelry on your bed. Throw away anything that is broken beyond repair or not worth fixing. Chances are, you have some things you know you won't ever wear again because they've gone out of style or your tastes have changed. Why hold onto it? Donate it to a local charity, sell it on consignment, or give it to your children or grandchildren for playing dress-up.

Off-Season Storage

Storing out-of-season clothing separately from in-season clothing allows you to find appropriate clothing without having to sort through the clothes you can't wear right now. But often, the big question is where to store seasonal clothes and linens. Some dwellings offer more options than others, especially those that have spare bedrooms with closets, and humidity-controlled basements. What's important is that you choose a place that is dry. Also, be sure that materials are completely dry before storing, to prevent mildew from forming.

Ideally, you'll have the space to move out-of-season clothing from your closet into another closet. If you can't do this, however, move out-of-season clothes off to one end of the closet and rotate them back in as the seasons change. A cedar storage trunk or closet is a great investment to keep moths and other insects from damaging garments or linens made of wool or wool blends. If you don't have one, put a cupful of cedar chips in a pair of old, clean panty hose and place in whatever storage containers you use. You can also use cedar blocks, mothballs, or moth crystals. Be sure that these repellents are fresh; otherwise, they won't work. Always clean clothes and linens before storing them for the season; the scent of your body is what attracts insects. Plan to thoroughly air clothes when you bring

"HOLY" CLOTHES!

With hundreds of dollars' worth of clothing and linens in your closets and drawers, it's wise to invest in pest protection products, such as cedar blocks and hangers, sachets, and sweater bags. Under the right (or wrong) conditions, virtually any fabric, cotton and synthetics included, can become dinner for a variety of pests. Without proper protection, clothing moths, carpet beetles, and even crickets can destroy an entire wardrobe in one season.

—*Staff, The Container Store*

them out of storage to get rid of the cedar/mothball odor.

If you have room in your bedroom, guest room, hallway, or finished basement, consider purchasing a freestanding closet for off-season storage of linens and clothes. Another option is to lay a broomstick or long pole over the backs of two same-size chairs for hanging shorter items, such as pants, jackets, and blankets. Cover with a sheet to keep the dust off.

Use a bed skirt to conceal convenient off-season storage under your bed. Store seasonal clothes or linens in suitcases, labeled storage bins, or drawers that fit under your bed; cedar drawers on wheels are even available. To create a little more storage under your bed, raise the height of your bed with risers. Be creative: Extra canned goods or paper goods can also be stored under a bed.

Items That Need Special Care. The following items require special care when they're stored for any length of time.

- **Blankets and comforters.** Make sure that blankets are clean and dry before storing. Down comforters should not be rolled too tightly or stored under heavy items, as this will compress the down. It's best to store these on a shelf, in a chest, or in a roomy bag. Tuck a few fabric softener sheets or cedar blocks between comforters and blankets to keep them smelling fresh.
- **Sweaters and casual clothing.** Wash or dry-clean sweaters and casual clothing. Sweaters should be stored flat. If you're storing them in the basement or attic, keep them in large plastic containers with tight-fitting lids to keep out mice and insects. If you're storing them elsewhere in the house, boxes or bags are acceptable. Label each box with its contents, and use separate boxes for each family member. You may find it easier to store children's clothing in boxes labeled by age or size and sex.
- **Suit jackets.** Hang suit jackets on sturdy hangers. Close all buttons. Stuff tissue paper into the sleeves of jackets to prevent creasing.
- **Leather, suede, and fine fabrics.** Do not store leather, suede, or silk in plastic. Plastic will cause leather and suede to dry out and other fine fabrics to develop yellow stains, rotting threads, or discoloration of buttons. If you want to keep clothing free of dust, hang items in canvas garment bags or cover each item with an old T-shirt, button-down shirt, or sheet of brown wrapping paper pulled down over the top of the hanger and folded in half over the shoulders.
- **Coats and accessories.** Hang clean, out-of-season coats on sturdy hangers. Hang out-of-season coats off to one side of your coat closet or in your off-season storage area. Mittens, gloves, and hats should also be cleaned at the end of the season. Store in a box on an upper shelf in your coat closet. Toss in a few cedar blocks for protection from moths, or pierce a small resealable plastic bag, fill it with mothballs, and put it in with clothes. If you store mittens, gloves, and hats in the basement or attic, keep them in a plastic storage bin with a tight-fitting lid. Label the bin.
- **Boots and shoes.** The end of the season is the ideal time to clean, polish, and waterproof boots and shoes. That way, they will be ready to wear at the start of the next season. Purchase an extra shoe rack for your off-season shoes. To prevent shoes and boots from getting dusty

ONE FOR THE ROAD

Keep an empty container under your bed for charity, filling it as clothing becomes outgrown or is no longer needed. When the box is full, take it to the charity of your choice. If you're really efficient, you'll itemize the contents of your box before dropping it off so that you will have a complete receipt for your tax records.

—*Debbie Williams, Let's Get It Together*

in storage, cover your shoe rack with an old sheet. Or wrap each pair of shoes and boots in a plastic grocery bag, tie the ends together, and toss them all into a large trash bag labeled "Sally's Summer Shoes" or "Jimmy's Boots." Off-season shoes and boots can also be stored in a large box or plastic storage bin with a lid. Because leather is particularly susceptible to mildew, avoid storing shoes and boots in your basement unless it is humidity controlled.

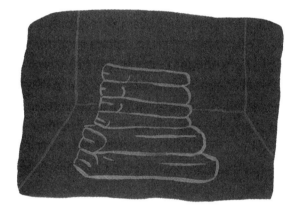

Linen Storage

Most people have more linens than they use or need. How many sets of sheets is enough for your household? It's nice to have extras, but why keep them if they're just taking up space? Sheets in good condition can be donated to several charities, including domestic violence shelters. Recycle old sheets into Halloween costumes for your kids, drop cloths for painting, or polishing rags. Or tear them into strips to be used in your garden to tie plants to stakes.

Organize your linen closet shelf by shelf. Arrange sheets by size: twin, full, queen, and king. Refold (if necessary) and stack same-size

> *Go to the library and look at decorating books. You'll find dozens of creative storage ideas. Then go home and analyze your particular needs in each room.*
>
> —Melinda Louise, Organize It

sheets. Labeling each section of each shelf will make it easy to find the sizes you need and also helps keep the closet organized.

Store sheets as sets by wrapping the fitted sheet and pillowcases in the flat sheet. Then, when you need a new set, you can just grab it with one hand. If you prefer to store sheets in stacks, store them folded side out. To fold fitted sheets, place a fist in one corner of the fitted sheet and then draw the opposite corner of the sheet over your fist. Now move your fist from the back to the front and lift the bottom elasticized corner up over your fist. Lay sheet down on a flat surface with the elasticized corners facing up. Fold edges in to form a square. Fold in half, and fold in half again.

It's nice to have a linen closet, but it's actually more efficient to store sheets in the rooms in which they are used. This way, when you're changing bed linens, you don't have to go somewhere else to get a clean set.

Store linens on a shelf in your bedroom closet, if you have the room. If not, a wooden chest or hall bench makes a convenient storage place for sheets, blankets, and comforters. It also makes a great place to sit when putting on your socks and shoes, which helps save your mattress from needless wear.

Another option is to buy underbed drawers that attach to your bed frame. You can use these drawers to store linens, pajamas and nightgowns, and out-of-season clothing. Plastic storage bins and drawers with or without rollers are also available. You can even store linens in a large, plastic zippered bag under your bed. These bags are often used as packaging for new quilts and comforters, and you might have some already. They're great for storing and keeping linens clean and dust-free. Be aware that you should *not* use a sealed plastic bag to store Vellux blankets because Vellux must breathe.

If you decide to buy a wooden chest or underbed drawers for storing linens, look for chests and drawers made out of cedar. They're a little more expensive but well worth the extra cost because cedar naturally repels moths and other insects. If you already have a noncedar storage box or drawer, slip in a couple of cedar blocks or fill a muslin pouch with cedar chips to protect against moth and insect damage.

Store extra bedspreads or blankets on upper shelves in your clothes closet, or hang them on hangers and keep them at the back of the closet. Another solution is to hang them from an over-the-door towel rod on the back of your bedroom door.

You say you have absolutely no place to store bed linens? Pare your collection down to two sets for each bed and store the extra set between the mattress and box spring or foundation. To do this, fold sheets in half horizontally and then several times lengthwise. Or keep only one set of sheets that you wash and put back on, eliminating the need for storage space altogether.

survey results

According to a recent customer survey conducted by The Container Store, people would be willing to give up bedroom and bathroom space (and even a spouse!) to have more room in their closets. The most common nonclothing items respondents reported storing in bedroom closets were handbags (70 percent), linens (30 percent), and gift wrap (21 percent). Receipts, tax information, board games, toys, household files, jewelry, and even silverware were also included in the mix.

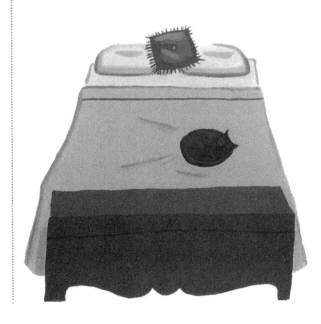

CHAPTER 9

KIDS' ROOMS

You've probably resigned yourself to the fact that you will never be able to eliminate "kid clutter" completely. But you can control it, with a little creativity, patience, and a few proven techniques and systems. The key to minimizing the mess in kids' bedrooms and playrooms is to create a home for everything and to design storage spaces that make it easy for kids to put things away.

For Starters

It's important to get your kids involved in the process of uncluttering and organizing their rooms. You'll do them a big favor by helping them to learn organizational skills that will come in handy throughout their lives. Plus, allowing them to have input in the process of getting organized also helps to ensure that they will *stay* organized.

Be sure to unclutter your own bedroom first to set a good example. Then, when you are ready, you can say, "Okay, my room is organized. Now let's organize *your* room!" The more enthusiastic you are, the more likely your children will want to help. You might even promise a fun reward later. At the very least, be sure to praise children for their accomplishments.

There are three basic principles to keep in mind when organizing kids' rooms:

1. **Make it easy to put things away.**
   Provide plenty of containers for putting like items together, so kids can see at a glance what goes where.

2. **Organize from the bottom up.** Keep frequently used items accessible on lower shelves and in bottom drawers. Store less frequently used items higher up.

3. **Label everything.** Label shelves, drawers, and containers. For children who can't read, label with drawings, photographs, or pictures cut out of magazines or catalogs.

Do Some Weeding

Step one is to reduce the amount of clutter by weeding out clothing and toys that your children have outgrown. If you're planning to donate these items, explain to your children how they can help make a less fortunate child very happy by sharing the things they aren't using anyway. You might even give children a choice of charities to donate to so they feel more involved in the donation process. If you have a garage sale, let the kids keep the money they get for selling their toys and clothes.

A good time to weed out toys is just before a birthday or other gift-giving holiday. Explain the weeding-out process to your kids as making room for new things. With children who are reluctant to part with their toys, it helps to focus their attention on what they want to keep rather than what they are willing to get rid of. Ask them to choose their favorites and set these aside. Then ask, "What else do you like to play with?" Put what's left in a box or bag for donation or a garage sale.

Sort through clothing just before you go shopping for back-to-school clothes or at the start of a new season. Start by going through the current season's clothes and shoes. Pull out everything in the closet and then move on to drawers. Discard worn-out and stained items, as well as anything that's not worth mending. Have children try on clothes and shoes for the upcoming season to see what fits and to find out what clothing they do and don't like. If they don't like it, it probably won't get worn. Make a shopping list for each child by using separate pages in a small, spiral notebook that you can bring with you to the store. Be sure to include sizes.

Store items only if you are saving them for younger children, planning to have a garage sale, or planning to take them to a consignment shop before the start of the season next year. Box or bag up everything else, put it in your car, and make a note to take it to a local charity sometime during the next week.

For Simplicity's Sake

Store children's seasonal clothing and shoes in stackable storage containers or boxes labeled with season, sex, and size rather than by child's name: for example, "Summer — Girl's Size 10–12." That way, you'll know what's in the box without having to open it. Organize boxes by season or sex. Or put separate categories into plastic bags, seal them with twist ties, and toss into a 55-gallon trash can for storage in your basement, garage, or shed. Just be sure to label the lid!

Closets and Drawers

If you want kids to hang up their clothes, put hanging rods within their reach. To make an inexpensive child-height clothes rod, run a length of chain through a piece of sturdy plastic pipe that will accommodate hangers. Attach each end of the chain to a shower curtain ring and hang the rings over the original clothes rod. Or install a tension rod at the appropriate height and raise it as the child grows. Use the upper rod for hanging special occasion or out-of-season clothes or for a hanging shelf unit.

Divide your child's closet into sections for school, play, and dress clothes. For children who can't yet coordinate colors, hang matching outfits together. Use child-size hangers for younger children. Children's clothing fits better on these hangers, and they're easier for small hands to handle. Screw hooks or pegs on the back of the bedroom or closet door or along one wall for hanging everyday items, such as backpacks, sleepwear, or sports attire. Be sure to put these hooks at a height your child can reach easily.

Invest in a shoe rack with enough space to store all of your child's shoes. Show your children how to organize their shoes by keeping pairs together. If children are sharing closet space, assign one shoe rack to each child or assign separate shelves on a multi-shelf unit.

To organize collections of accessories, such as baseball caps or pocketbooks, look for an accordion-style coat or tie rack. Hang it on the back of a door or on a wall within easy reach. Organize barrettes by clipping each one to a length of hanging ribbon.

Designate specific dresser drawers for specific items, such as socks, underwear, shorts, T-shirts, pants, and shirts. Use drawer organizers to keep such items as socks and underwear separate from each other. You might also consider storing socks and underwear in a shoe bag with clear plastic pockets that you can hang in the closet.

make your own

Mini-Closet

What You Need:
- Old wood chest with hinged top
- Four screw-on furniture legs
- Tension rod
- door pull
- Friction catch

Make a child-size closet. Screw legs into one end of an old wood chest with a hinged top; this will become the bottom of the closet. Stand the chest up, put a rod across the inside, and install a pull on the door. For safety reasons, install a friction catch to keep the door closed.

For Simplicity's Sake

Put a hamper in each child's bedroom for collecting dirty laundry. For the sake of efficiency, make it a basket that you can pick up and carry to the laundry room and use to return clean and folded laundry. Make it fun for kids to throw dirty laundry into the basket by hanging a wall-mount or standing basketball hoop over the basket.

Double or triple drawer space by installing slide-out drawers under your children's beds. Or put colorful, stackable crates or a ventilated wire bin system in the closet. These ideas are especially useful for younger children, who may have trouble opening heavy drawers or reaching the top drawer of a standard dresser. Cardboard and clear plastic drawer organizers are another alternative.

Tape pictures or photographs of what goes in each dresser drawer to the outside or bottom of drawers, so that even very young children can put clothes away. As they learn to read, you can replace the pictures with words.

Create Activity Centers

Take a cue from kindergarten teachers and organize your kids' room into sections designed for specific activities. Activity centers create natural homes for things and provide children with visual cues for where things can be found — and where they belong when it's time to put them back. Examples of activity centers include:

- Reading center
- Play center
- Arts and crafts center
- Projects center
- Music center
- Computer center
- Homework center
- Entertainment center (television, stereo)
- Dressing center

How you divide a bedroom or playroom will depend on your children's ages and interests, and the size of the room. In each activity center, store all items that are related to that activity. In the arts and crafts center, for example, you might set up a table and chairs and store supplies (paper, crayons and markers, stickers, tape, and scissors) in a cardboard drawer organizer under the table or in open bins on a nearby shelf.

Toys and Books

When organizing toys and books, think "open" and "visible." A proven technique for organizing toys is to use shelves wherever possible instead of a toy box. Things tend to get thrown into toy boxes and end up broken or buried. Storing on shelves make it easy for children to find the toys and books they want without having to pull out everything.

Organize toys on shelves by categories. Use colorful plastic dishpans on shelves to contain like items, such as building blocks, doll clothes, books, or small toys. Or use clear plastic, lidded bins that allow kids to see what's inside without opening them. Very young children may need assistance opening the lids; this may help parents teach the practice of getting out one toy at a time.

An alternative to using shelves for storage is to create cubbyholes for books, toys, and games with colorful, stacking crates. Interlocking crates are best, but you can secure non-interlocking crates to each other by using clear packing tape. Arrange the crates along one wall or in a closet.

If several children share a bedroom or playroom, consider keeping their toys and books separate. Use lower shelves and crates for younger children and higher shelves for older children. When children are very young, keep toys where they are convenient for you to access and put away. Store heirloom toys and toys that require adult supervision on "special" shelves that only you can reach so children have to ask for them. Or keep them tucked away in a "secret" place.

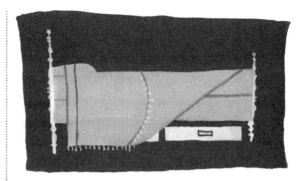

Designate and label specific spots for storing toys. Tape a little picture of the toy in its spot. This practice is also educational for toddlers, as it helps them with memory and matching skills.

Use the space under the bed for storing smaller items, like doll clothes or miniature cars. Look for plastic storage boxes with drawers. This is also a great place to store keepsakes. Provide each child with one lidded box for storing mementos. Make it large enough to hold all of their current keepsakes with room to add some more. When the box is full, help children go through the box to pare down the contents to the items that are most meaningful.

Stack game and puzzle boxes on shelves. If game boxes are falling apart, use empty egg cartons or recycled margarine tubs to store game pieces. Label the cartons or tubs with the name of the game and stack them on a shelf. Write the name of each game on the back of each game board along one side of the spine, and then fold and stack the game boards with the names facing out. Place instructions inside the folded board or inside a resealable plastic bag secured to the back of the game board with tape.

Reduce excessive toy clutter by putting some toys in storage for a few months. Bring them out on a rainy day or a day when your children could use a nice surprise. A good time to do this is right after a major gift-giving holiday when children are less likely to put up a fuss about your packing up a box of older toys.

The more you can keep things off the floor, the less cluttered a room looks and the easier it is to clean. Use hanging shoe bags on the back of a door to store beanbag toys, action figures, and other small toys. Hang it low enough so that kids can reach into all of the pockets. A great way to corral stuffed animals is to hang a nylon hammock in one corner of the room. Or hang a length of colored string or ribbon between two hooks at either end of a bare wall, and clothespins to clip beanbag toys and small stuffed animals to the string. You can use this same method to display artwork.

make your own

Comedy Central

What You Need:
- Magazine storage boxes *or* cereal boxes

You can buy magazine storage boxes to store collections of comic books, or you can make your own from empty cereal boxes. Use scissors to cut out a section of the right side panel of the box from the top down to about four inches from the bottom. Then cut diagonally from the top left corner of the front of the box down to that point. Cut out the back of the box to match the front. Store books with spines facing out. Store boxes side by side on a bookshelf. You can have kids make labels for the boxes, too.

Artwork and Loose Papers

Designate one space, such as the front of your refrigerator, as a "gallery" for displaying your children's drawings and paintings. Limit "shows" to one piece of artwork per child per week. Store post-show and unshown artwork in a sturdy portfolio that slips between the countertop and refrigerator. Or store artwork under your children's beds in boxes.

Ask your local pizza delivery store for a couple of clean pizza boxes. Give one to each child for storing their artwork. Have children write their names on their boxes and perhaps even decorate them. Make it their responsibility to file everything they bring home. At the end of the school year or when the box is full, have your child select his or her favorite, or select yours.

For long-term storage of favorite pieces, roll artwork in a paper towel or gift-wrapping tube. Write your child's name on the outside of the tube along with your child's age and the year. Or purchase an art portfolio or scrapbook for each child to save these treasures.

Consider recycling your children's artwork. Choose your favorites each year to create calendars that you can keep or give as a gift to grandparents and relatives. Create the calendar pages on your computer and then have the artwork and calendar pages laminated and spiral bound by an office supply store.

Loose school papers can quickly create a mess. It's important to contain them somehow, preferably in a place accessible to kids so that they can put them away after showing them to you. Following are three ideas for storing graded tests, school papers, photos, cards, certificates, artwork, and other loose papers. Whatever method you choose, be sure to put a large trashcan in each child's room to collect waste paper.

- **Purchase a large three-ring binder for each child.** Label the spine with your child's name. Have your child punch each paper and file it in chronological order throughout the school year, adding new papers to the top. Store nonpunchable items in the front or back pockets of the binder. Or purchase three-hole punched dividers with storage pockets for these items. Purchase additional binders, as needed, throughout the year.
- **Use a heavy-duty cardboard chest with drawers as a filing center.** Sort your child's papers into categories such as school papers (homework and tests); greeting cards and letters; and report cards, certificates, and awards. Then label and organize drawers by category. It's not quite as neat as filing, but it does make it easier to find things.
- **Invest in a small filing cabinet for storing all kinds of loose papers.** Show your child how to use hanging files and folders to organize by grade, classes, and projects — and how to purge files at the end of the school year. Buy colorful file folders and use color-coding for separate categories. If children share a room, assign one drawer to each child. If you are planning to buy a desk for doing homework, consider purchasing a desk with a drawer that will accommodate hanging files.

EVERYBODY'S A CRITIC

Keep children's art and school papers in an under-the-bed tub. Then, at the end of the year, you can sit down with your child and enjoy a little reminiscing as you go through the year's papers. Set a numeric limit (10 or 20 or whatever) or a spatial limit (whatever will fit in this manila envelope) and pick out your favorites together. It's a nice bonding activity, and it's easier to be discriminating about what you will keep when you view the entire collection all at once.

—*Ramona Creel, OnlineOrganizing.com*

CHAPTER 10

BATHROOM

Next to the kitchen, the bathroom gets more regular use than any other room in the house. With use comes more potential for clutter and disorganization. Happily, because the bathroom is generally the smallest room in the house, it's one of the simplest and easiest to organize. Start here if you want to see results fast.

Uncluttering

You may have more than one bathroom. If so, think about each bathroom as a large storage unit. Assign each unit to individual household members, groups (such as children), or guests. Then you can organize each bathroom in the manner best suited to its primary users. Having his and hers bathrooms is a good strategy to use if your partner's organizational style is vastly different from yours: for example, you like everything neat and tidy and your partner is oblivious to clutter. That way, your differences won't come between you every day.

Before you start organizing the bathroom, take a look around. What are your biggest challenges? A cluttered sink top? Messy drawers or shelves? Things on the floor that shouldn't be there? All of these challenges can be addressed with a thorough uncluttering, simple organizational techniques, and some inexpensive organizing products.

Your first step is to unclutter. How many toothbrushes do you have? How many do you need? Throw out worn toothbrushes. If you wish to save them for small cleaning jobs, keep only as many as you need — probably one — and put it with your cleaning supplies.

As you go through your medicine cabinet and drawers, you'll probably find duplicates of things like antibiotic ointment, adhesive bandages, makeup, and other partially used items. Consolidate whatever you can, but do *not* consolidate newer products with older products that may be approaching their expiration dates. Use the older product first, then the newer product. Some items, such as opened bottles of shampoo can be put to use in another bathroom. You can also use duplicates to create a first aid kit for your car or a toiletries bag for traveling.

To keep the sink top free of clutter, you'll need to create a home for everything. If you have enough drawers or shelves in your bathroom, assign one to each household member. Otherwise, organize drawers by categories, for example: makeup, hair care, and bath supplies. To keep drawers from becoming a jumbled mess, use ready-made drawer organizers to keep like items together, or make your own organizers from boxes, zippered or drawstring bags, baskets, or bins.

If your bathrooms could use more drawers and shelves, there are some simple solutions. If you're handy, you could install a few shelves along one wall. Another solution is ready-made storage units, including wall cabinets, freestanding shelf units and cabinets, and corner shelf units. Wire wheeled carts work well for storing extra towels, soaps, and other small items.

Eliminate clutter in the shower and tub with caddies designed to hold shampoo, soaps and bath gels, and razors. This will reduce clutter and make it easier to clean the shower and tub. If you have a lot of bottles, look for a tension-mounted shower caddy, which tends to offer

more shelf space than the kind that hang over the shower nozzle pipe. You might also consider installing wall dispensers for shampoo and liquid soap. Store bath toys in a nylon mesh bag that you can hang from the shower nozzle pipe, shower curtain rod, or a large hook attached to the shower wall by a suction cup.

The Medicine Cabinet

Empty your medicine cabinet and begin to sort through what you've got. Set aside expired prescription and nonprescription medicines, as well as antibiotics, regardless of expiration date. (Not completing a course of antibiotics places you at risk for developing resistant strains of bacteria, reducing the efficacy of the drug when it's needed most.) Also set aside any nonprescription medicines that are more than two years old or past their expiration date. Changes in chemical makeup over time causes them to lose their potency and, hence, their effectiveness. The same is true for sunscreens. Dispose of all old and outdated items properly (see the box at left).

Organize your medicine cabinet like you would any cabinet. Store the most frequently used items on the shelves that are easiest to reach, and store like items together. Group prescriptions and vitamins together by family member so that you don't have to search through all the bottles to find yours. Other

For Safety's Sake

Flush outdated and expired medicines down the toilet, or collect and return them to your pharmacist for disposal.

efficient groupings include cough and cold remedies, sunscreen and insect repellents, pain relievers, and first aid supplies.

Restock your medicine cabinet with labels facing outward. Use small plastic bins to contain small tubes and things you use together, such as antibiotic ointment and adhesive bandages. Consider labeling shelves so that you don't have to think about what goes where.

If your prescription plan requires you to bring refill labels to your pharmacist, keep them in the medicine cabinet along with your prescriptions. That way, when you need a refill, you know exactly where to find the label. When you get down to a one-week supply of a prescription, put the refill label in your wallet or purse and make a note to yourself to go to the pharmacy. Better yet, if your pharmacy offers an automated refill service, simply call, enter the refill number, and select the time and day you'd like to pick up the prescription; it will be ready when you are.

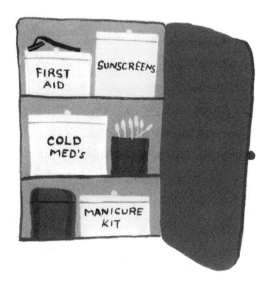

For Safety's Sake

Garbage disposal. Be careful when disposing of medicines, vitamins, cosmetics, and any potentially hazardous materials. Do not put them in the bathroom trashcan where children and pets may find them. Flush down the toilet what you can. Put everything else into a bag, tie up the bag, and put it into a lidded trash can out of reach of children.

Organizing Toiletries

The biggest challenge with toiletries, especially those you use daily, is being able to find what you need among the chaotic array of bottles, jars, and tubes. The best way to organize toiletries is to go through your shelves and drawers one by one, removing all containers of makeup, skin and hair care products, and other toiletries. Then sort by categories, which might include the following:

- Makeup
- Dental care
- Skin care
- Hair care
- Nail care
- Perfumes, powders, and deodorants

Examine each item carefully. Discard old, sticky nail polishes, makeup that is more than six months to one year old, and any empty bottles or jars. Discard or give away items that you no longer like or use. They're just taking up space that you can put to better use.

Where you store these things will depend on the set-up in your bathroom. How you store them may be as simple as grouping like items together on a shelf or in baskets or bins in a drawer. For a neat and uncluttered appearance, use same-size or same-style containers, especially if they will be placed on open shelves. When you store similar items together, it's not only easier to locate what you're looking for, but it also reduces the chance that you will buy duplicate items. If you like to keep extra supplies on hand, store them in back of the opened items. Keep in mind that most toiletries should be stored away from direct sunlight and heat, which can shorten their life.

How you store makeup will depend on how you use it. If you use the same few items daily, keep these items in a small basket, bin, or bag that is easily accessible. Store less frequently used items in a separate container. If you use a variety of makeup on a regular basis, contain it all in a makeup box designed like a fishing tackle box, with individual compartments for smaller items and a large storage compartment for larger items. Find one that will hold all of your makeup *and* fit neatly in its storage place. Take it out when you need it and put it back when you're done.

Hang It Up

If towels and clothing often get left on the floor, it's not necessarily because the previous occupants are too lazy to hang them up. It might be because there aren't enough places to hang wet towels or it's too difficult to do so. Both of these problems are easy to fix. From

the few suggestions below, choose the ones that will work best in your situation:

- Add more towel rods behind the door or on the wall. If you have children, mount a few at child height.
- Hang an over-the-door towel rack.
- Bring in a freestanding coat rack to use as a towel rack
- Install hooks or towel rods near the sink for hanging washcloths and hand towels.
- Install pegs or hooks, at adult and child height, on the back of the door or along one wall for hanging pajamas and robes.
- Hang a mesh bag behind the door for collecting dirty towels.

All of these products are readily available through catalogers and retailers that specialize in home organization products and at discount stores. (See Resources, page 281.)

Towels and clothing aren't the only things you can hang in the bathroom. Take a tip from hair styling professionals and hang hairdryers and curling irons. Most of these appliances have hooks for hanging. All you need to do is tap a nail or screw a hook on the inside or outside wall of the vanity. Or hang a flat-backed basket with handle from a hook on the vanity, wall, or door and store all brushes, combs, styling products, and accessories along with electrical styling appliances.

Storing Bathroom Necessities

It may seem logical to store towels with sheets in a linen closet (if you have one), but because

the bathroom is where you use towels, it's the most efficient place to store extra sets. If you have few or no shelves, consider adding a free-standing, ready-made shelving unit over the toilet. If you need something to fit a narrow space, try a baker's rack. Here are a few more space-saving ideas for towel storage.

- Roll towels and washcloths and store them in a basket near the bathtub or shower.
- Use a wine rack for storing rolled hand towels and washcloths.
- Hang a three-tiered wire basket from the ceiling for storing extra washcloths, soaps, and bath products.

Whether you store towels on shelves in your bathroom or in a linen closet, consider folding towels as sets. Lay the hand towel and washcloth on top of the bath towel and fold all three together simultaneously. Then you can easily grab a full set when you need it. If you choose to fold and store towels individually, fold them all the same way to make them easy to stack and retrieve.

Sort through your towels and pull out any that are worn or frayed. Discard them or recycle them as rags, for pet baths, or for emergency use in your car. (If your vehicle gets stuck on ice, placing a towel in front or behind your wheels might provide enough traction to get you out.)

Consider storing bathroom cleaning supplies where you use them — in the bathroom. Keeping these items handy eliminates having to go get them from somewhere else when you need them. Use wire baskets that stack and slide for easy access. If your sink is the type with only a pedestal or legs underneath it, wrap it with a sink skirt under which you can hide cleaning supplies. If you have young children, be sure to use child-safety latches on cabinets and store cleaning supplies out of reach.

Store extra toilet paper and feminine products as close as possible to the toilets. Look for a decorative basket or canister with lid to keep these items accessible yet out of sight. Near the toilet is also a good place for a magazine rack if occupants enjoy reading in the bathroom. If extra toilet paper doesn't fit in storage near the toilet, hide it under the bed in the nearest bedroom.

In the guest bathroom, provide several sets of towels as well as basic toiletries such as soap, shampoo and conditioner, and hand or body lotion. It's also a good idea to provide at least one extra roll of toilet paper. Additional "nice-to-have" items in the guest bathroom include a hair dryer, an unused toothbrush (still in its original packaging), toothpaste, dental floss, and air freshener.

CHAPTER 11

THE OFFICE

Whether you are managing your home or pursuing a home-based career, you need a place to do your job. It might be a "corner office" in your dining room or a suite of rooms in your basement. The size of the office doesn't matter. What's important is that your office space is organized to accommodate your needs so that you can perform your work as efficiently and productively as possible.

Location, Location, Location

Where do you pay bills and file important papers? Do you keep bills to be paid in one place, pay them in another, and file receipts in yet another place? Having a designated office space makes it simpler and easier to handle incoming mail and paperwork, organize bill paying, and manage your household. You don't need a full-fledged office for home management, but you do need a work surface, something to sit on, somewhere to file important papers, and a place to store basic office supplies.

For many home managers, the kitchen is the ideal place to set up a household office. Your kitchen table or countertop may be the perfect work surface; all you need is a place to store files and supplies. Use the tips in chapter

3, "Organizing Basics," and chapter 6, "Kitchen and Dining Area," to make some room in a cabinet below the counter near the work surface. On one shelf, place a crate or bin that accommodates hanging files. Use the space alongside your filing box to store envelopes and paper, a calculator, and stapler. Store loose items, such as pens and pencils, paper clips, and rubber bands in coffee cups and place them on a turntable for easy access. Or put all of your office supplies in a portable, lidded bin that you can pull out when you need it and put back when you're done. Use a napkin holder on the counter for outgoing mail.

Since you really don't need much space for a simple household office, you may find that you can set one up in the corner of the dining room, family room, or bedroom by using a secretary desk or other furniture that blends with your decor. Or you can hide your office area behind a couple of room dividers.

You may even be able to use a closet for your office. Build in a tabletop and shelves and add an electrical outlet or phone jack if needed. Or simply use the closet as a place to store a rollaway desk and file trolley that you pull out into a hallway or spare room when needed. You can also create a compact office center in an armoire. Open the doors, pull up a chair, and voilà! There's your office. Close the doors, and all you see is a beautiful piece of furniture.

Setting Up a Home Office

A work-at-home office requires more space than a household office because it needs to hold project and client files, reference books and materials, and office equipment. Location is also more critical. Ideally, your office is in a room with a door to afford privacy, and it's

located away from high-traffic areas, such as the kitchen. A separate entrance is good if you have business visitors.

Organizing for comfort can improve productivity — and your bottom line. Start with the basics: a good chair and proper lighting. A comfortable, supportive chair is a must. When shopping for a chair, try out different models to see how they feel. Look for a chair with lots of adjustability to create a perfect fit for your body. Pneumatic height adjustment lets you alter your seating position throughout the day with just a touch. A wheeled chair is great for rolling from one work area to another, but if you spend most of your day sitting in one place, consider getting a kneeling chair that helps to keep your spine in proper alignment.

Lighting is also critical for comfort. There are two types of lighting: ambient lighting for the room and spot lighting for office tasks. The best ambient lighting for computer work is indirect lighting suspended from the ceiling. Spot lighting is a must for focused paperwork. Desk or table lamps should be positioned to light work areas. A fluorescent lamp fixture mounted under a cabinet is another option for office task lighting. To reduce glare and reflections from nearby light sources and relieve eyestrain, mount a glare screen on your computer monitor. And keep it clean. Some kits with antistatic wipes and cleaner mount on the side of your monitor for easy access.

Efficiency begins at your desk. If you have only a standard desk, you're probably cramped for space. An L-shaped configuration is a more efficient set-up; a U-shaped configuration can accommodate an assistant or guest. A modular desk is a good choice because it allows you to reconfigure to adapt to future needs. When shopping for a desk, look for furniture that is easy to assemble. And make sure that your desk has at least one hole to collect computer and telephone wires and keep them out of the way. Make a sketch of your office layout before purchasing furniture, and take it with you when you go shopping. It's also a good idea to take measurements of the room, so you know the parameters of the space you're working with.

The right technology can also increase productivity. Invest in whatever office equipment you need to do your job well. Remember, it's tax deductible. If you can't buy it outright, consider leasing. Keep your future needs in mind when selecting equipment. And be sure to buy from a company that provides good technical support and quick turnaround on repairs. Avoid buying multifunction equipment, such as fax/copier/printers and telephone/answering machines. They save space, but if one function goes on the blink, you have to remove the whole unit for repair. If your budget is tight, look for rebate offers or check out reconditioned equipment. And if you're not sure if you really need a piece of equipment, wait sixty days and then reassess your needs.

Set up a phone number for your business that is separate from your home number. Consider getting at least one other line for your fax and Internet connection. Choose a telephone that has hold, redial, speakerphone, and caller identification features. It's also a

Put a period between the words home *and* office *to keep them separate.*

—Barbara Fields, PAPERCHASERS

good idea to get a phone that enables you to add a headset to keep your hands free for typing or writing.

Finally, stock up on office supplies so you won't have to waste time running out to buy an ink cartridge for your printer in the middle of an urgent project. But don't go overboard on supplies, especially if your storage space is limited. Many office supply companies will deliver just about anything within 24 hours with no shipping fees on orders more than a certain dollar amount. Set up an account with the company of your choice and keep a running list of supplies needed so that you can order them all at once.

Uncluttering Your Office

Your office probably contains more stuff than you need or use — everything from outdated computer equipment to invitations left over from an event that took place five years ago. Most of this stuff gets saved "just in case," but meanwhile, it's taking up valuable space. And the thing that generally takes up the most space is paper.

Start by moving all inactive files into storage. Your inactive files might include past client projects, the previous year's bookkeeping and tax records, research or coursework materials, and any files you do not need to access on a regular basis. Go through your filing cabinet drawers and piles of folders and pull out all of your inactive folders. Group them into categories, such as tax records or client projects, and put them in a lidded cardboard storage box that accommodates hanging folders. You can get these inexpensively at office supply stores and many discount department stores. Use a wide-tip marker to label the box. Store these boxes in a closet, attic, basement, garage, or off-site storage area. Or stack boxes on top of each other in one corner of your office and hide the whole lot behind a decorative screen.

Next, collect all of your office supplies in one place. Sort supplies into two categories: things you use and things you don't use. Give the things you don't use to charity. Then sort the ones you do use into categories by use, such as computer supplies, desk supplies, and paper supplies. Create a supply center, where you contain and store like items together by using labeled boxes or stacking trays on shelves.

For instant shelving in a closet, use a freestanding bookcase or shelving unit. If you don't have a closet, you can use an open bookcase (hidden behind a screen if you prefer) or a freestanding cabinet with doors. Or store supplies under your desk, out of kicking range.

You may be able to use the space behind your office door for storage. Hang a shoe bag with clear plastic pockets for containing smaller items, such as boxes of staples, paper clips, and diskettes. Or hang an over-the-door rack for storing videotapes, magazines, and file folders.

IT'S YOUR DECISION

When setting up a home office, you need to make lots of important decisions. Carefully consider your needs, then choose what's best for you.

- ❏ **PC or Macintosh computer?**
- ❏ **One, two, or three phone lines?**
- ❏ **Voice mail, answering machine, or answering service?**
- ❏ **Which long-distance service?**
- ❏ **Call waiting?**
- ❏ **Do you need a copier? Or will the fax machine suffice?**
- ❏ **Do you need a postage machine?**

Sell or donate computer equipment you are no longer using. If you donate it to charity, you may be able to take a tax deduction. In the Resources (see page 285), you'll find contact information for several companies that accept computer donations. You also might be able to donate your computer to a local nonprofit organization or to a technical or vocational school where students are learning to repair computer equipment.

Now, about your desk drawer. Do you really need everything that's in there? Take everything out and put back only what you use on a regular basis. Store extra pens, pencils, and other supply items in your supply center. Make sure they work first! Discard any junk you find. Uncluttering your drawer will create more space, but if you make a home for everything in your drawer, you'll be able to find whatever you need without having to rummage through everything. A drawer-organizing tray may suffice to organize pens, pencils, scissors, stapler, staple puller, postage stamps, paper clips, and other items. If you happen to have an extra cutlery tray, that works well too.

Finally, unclutter your computer. Start by backing up your files. Then empty the trash can on your desktop. Run a disk clean-up program if you have one. Uninstall programs and components you aren't using. Run the disk defragmenter utility, which reorganizes your hard drive, making it quicker and easier for your computer to find files. To make it easier for *you* to find files, set up or reorganize your computer system by using the folder system to keep related files together. Create folders within folders; if you don't know how, consult the Help feature. Move files where they can be more readily found. Rename files or folders if necessary. Delete documents that you no longer need.

Organizing Your Workspace

Make a list of the things you use daily or weekly or collect them all in one place. Then sit in your office chair, pull yourself up to your desk or computer in your usual seated position, and extend your arms out from your sides. Now sweep your arms together in front. That semicircle you have just circumscribed is your primary workspace. This is where you want to keep the things you use at least several times each week.

Organize your primary workspace to accommodate the flow of work. For example, you might keep your incoming mail and "Bills to Be Paid" folder on one side of your primary workspace and your out box on the other. If you are right-handed, position your telephone to the left of your seated position. Lefties should position the telephone to the right. Keep your appointment book, notepaper, and writing implements within easy reach of your telephone.

Next, use your imagination to draw concentric circles around your primary workspace. The things you use occasionally should be closest to your primary workspace, and items you use less frequently should be farthest away. If you find yourself regularly getting up to retrieve certain files, use a vertical desktop file organizer to create an interim holding place for current project or client folders. Or get a rolling cart that you can keep close to your desk.

corraling your cords

Organize the cords that come out of your computer, telephone, fax, and answering machine. Get some plastic garbage bag fasteners, cable organizers, or hook-and-loop straps. Take a few minutes to straighten out all the cords. Fasten them together so that they form one big rope. If possible, drop the whole bundle through a hole at the back of your desk. You can do this with the wires of your television, VCR, and stereo equipment, too.

One Challenge . . .

I need help uncluttering my desk. I clean it off one day and within one week, it's a mess again. What can I do to keep my desktop organized?

Three Solutions

❶ FROM DEBBIE GILSTER, ORGANIZE & COMPUTERIZE: Put all loose papers, magazines, receipts, business cards, and other paper items in a box. Create "Action Files" using bins, hanging folders or stacking trays. Set up "In" and "Out" baskets. Label files "File," "Read," "Pay," "Do," and "Pending." Now sort your papers, one small pile at a time, until the box is empty. Just move each item into its new home based on what the next action is. Don't forget to use the trash can as much as you can.

❷ FROM JAN JASPER, JASPER PRODUCTIVITY SOLUTIONS: Set up a system for your working files by using a small, inexpensive file holder that you keep right on your desktop. Sort your current and pending papers into categories. Many people need folders for the following categories: papers to photocopy, papers pertaining to a meeting, an upcoming business trip, bills to pay (or expense receipts to turn in), things to read and decide about, several folders for current projects, and a "pending" folder for things on which you're waiting someone else to act. Label folders clearly so you'll know at a glance what's where. Once you get in the habit of using these folders in tandem with your reference files, you can keep your desk clear. The hard part is getting started. But once you start, you'll see immediate results, which will provide the motivation to maintain the system.

❸ FROM RONNI EISENBERG WITH KATE KELLY, AUTHORS OF ORGANIZE YOUR OFFICE! (New York: Hyperion, 1999): Set aside a block of time to unclutter your desk. Have on hand a trash can, a pen, file folders, and labels. Clear the space you want to organize. Then make a big pile of all the paper. Evaluate each item, categorize it, and put it away in a desk drawer, file folder, or a desktop organizer. Throw out as much as possible. Even when you are feeling overwhelmed, just keep sorting and categorizing. If you devote the necessary time, your desk can be cleared. You might want to enlist the help of a partner — a spouse, secretary, or someone who can help you keep going.

Organizing your workspace can greatly enhance your productivity. Making simple adjustments to your workstation can do the same. Position your computer monitor a full arm's length away from your seated position. If you can read the screen, it's not too far away. As much as half of the viewing area should be below eye level. Tilt the top of the monitor slightly farther back than the bottom. If you have to reach for your computer mouse, move it closer. Keep the feet of your keyboard up.

Controlling Paper Chaos

Wasn't the introduction of the computer supposed to be the dawn of the paperless office? Instead, we have more paper than ever — and more misplaced files and lost paperwork as well.

Gather all loose papers in one place. Pick up the first piece of paper and make a decision: Do I need this? Keep it only if it serves a purpose. File it only if you will need to refer to it at a future date. If it is something that requires action, such as replying to a letter, or if you need the information to write a report, make a note on your "To Do" list. Then put the paper item in a folder labeled "To Do" or note on your "To Do" list where to find it. Tackle your filing one stack at a time or for ten to fifteen minutes each day until it's all done. If you're really uncertain about whether to save a paper, ask yourself what's the worst possible thing that could happen if you threw it away. Keep in mind that often, all you really need to keep is the information, not the paper. Make a note of favorite URLs or the name of a reference book, for example, and throw away the paper.

TIME-SAVER 60

File only what you really need to file. Research has proven that 80 percent of what is filed is never looked at again. So if you spend a total of one hour each month filing *everything*, you are wasting 48 minutes every month. If you know where to go to get that information should you need it in the future, don't file it.

Avoid piling paper. Use hanging files and vertical files that allow you to flip through papers more easily. Even your "To File" folder can reside in a hanging file until you get to your filing. The one exception to piling may be your in box and out box. It's easier to toss these items into baskets than it is to put them into file folders.

Use paper organizers to keep stationery and envelopes handy. Stacking paper trays do the trick. Use one tray for storing recycled paper. That way, you'll always know where to find a piece of paper to jot down a note, and you'll have less paper trash. If you're short on desk space, consider buying a paper organizer that resides under your printer or fax. You can also file stationery in hanging folders in a desk drawer.

Filing Systems

Files can be classified as active and inactive. Active files should be stored within arm's reach or very close to your primary workspace. Inactive files, also known as *archive files*, should be stored away from the main work area in a separate filing cabinet or labeled storage boxes.

The secret to a good filing system is to keep it simple. Whatever filing system you use should make it easy to find what you need, be easy to maintain, and make sense to everyone who needs to use it. One of the easiest systems is the A-B-C system. Label a set of hanging folders with tabs for each letter of the alphabet. Then use interior manila file folders with subject labels, such as "January Receipts," that you file under "R" for receipts. File the interior folders in alphabetical order within each lettered folder.

TO PRINT OR NOT TO PRINT

Has the computer brought more paper into your life because you print out your e-mails? Most e-mail messages (if they need to be saved) should be stored on your computer. Create folders in your e-mail program so you can file them by client, project, or subject. Better yet, use a contact management software that automatically links every e-mail to the record of the person who sends it to you. Not printing e-mails reduces filing time, speeds finding messages later, and reduces paper clutter. If you need to bring an e-mail to an off-site meeting, you can print it out, but that should be the exception, not the rule. Try it. It's amazing how much time and space you'll save!

—Jan Jasper, Jasper Productivity Solutions

Another system that is easy to set up is a simple numeric system with master index. Label a hanging folder with the number "1." Pick up the first piece of paper you want to file. Write "1" in the upper right hand corner and put in the hanging folder labeled "1" Then write "1" at the top of a sheet of paper that will become your master index. Write a three- to five-word description of the paper you just put in the folder; for example, Directions to Boston. Continue filing in this manner until you have about a dozen papers in the folder labeled "1." Create a folder labeled "2." Start filing papers in that folder. It doesn't matter that the papers are unrelated.

Type your index into a word-processing document on your computer and store it on your hard drive. When you need to find a particular document, use the search feature on your computer to locate the document and corresponding folder number by searching for a keyword, such as "directions."

Although alphabetical and numerical systems are the easiest to set up and work well for many people, subject files are generally the preferred method of filing. Set up hanging files for broad categories, such as "Accounting" or "Prospective Clients." Then set up interior file folders for papers to be filed within each category. For example, in the accounting category, you may have separate folders for accounts receivable, accounts payable, and monthly receipts. (*Hint:* Use box-bottom hanging folders to accommodate thick subject files.) File subjects alphabetically, or group related folders together in each drawer.

Remember that the reason you file something is so that you can find it again if you need it. When naming a new file, think of what heading you are likely to look under should you need a document in the future, not "Where should I put this?" Don't think too long about this. The first name that springs to mind is probably the best file name. Use a noun (person, place, or thing) as your file name.

Label all new folders immediately. Avoid labeling files and folders "Miscellaneous." Documents are either important enough to have their own label or not important enough to save.

Try using different-colored file folders to classify different categories of information. Color-coding makes it easier to identify which files are which without even reading the file name and makes finding the appropriate files a split-second task. It also looks nice, which makes filing a more pleasant task. If you color code files, keep your system simple. Limit the number of colors you use to four or five. For example, you could use green for accounting files (bills, receipts, and copies of invoices), blue for administrative files, and a few different colors for each client.

When filing by subject, try to sort everything into ten to fifteen categories or fewer. You can always add or eliminate categories later. Use broad headings for file folders that will allow room for several subcategories. For example, use "Advertising" as the name for one hanging file, and in that file, hang folders labeled "Yellow Pages," "Trade Journal," and "Newspaper."

For Simplicity's Sake

If you were going to build a house, would you begin by going out, buying supplies, and dropping them off at the building site? Probably not. You'd start with a plan. The same is true for setting up a filing system. Start by making a blueprint or outline. List all of your current file names in their disorganized or organized state. Then look for natural groupings and start rearranging your list according to those groups. It's critical that you be involved in the planning stage. The "doing" stage, or physical act of setting up files can be delegated if that's an option.

—*Harriet Schechter, The Miracle Worker Organizing Service*

Use separate drawers for separate broad categories. You may want to reserve one entire drawer for current client projects and another for business-related files, such as expense receipts, vendor account information, and membership files. Create "hot files" for those files you access frequently. Make space in a filing cabinet or desk drawer that is within arm's reach, or use a vertical desktop file or rolling cart file.

Once you have your filing system in place, align hanging file tabs in a zigzag pattern. Use the slot on the far left, then the middle slot, then the far right and repeat so you have just three columns of tabs showing and all tabs can be seen. (Use clear tabs for easy readability.) If you position tabs on the fronts of hanging folders, it makes folders easier to open; just grasp the tab and pull forward. Do not overstuff drawers; leave a couple of inches free so that it's easy to open folders without having to remove them.

Always put new documents in the front of the folder, so all your files are in reverse chronological order. Periodically, go through all of your folders. Throw away anything that's obsolete, and consolidate or add file folders as needed.

File papers in a loose-leaf binder only when you need to keep similar topics together for quick and easy reference or need to bring that information with you to a meeting. If you want to keep a binder in your filing cabinet along with related items, look for hanging binders in an office supply store. These are especially handy for storing newsletters, phone lists, manuals, or other reference materials.

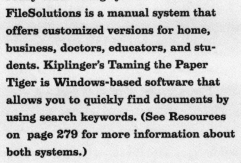

TIME-SAVER

Set up the perfect filing system for you by using a ready-made filing system. FileSolutions is a manual system that offers customized versions for home, business, doctors, educators, and students. Kiplinger's Taming the Paper Tiger is Windows-based software that allows you to quickly find documents by using search keywords. (See Resources on page 279 for more information about both systems.)

For detailed information about organizing financial records, see page 125. Following are some general filing suggestions for personal records.

• Keep receipts and other tax documents in one place, so that they're handy when you're ready to do your taxes.
• Set up a file for automotive service and repairs. Keep it for as long as you own your vehicle.
• Set up a file for each child that includes Social Security numbers, medical forms, report cards, and any other records you wish to keep.
• File operating manuals and warranties in a hanging folder. If you wish, you can set up interior manila folders and file manuals and warranties by room. The important thing is to keep them all together in one place. Staple the receipt to the documentation. This will make it easier to follow up with the store or company if there is a warranty problem. Keep the warranties, manuals, and receipts for as long as you own the item. Or, if you prefer, file manuals, warranties, and receipts in an accordion-style folder that you can store on a shelf.

Table It. Debbie Gilster of Organize & Computerize recommends making a master index for your files. You can make this list by creating tables with word-processing software or spreadsheet software. Create a table with two columns. Think of a short name for each of your filing cabinet drawers. In the first column, list the name of the drawer. In the second column, list all of the file names in that particular drawer. (Judy Stern of Organize NOW recommends doing this with two people: one to read off the names of the files and one to type the names.)

Use the sort feature to alphabetize the list. You can do a sort within a sort to see only the files for a certain drawer, or you can do a single sort and see all of your files. When filing, refer to the master index to determine where a paper should be filed. Write the location and file name in the upper right hand corner of the paper and store it temporarily in your "To File" bin. With a master index, you can do your filing from anywhere. Just take the stack of papers and master index with you. You might even be able to delegate the physical filing of papers.

One Challenge . . .

What's the best way to organize reminders and little pieces of information I don't want to lose? I've got little scraps of paper and sticky notes everywhere, and still I can't find what I'm looking for when I need it.

Three Solutions

1 FROM MITZI WEINMAN, TIMEFINDER: I recommend creating a paper fact file by using a small, three-ring notebook with tabbed separators, A through Z. Put a few sheets of paper in each section. Write important bits of information directly into your notebook under the letter where you are most likely to look first for this information such as "D" for directions, "P" for passwords, or "B" for books you want to read. Once you've entered the information, you can discard the paper.

2 FROM PAT VOYAJOPOULOS, OASIS: Save bits as bytes! Create an electronic version of the paper fact file described by Mitzi Weinman using your spreadsheet program. Set up twenty-six worksheets, one for each letter of the alphabet, within one workbook. As you receive information, type it into your spreadsheet on the appropriate page.

3 FROM STAFF, THE CONTAINER STORE: The solution may be right at your fingertips. If you use a revolving card file for phone numbers and addresses, you can use it to record other information as well. Simply file it under the appropriate letter of the alphabet. Record deadlines and birthdays on your calendar. This will prevent little scraps of paper from piling up on your desk.

CHAPTER 12

STORAGE AND UTILITY AREAS

The basement, attic, and garage are often the most disorganized rooms in the house, because that's where we dump everything we don't want in the living area. The same goes for the back porch, sheds, off-site storage areas, and for utility rooms — workshops, laundry rooms, and cleaning closets. Organizing these rooms can save time, reduce frustration, and make household tasks easier.

Organize a Cleanup

Schedule some time to clean up and clean out storage areas. If you have adult children no longer living at home, let them know that you are planning to unclutter and organize your storage areas. Give them a deadline to come and get their stuff. Donate or throw away whatever is still there after the deadline.

You'll need all the help you can get in the cleanup, so get your family involved. Or invite a few friends or relatives to help you in return for helping them clean out their basements, attics, and garages. Once you get the job done, keep storage and utility rooms uncluttered by getting rid of things you are no longer using instead of storing them. Following are some suggestions for getting started.

- **Be prepared.** Before clean-up day, look at each area and make a list of what needs to be done and what you will need to do it. For example, you will need bags for hauling away trash and boxes for packing up donations, garage sale items, and things that belong somewhere else. Label these boxes clearly and set them up in the middle of the room, along with a supply of trash bags. You'll also need felt markers for labeling these boxes and storage boxes. You may need extra lighting so you can see what you're doing.
- **Plan to spend one entire day in each room.** If you're not done by the end of the day, you should have a pretty good idea of how much more time you need to finish. Schedule another clean-up day if necessary.

- **Wear comfortable clothing and shoes.** You'll be on your feet and moving around most of the day. Expect to get warm from your exertions (just think of all the extra calories you'll be burning!). And expect to get dirty.
- **Work in one room at a time.** In larger rooms, clear one section at a time. Assign sections to individual helpers or pairs of helpers.
- **Go through everything.** Open every box. Take everything off every shelf. Put back only what you want to keep. Consolidate boxes of similar items and label your boxes. You might even want to print out an inventory list and tape it to the outside of the box. Haul away what you decide to trash, donate, sell, repair, or move somewhere else.
- **Make clean-up more fun.** Let's face it. The last thing anyone *wants* to do is spend the day in a dark, musty basement, hot attic, or dirty garage. Make it more of a party. Play music, have refreshments on hand, and plan to take a lunch break. Also plan your reward — think of something fun that you and your helpers can do together when the work is done.

Basement, Attic, Garage, or Shed?

Should you store things in the basement, attic, garage, or shed? Base your decision on accessibility and climate. Easy accessibility makes a garage or shed ideal for storing frequently used sporting equipment, such as bicycles; lawn, garden, and snow removal equipment; trash cans and recycling bins; and automobile-related items. Basements also generally allow easy access to stored items. The attic is typi-cally the least accessible storage place, especially if it's just a crawl space or if you have to climb a pull-down staircase to get up there. Limit attic storage to things you need to access only occasionally, such as holiday decorations, moving boxes, and tax records.

Don't put things in storage that should really be trashed, donated, or sold. Do store things you use only once a year or less in the back or bottom of your storage area. Store items you need to access more frequently in the front or on top. Label everything using wide felt tip markers. Store boxes and bins with labels facing out so you can find what you're looking for without having to move heavy boxes. Folks who are super-organized may even want to tape an itemized list of the contents to the front of the box.

Basement Storage. Basements tend to be very humid, which creates a breeding ground for mold and mildew that can damage clothing and furniture. Some basements may also flood, or you could end up with water in your basement because of a sump pump failure, leaking washing machine, or broken pipe.

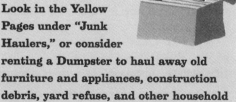

GOT JUNK?

Look in the Yellow Pages under "Junk Haulers," or consider renting a Dumpster to haul away old furniture and appliances, construction debris, yard refuse, and other household junk for disposal or recycling.

a word about off-site storage

Off-site storage should be a last resort. If you are currently renting storage space, think carefully about the items you are storing. Is it really worth the money to store this stuff? Or could you get rid of some or most or even all of it? Periodically, sort through items in your off-site storage area and reevaluate what you really need to keep.

Designate one area for all stored items. Unless you have a heat- and humidity-controlled basement, don't store anything directly on the floor. Place boxes on shelves or pallets and furniture on pallets. If you buy or build shelves, make sure they're deep enough to store boxes safely and high enough to let you sweep or vacuum underneath. Hang clothes in a freestanding closet or canvas garment bag.

Store like things together in boxes or crates, and label everything. Open crates on shelves are great for things that require frequent access, such as camping or sporting equipment. If flooding is a possibility, store everything in watertight plastic tubs. Cardboard boxes are fine for dry, well-ventilated basements.

Attic Storage. Although the attic is often the driest storage area, its contents are subject to extreme heat, especially during summer. Heat can damage photographs, audio and video cassettes, albums, and some clothing. Your attic may also be a winter home for mice and a year-round home for insects that can do damage. Use plastic containers with tight-fitting lids to protect clothing, books, and paper products. Cover furniture with old sheets to keep the dust off; if water leaks are a concern, use waterproof tarps instead. Stack or flatten extra boxes and store them at the far end of your attic, along with other long-term storage items.

Garage and Shed Storage. Storage space is often limited in the garage or shed, but you can maximize it by using vertical storage systems. Use vinyl-coated hooks to hang bicycles, sleds, winter tires, folding lawn chairs, and ladders from the rafters. Look at what items you might be able to hang and then figure out how many hooks you'll need to buy.

Use wall-mounted long-handled-tool holders to hang brooms, rakes, shovels, and other long-handled tools, or simply use two well-spaced nails that support the head of these tools. Another variation is to cut the top and bottom off of any size can and nail the can to the wall with the open ends facing the floor and ceiling. Slide the long handle of a tool down through the can; one tool per can works best for easy access.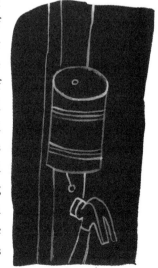

You can also create storage for long-handled tools between exposed studs. Purchase two 2 x 4 boards. Nail one board horizontally across the exposed studs approximately one foot off the ground and the second one approximately three feet off the ground. You can then slide long-handled tools in between the outside wall and the boards. Set up a metal or wood shelving unit along one wall for storing assorted loose items, such as automobile maintenance products, recycling bins, and in-line skates.

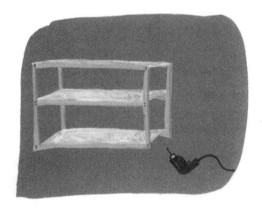

Workshop. Have you ever bought something from the hardware store only to discover days or weeks later that you already had it right there in your workshop? Is your workbench so cluttered that you have to push things aside to do anything? Once you get your workshop organized, your work area will be uncluttered and it will be easy to find the tools and supplies you need.

Before you start organizing, think about the way things are arranged in a hardware store. Broad categories of materials, such as plumbing and electrical supplies, are stored in separate sections. Hand tools are grouped by use. Screws, bolts, nails, and fasteners are organized in different compartments according to use and size.

Start organizing your workshop by sorting tools and supplies into major categories: electrical, plumbing, woodworking and building, household, and painting. Then sort within categories; for example, screwdrivers, wrenches, chisels. Use a box to collect tools and supplies you know you never use. Maybe you know someone who can use them, or perhaps you'll put them with other items you've been collecting for your next garage sale. Throw away all garbage, including broken tools and rusted hardware.

Next, designate storage areas for each of the major categories and find a place for everything. Try to keep categories as separate as possible.

THE ORGANIZED WORKSHOP

It's easier to get organized when you have items that will help you get organized.

- ❑ Sorting table (a sheet of plywood or an old door over two sawhorses works well)
- ❑ Large box for collecting giveaways
- ❑ Trash can or box for garbage
- ❑ Cardboard boxes or crates for containers
- ❑ Hardware organizer or assortment of lidded containers
- ❑ Label maker, or masking tape and wide-tip marker

You might assign separate shelves, separate cabinets or drawers, or even separate walls.

Accessibility is the key to an organized workshop. Keep the tools and supplies you use most often within easy reach. Store less frequently used items on upper shelves, under your workbench, or at the back of cabinets. If you can hang something, do it. Hanging is preferable to shelving because it keeps things more visible and accessible. Following are some storage ideas for your workshop.

- **Hang it up.** Use pegboard and pegs to hang power tools and large hand tools, such as saws and hammers. Use a marker to trace the silhouette of each tool onto the pegboard, for a visual reminder of where it goes. For tools with wooden handles, insert large eye screws at the end of each handle and hang them from hooks on the wall. If your ceilings are low, you might be able to attach wire shelving horizontally to the ceiling rafters and use S-hooks to

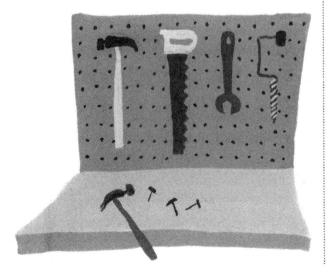

For Simplicity's Sake

Keep a master storage list, preferably on your computer. Update the list when you add to or retrieve an item from storage. If you use spreadsheet software to prepare your master storage list, you can alphabetize your list and sort by storage place.

hang tools. You can also hang a length of heavy-duty chain from a stud in the ceiling and place S-hooks at intervals on it. Keep lumber in racks that hang from the ceiling. Color-code the lengths like they do at the lumberyard by painting the ends of the boards: red for 10 foot, green for 12 foot, and so on.

- **Divide and conquer.** Use cardboard boxes, empty joint compound buckets, and plastic crates or bins to store similar items, such as plumbing supplies, on shelves. Label containers and shelves. Use glass jars (such as those from peanut butter, spaghetti sauce, or baby food) to store hardware. Divide hardware by type (nuts, bolts, screws, nails, picture hangers, and fasteners) and size. Screw the lids to the underside of a shelf, then screw the filled jars into the lids. You can also use lidded coffee cans. Lay the cans horizontally with the lid facing out. Label the lid, or tape a sample of what's inside to the lid. Drive a long nail or furring strip into each end of the shelf to keep the cans from rolling off.

- **Contain yourself.** Use a hanging shoe bag with clear plastic pockets to store small hand tools, such as screwdrivers and wrenches, and other small items, such as tape measures and pencils. Or nail coffee cans to the wall at about waist height, so that you easily see what's inside each one. To organize and contain small items in drawers, use recycled margarine tubs, spray can tops, resealable plastic bags, or an old cutlery tray.

Laundry Room

Do you have piles of dirty laundry on the floor of your laundry room? Nowhere to put clean clothes when they come out of the dryer? In a well-organized laundry room, there's a place for everything.

To eliminate the piles of laundry on the floor, set up "in" baskets for dirty laundry and "out" baskets for clean and folded laundry. See page 216 to learn how to set up a color-coded system for sorting dirty laundry and a system for returning clean laundry to its owners.

Mount a shelf directly above your washer or dryer for storing laundry detergent, bleach, stain treatment, fabric softener, and other laundry supplies. (If you can mount additional shelves, this might be a good place to store miscellaneous household items, such as extra paper goods, cleaning supplies, and flower vases.) You can buy an upright wire shelving unit that fits over your washer and dryer or a space-saving, coated wire shelf that hooks over the control panel of your washer or dryer and braces to the back wall. If there is no space above your washer and dryer, invest in a washer/dryer caddy that fits between or to one side of your appliances. Or keep a wheeled

organizer in a cleaning closet and roll it into the laundry room on wash day.

The laundry room is generally the best place to fold and sort laundry. If you have side-by-side appliances, keep the tops clean and clear so that you can use them for folding and sorting. Set up your ironing board for additional folding and sorting workspace, or keep a folding card table handy.

Get the organizing tools you need. Use a wall-mounted or over-the-door hanger that will hold your iron, ironing board, spray starch, and mister. Another handy gadget is a hanger holder that screws into a wall or door, giving you a place to hang pressed clothes and clothes that come out of the dryer. If you need a drying rack for fine washables, choose from stackable racks or pop-open racks that fold flat for storage. If space is limited, get a wall-mounted drying rack that you can pull out when you need it.

For tips on doing laundry, see page 216.

The Cleaning Closet

Cleaning closets tend to have their share of clutter — everything from cleaning products you bought and didn't like to things that got thrown in the closet when visitors arrived unexpectedly one day. The first step in organizing the closet is to take everything out and look at it critically. Put back in the closet only the tools and supplies that you use. Give away or discard everything else. If you have many old towels and rags for cleaning, keep only the number you need. Remember, there's more where they came from.

Organize your cleaning tools for easy access. Use wall-mounted long-handled-tool holders to hang your mop, broom, and carpet sweeper on the wall. Screw in hooks nearby to hang your dustpan, whisk broom, and feather or lambswool duster. Invest in an over-the-door wire rack for storing cleaning supplies, or hang a shoe bag with clear plastic pockets on the wall just inside the door. Organize cleaning products by category, and store similar items together. If you have shelves, use stack-and-slide baskets or clear plastic boxes to store small items, such as shoe polishes. Store the most frequently used cleaning products in a bucket that you can carry from room to room.

If you don't have a cleaning closet, store cleaning tools and supplies under a bathroom or kitchen sink. Keep your vacuum cleaner in the hall closet. Hang brooms and mops on a wall in your mud room, in a hidden space in your kitchen, or on the wall along the cellar stairs. Hide furniture polish and a rag in your living or dining room.

Label all shelves, drawers, cabinets, containers, and areas in storage and utility rooms. Labeling not only helps everyone find what is needed, when it's needed, it also enables everyone to participate in maintaining these areas.

— Donna Cowan, Cowan & Company Professional Organizing

Organizing Your Car

Your car is much smaller than your home, but it has an incredible amount of storage space per cubic foot. There's the trunk (or the back of a truck or van), glove compartment, and space under your front seats. You also might have seat and door pockets and between-seat storage compartments. Organize this storage space well, and you can say farewell to car clutter. Keeping your car neat and organized not only makes it look nicer, it makes you feel better about driving it. And it can help to maintain the value of your car.

The first step to organizing your car is to clear out the clutter. Bring out a trashbag to collect garbage and a box or laundry basket to collect things that do not belong in the car. Open the glove compartment. Do you really need to keep the car stereo manual, or even the car manual, there? Maybe you could use that space to store a bottle of water and some nonperishable food items, in case of an emergency. Go through your trunk and decide what you want to keep in there. Put everything else in the trash or the "Store Elsewhere" box or basket.

Now you're ready to start organizing each storage space. Look at the spaces that are most convenient to the driver's seat: behind the visor, on the dash, in the door, between the front seats, and under the seat. These are the best places to stow your cell phone, CDs and tapes, sunglasses, umbrella, and anything else you need to keep handy. Remember that valuables should be stored out of sight or, better yet, not left in the vehicle.

Many products have been designed to help you organize your essentials in the car. You can buy an inexpensive cell phone holder that attaches to the dashboard, so that you won't have to search for the phone when it rings. Portable carry cases provide easy access to the music of your choice and make it easier to exchange CDs and tapes with music from your main collection. A visor organizer is great for collecting gas, toll, and meal receipts or stashing a couple of business cards. You can also buy a pocketed bag that hangs over the back of a front seat to store children's essentials, such as toys or extra diapers. Or store these things in a tote bag on the floor behind the front seats.

If you don't have a door pocket, use the space under your seat to store such things as your CD carrying case, umbrella, flashlight, and maps. Buy a map case, or store maps in a zippered plastic bag. Use the compartment between seats or the glove compartment to store a small pad of paper and a couple of pens, napkins, a travel pack of tissues, wet wipes, or a small bottle of antibacterial soap that doesn't require water.

To keep your car litter-free, keep a small plastic bag in there for collecting trash. Hang it around the cigarette lighter, or secure it to a side window by using a suction cup hook. Organization, etc. (see Resources, page 281) sells a lidded leak-proof bag that hangs over the back of your seat. Get in the habit of picking up trash every time you get out of the car and emptying the trashbag every time you fill up your car with gasoline.

For Safety's Sake

Emergency kit for your car. Be prepared for emergencies and keep the following emergency essentials in the back of your vehicle. Some items, such as bottled water and non-perishable food, could save your life if you are stranded.

- Spare tire
- Car jack
- Tire iron
- Can of flat fixer
- Wheel chock
- Emergency road flares
- Jumper cables
- Work gloves
- Old towel or rag
- Wire and wire cutters
- Bottled water and nonperishable food
- Flashlight and extra batteries

- Cigarette lighter
- Gallon jug of water for radiator
- First-aid kit
- Pocket knife

Further essentials for cold, snowy climates include:

- Blanket, hat, scarf, and mittens
- Small bag of cat litter, sand, or rock salt
- Shovel
- Ice scraper
- Wiper fluid

If you have room, leave your cooler in the car throughout the summer months. When you go grocery shopping, pick up some bagged ice and use the cooler to keep refrigerator and freezer items cold until you get home. To keep the cooler from sliding around in the trunk, set it on an old bathroom rug with the "grippy" back side faceup.

Since your car goes just about everywhere with you, it's a great place to keep things you might need while you are out and about. This includes the following items.

- A couple of rain ponchos
- Sunscreen and insect repellent
- Bungee cords or rope, for tying down large purchases
- Telephone book
- Change of clothes for each child
- Extra diapers, baby wipes
- Blanket
- Travel toys and books
- Small bag of toiletries including a toothbrush and toothpaste, dental floss, deodorant, nail clippers, nail file, and feminine products

Stash these just-in-case items in a crate, lidded storage box, duffel bag, or diaper bag in your cargo area. You might also want a separate container for automotive items, such as windshield washer fluid, oil, and a rag for checking oil.

If you use your car for business, consider getting a hanging file box for papers and files you need to have with you. You may also find it useful to keep some office supplies handy. A tackle box makes a nice portable storage box for postage stamps, paper clips, pens, pencils, markers, and notepaper.

Sports Equipment

Store only sports equipment that is being used regularly. Donate or sell outgrown bicycles and skis. Throw away broken equipment, or have it repaired. Get rid of exercise equipment that is not being used; sell it at a garage sale or through the classified section of your local newspaper.

If there's enough room in your garage, designate one wall as an indoor "parking" area for children's bicycles and riding toys. Ask children to "park" there whenever they're done riding. To encourage them, you could make parking signs with their names on them. For quick clean-up of smaller outdoor toys, designate a large, clean trashcan in the yard or garage.

Assign one area of your garage, basement, or shed for storing all sports equipment. Hang bicycles from the rafters or on the wall, or install a bike storage pole that extends from floor to ceiling and requires no mounting. Snowshoes, ice skates, and bicycle helmets can be hung on the wall. Store baseball bats, lacrosse and hockey sticks, fishing poles, skis and ski poles between exposed studs (see page 105). Or buy an organizing product specifically designed for sports equipment that has space for tall stuff and shelves and drawers for smaller stuff.

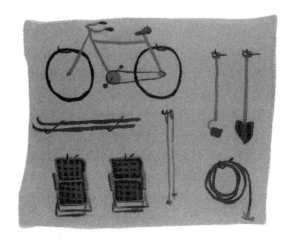

Keep balls in a large netted bag that hangs from the wall or ceiling of the garage, in a clean trashcan, or on a narrow shelf with a piece of wood or large nail at each end to keep them from rolling off. Another idea is to string a nylon hammock across one corner of the garage. You can use it to store balls, baseball gloves, bicycle helmets, and hockey pads.

Holiday Decorations

What do you do with a half-used roll of Valentine's Day tissue paper, the reusable Easter decorations, or a dozen cups and napkins with jack-o-lanterns on them that are left over from your Halloween party? Why, save them for next year, of course. But this year, store them so that you can find them again next year.

Gather all decorations and supplies for every holiday. Then place them into one box for each holiday. Get same-size boxes that you can store individually on shelves (the ideal situation) or stack in order of holidays and rotate as the holidays pass.

Label boxes in big bold letters on the side that faces out or decorate each box with wrapping paper, artwork, or colors from each holiday. This is a great project for young artists. If you decide to buy large plastic storage tubs, select tubs with different colored lids for easy identification. These tubs are a good choice if you plan to store holiday decorations in a damp garage or basement or in an attic that harbors mice.

Holiday ornaments require care when packing. Protect your ornaments from break-

HANG IT UP

Cover hanging decorations with clear plastic trash bags, tape the bags shut, and hang them from rafters in your basement, garage, or attic.

age by using ornament boxes, which are available wherever organizing products are sold. Or wrap ornaments in tissue or newspaper and store several in each partition of a cardboard liquor or wine box; your local liquor store will be happy to give these to you. Very small breakable ornaments can be stored in empty egg cartons secured with a rubber band around each end. To keep strands of holiday tree lights or garland from becoming a tangled mess, wrap them around empty wrapping paper tubes.

Keep year-round wrapping paper in an accessible yet out-of-the-way location, such as a shelf in your laundry room or cleaning closet or under your sofa or bed. If you have many rolls of gift wrap, a cardboard map/plans box from an office-supply store can help keep them organized. Keep the paper clean by putting several rolls in a clear plastic trash bag that's secured with a twist tie. Keep rolls of paper from unraveling by slitting an empty wrapping paper tube from end to end and sliding it over the new roll. With this system, you can also dispense paper neatly and easily through the slit. Or slip one leg cut from a pair of old pantyhose over one or more rolls and secure the open end with a twist tie. Consider limiting yourself to one or two kinds of gift wrap and one or two colors of ribbon and bows that will work for everything. A pretty pastel print will work for showers and weddings, and a brightly colored print makes a fine wrap for birthday presents for children, men, and women.

Managing Memorabilia

As you unclutter your storage areas, you will come across some (or many) things with sentimental value. What should you do with them? Do what feels right to you. You may look at some stuff and say, "What am I saving *this* for?" and not hesitate to throw it away. Or you may say, "I couldn't possibly part with this" — so don't. But do find a suitable home for the things you wish to keep.

Decide how much space you are willing to give to memorabilia; it might be a box or a shelf or an entire closet. When your stuff expands beyond that space, you'll know it's time to pare down. If space is at a premium right now, choose to keep the items that are most precious to you and offer the rest to your children or siblings. Or bring memorabilia out of hiding and out in the open, where you can see and enjoy it. Here are a few suggestions:

• Take photos of your children's artwork. Put the photos in your photo album and let go of the physical memento. (Remember, don't store photographs and scrapbooks in the attic or basement, where they are exposed to intense heat or high humidity. Store these in the main area of your home, away from light and heat.)

• Make a keepsake quilt from scraps of clothing, such as your father's flannel shirts, your favorite baby clothes, or your T-shirt collection. Or trace children's artwork onto cotton squares, sew them together, and use fabric paint to color them exactly like the originals.

• Drape one of your mother's pretty scarves over your dresser, use one to hang a decorative wreath, or artfully arrange a few over a curtain rod to create a unique valance.

• Laminate and use event tickets as bookmarks. Store them in a basket or box on a bookshelf.

• Create a mosaic plant pot or a picture frame from pieces of a broken vase or chipped dishes.

TRAVEL SOUVENIRS

If you're a born collector like I am, you enjoy keeping souvenirs from your trips. But then what do you do with them once you get them home? When it comes to inexpensive souvenirs such as lapel pins, coins, and matchbooks, I recommend collecting only one of each item from each place you visit. To keep souvenirs organized at home, invest in organizers designed for collectibles. Display pins in shadow boxes, using foam and black velvet to fill the frame. Arrange and display postcards in large picture frames or in scrapbooks or photo albums. Look for a nice display case for storing collections of items such as matchbooks, spoons, golf balls, and shot glasses.

— Stephany Smith Gonser, Put Simply Consulting

PART III

Organizing Finances

Whether you are living from paycheck to paycheck or off the interest from an inheritance, it pays to get your financial house in order. Whatever your financial situation, you can always improve it by learning to manage your money better, taking steps to reduce your debt (and spending), and developing strategies to increase your savings and investments.

Organizing your finances can have a profoundly positive effect on your life. In chapter 16, "Living on Less," you will find dozens of ideas for simplifying your life and gaining financial freedom by organizing your spending around needs rather than wants.

You would do well to consult with a certified financial planner who can evaluate your financial fitness, develop a plan for reaching your goals, and recommend specific steps for achieving those goals.

CHAPTER 13

MANAGING YOUR MONEY

Many think that managing money means making ends meet, but it's also about making the best use of your assets so that you can achieve your financial goals. Do you have a personal financial plan to achieve those goals? Are you and your assets protected? Do you have a budget and a system for paying bills? Are your financial records organized in one place?

Assessing Your Situation

Start taking control of your finances by looking at your current financial status and developing some goals. Put your goals in writing. Make them specific and quantitative: for example, "I want to become debt-free in two years" or "I want to retire by age sixty and have an income of $3,000 a month." Once you know where you are and where you are going, you can develop a personal financial plan.

Get a snapshot of your financial status by preparing a balance sheet or net worth statement. This is a simple financial planning tool that weighs everything you own (your assets) against everything you owe (your liabilities). Liabilities include mortgages, charge accounts, and loans. Assets include the following:

• Cash and cash equivalents (cash on hand, bank and credit union accounts)
• Liquid investments that can be easily converted to cash (CDs, cash value of insurance policies, bonds, trusts, stocks and mutual funds, securities and annuities, gold and silver, employee savings plans, and money owed to you)
• Nonliquid investments (individual retirement accounts and other retirement funds, investment real estate, business interests and partnerships)
• Personal possessions (house, cars, antiques, jewelry, other)

To prepare a balance sheet, make a list of all of your assets and liabilities. Calculate a total for each of the four categories of assets listed above. Then add up your liabilities. Subtract your liabilities from your assets, and you will have your net worth. If the figure is negative, then you owe more than you own. In that case, you'll want to concentrate your energies on developing and implementing a personal financial plan to reduce debt. You'll find lots of information about reducing debt in chapter 14, "Spending and Debt."

If your net worth is positive, take a closer look at your assets. Do you have enough cash or liquid assets for emergency reserves, or are most of your assets nonliquid? Conventional wisdom advises us to have on hand the equivalent of three to six months' take-home pay. This fund is meant to cover your expenses should you lose your job or be unable to work because of injury or illness. It's also nice to have emergency reserves in case you need to pay for an unexpected house repair, car repair, or medical bill. Stockpiling an emergency fund is a good savings goal to work toward once you have eliminated your debts.

Conversely, if most of your assets are in low-yield savings accounts and your goal is to retire rich or at least comfortably, you will want your financial plan to include more higher-yield investments. You'll find more information about savings and investments in chapter 15, "Saving and Investments."

Protecting Your Assets

Part of managing your money involves insuring your assets as well as your intentions regarding your assets. Without adequate insurance, you could lose everything you own. And,

Keep systems as simple as possible so that things fall into place with little or no effort.

— Pat S. Moore, The Queen of Clutter

if you don't update your will or the beneficiaries on your insurance plans, your assets could end up going to an ex-spouse.

Following are seven types of personal insurance. You may not need all of them, but you should consider each one and determine whether it should be part of your financial plan.

1. Health insurance. Without health insurance, a major illness or lengthy hospital stay could deplete your nest egg. Worse yet, you could end up owing tens of thousands of dollars in medical bills. However, many people overpay for health insurance. If you have an emergency reserve fund, you may be able to bring down your monthly premiums by choosing a policy with a higher deductible. Consider all of your options, but don't consider going without health insurance, even if it's just major medical insurance that covers only hospital expenses.

2. Life insurance. If your death would cause hardship for your spouse or children, you need life insurance. If not, you probably don't, unless you want just enough coverage to take care of your final expenses. The next decision is whether to buy a term-life policy or whole-life policy with a cash value. Most financial advisers agree that you may be better off getting term life insurance, which is available for a lower cost, and investing the difference for long-term growth. Do some research and consult with your insurer of choice to figure out what's right for you.

3. Disability insurance. If you're younger than age sixty, your chances of becoming disabled are much greater than your chances of dying. If you are the primary breadwinner, it's worth investigating disability insurance, which would pay a portion of your regular income.

ANNUAL CHECK-UP

As a financial planner, I like to look at the big picture. This is why I ask my clients a lot of questions, including:

- **Who is named as the beneficiary on your life insurance policy?**
- **Who is the beneficiary of your retirement accounts?**
- **Do you have a will? When was the last time you reviewed it?**

Sometimes we discover that the person named as the heir on a will or the beneficiary on a life insurance policy or retirement account is an ex-spouse or deceased relative. Things change. That's why I recommend periodically reviewing your will and updating it as necessary. Also periodically check to see that the beneficiary designations on your life insurance policy and retirement accounts are correct, especially if you are or have been divorced.

—Bob Colley, Cornerstone Financial Advisors

This type of insurance is pricey, but you may be able to reduce your premium by selecting to receive benefits after 180 days rather than 90 days. This is another reason to have an emergency reserve of cash.

4. Long-term care insurance. This type of insurance covers long-term hospital and nursing home stays. The earlier you start paying for this insurance, the less you have to pay each year. Alternatives to long-term care insurance include saving specifically for this possibility, tapping into your home equity, or relying on government assistance.

5. Homeowner's or renter's insurance. Homeowner's insurance covers your home (structure and contents) against virtually everything except war damages, earthquakes, floods, and nuclear power plant accidents. Renter's insurance covers contents only. Both types of insurance include coverage for belongings you might take away from your home and also protect against most non-business-related lawsuits, except those covered by your automobile insurance. Be sure that your insurance plan will replace property at its current value, not what you paid for it. Valuables such as jewelry and furs must be covered separately.

6. Automobile insurance. Some states do not require automobile coverage, but it's a good idea to have it anyway because it will cover you if you're responsible for an accident or if your car is damaged by an uninsured or underinsured driver. Get quotes from several companies. If you have an emergency reserve fund, you may be able to reduce your monthly premium by increasing your deductible.

7. Personal umbrella insurance. If you are sued as a result of an automobile accident or injury sustained on your property, your automobile or homeowner's/renter's insurance will cover up to $300,000 and $100,000, respectively. (Check your insurance policies to make sure that you are covered to these maximum amounts.) An umbrella personal insurance policy extends these limits to $1,000,000 or more, depending on the coverage you choose.

Establishing a Budget

The most critical component of managing money is budgeting. A budget allows you to track what comes in and what goes out. It's also a great tool for learning where you can cut expenses, thereby freeing up cash to reduce debt or invest for your future. In short, a budget can help you gain control of your finances — and your life.

There are two types of expenses: fixed and variable. Fixed expenses include mortgage and rent payments, property taxes, car and loan payments, insurance premiums, tuition, and day care. If you pay a set amount on a regular basis, it's a fixed expense. Everything else is a variable expense. This category includes utilities, groceries, clothing, eating out, haircuts, and entertainment.

thy will be done

Do you have a will? If not, your property will be distributed according to the laws of the state in which you live. Having a will is the only way to make certain that your assets and personal possessions are distributed in the way that you want, without unnecessary delays. It's also important to have a power of attorney that authorizes someone you trust to manage your financial and legal affairs if you are unable to do so. This document cannot be drawn up after the fact. (See chapter 27, "Organizing Your Estate," for more information.)

One way to get a handle on your actual expenses is to review your checkbook register. List all expenditures for the past six months in a budget sheet like the one shown in the chart on the next page, or use a spreadsheet program. Then break your list into fixed and variable expenses. Total up all expenditures in each category, such as groceries or parking, and divide by six to get the average monthly expense for each.

To create a budget that really works, you also need to figure out where your cash goes. Although it's a lot of work, the simplest and best way to track cash expenditures is to write down every penny you spend and for what. Don't change what you normally spend. Just write it down in a small spiral notebook that you carry everywhere. At the end of one month, total up what you spent in each category. Then add these expenses into your budget as variable expenses.

monthly budget

Expense Item	January	February	March	April
Fixed Expenses:				
Rent or mortgage				
Car payments (list separately)				
Car insurance				
Other insurances				
Child care				
Prescription drugs				
Cable				
Internet access				
Savings and investments				
Variable Expenses:				
Credit card payments (list separately)				
Telephone				
Electric and heat				
Food (groceries, school lunches, snacks at work, eating out)				
Clothing				
Household furnishings				
Transportation (include gasoline, tolls, parking)				
Recreation and entertainment (include subscriptions, allowances)				
Personal grooming (include beauty, dry cleaning, laundry)				
Charitable contributions				
Memberships				
Other (pet care, gifts, cards)				
TOTAL				

May	June	July	August	September	October	November	December

Once you know what you're spending each month, compare it to what you earn each month *after* tax. Earnings include take-home pay, commissions or bonuses, tips, alimony and child support, rental property income, dividends and interest, Social Security benefits, and retirement funds. Then evaluate your financial health.

- If your earnings exceed your expenses, you can use the surplus to reduce debts or contribute to savings or investments.
- If your expenses equal your earnings, you are probably living from paycheck to paycheck. Take a look at your variable expenses to see where you might be able to make some cutbacks without seriously affecting the quality of your life. Consider bringing your lunch to work at least a few days a week, carpooling, eating out less often, or buying clothing at discount stores. Use any "found" money to build savings for unplanned expenses and for retirement.
- If your expenses exceed your income, reduce expenses to avoid getting deeper in debt. If necessary, investigate extra sources of income. Eliminate or reduce all nonessential expenses until you can balance your expenses and earnings. Also take a good look at your fixed expenses. You may be able to find a comparable apartment for less money or trade in your car for a less expensive one.

Maintaining Your Budget

Once you have established a realistic budget, make a conscientious effort to stick to it for at least three months. At the end of each month,

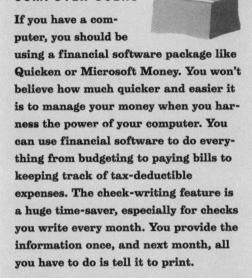

A MUST FOR COMPUTER USERS

If you have a computer, you should be using a financial software package like Quicken or Microsoft Money. You won't believe how much quicker and easier it is to manage your money when you harness the power of your computer. You can use financial software to do everything from budgeting to paying bills to keeping track of tax-deductible expenses. The check-writing feature is a huge time-saver, especially for checks you write every month. You provide the information once, and next month, all you have to do is tell it to print.

—*Karen Simon, PC Tech Associates*

compare your budget figures to actual figures. It may be helpful to make a chart that allows you to do this easily. If you are way off course after the first month, don't give up. Look at what happened and see if you can make a couple of adjustments during the next month to bring those numbers closer together. After a few months, you should need to make only minor adjustments.

Saving up for a major purchase or annual expenses, such as vacations or holiday gifts, can be tricky. The key is to plan ahead and set aside some money every month. Divide the amount you will need by twelve and add that figure to your monthly budget. Then write a check each month to your general savings account, or open a special savings account specifically for annual expenses.

Paying the Bills

Processing bills is a routine task that you can simplify with a system that organizes the whole process, from where to store bills that need to be paid to what to do with bills and receipts after they've been paid. Your system should also take into account when, where, and how you process bills.

Is bill-paying a chore you dread? Consider trading off this responsibility with one of your partner's responsibilities. Or find a way to make it more pleasant. You could, for example, make it a point to play your favorite music or tie a reward to paying bills, such as writing a check to your savings account or treating a friend to lunch on what's left of your entertainment budget.

Designate one area in your home as a bill-paying place, and keep everything you need to pay the bills there. Store bill-paying supplies in nearby drawers or cabinets, or put them in a portable storage bin that you can stash somewhere when not in use.

Scheduling bill-paying days also helps to streamline the process. Get in the habit of paying bills on the first and fifteenth of the month or on every payday. That way, you're more likely to pay bills on time and will avoid having to pay late fees and interest charges. Paying bills on time also maintains (or re-establishes) a good credit record.

Store bills to be paid in one place close to where you open mail or where you sit down to pay bills. If you pay bills twice a month, you might try storing bills in a folder with two pockets, one for bills to be paid on the first of

the month and one for bills to be paid on the fifteenth. Keep a running list of each bill you need to pay, along with the amount due and the due date. As you pay each bill, cross it off the list. Add new bills to the bottom of the list. Write check numbers on paid bills and file the stubs in folders labeled by category, such as "Telephone" or "Car Insurance." (See page 125 for more information about organizing financial records.)

What You Need

Typical bill-paying supplies include:

- ❏ Calculator
- ❏ Postage stamps
- ❏ Envelopes
- ❏ Return address stamp or stickers
- ❏ Pen
- ❏ Calendar
- ❏ Stapler
- ❏ Paper clips
- ❏ Blank checkbooks and registers

To reduce the number of checks you write each month, consider paying bills electronically. You may be able to set up an automatic withdrawal from your checking account to pay your telephone or electric bill, insurance premiums, or credit card bill. Paying electronically saves you the time (and expense) of writing and sending checks. Of course, this has to be something you are comfortable with. And you still have to remember to write the amount paid in your checkbook register.

Many banks and independent companies, such as Paytrust, also allow you to receive, review, and pay all of your bills on-line. You decide who to pay, how much, when, and from which account. Paytrust even allows you to make a payment to someone who doesn't normally send you a bill, such as your babysitter or gardener. The best part is that you don't have to file anything — they store all of your bills on-line (securely, of course) for one full year and off-line for up to eight years. At the end of each year, you can purchase a CD-ROM with all of your bill images from the past year.

If you prefer to pay all bills by check, consider setting up two separate checking accounts. Use one account to pay fixed expenses (including payments to your savings and investment accounts) and the other account to pay variable expenses. Take enough out of each paycheck to cover all of your fixed expenses and put the rest in your variable expense account to pay for groceries, clothing, and entertainment. If you and your partner split the bill paying, you could set up a joint money market account into which you deposit all income and two separate checking accounts in your names for paying bills. Each month, you and your partner would then write a check to your respective accounts to pay whatever bills are your responsibility.

One simple bill-paying system that works well for families with limited income is the envelope or cash system. When you deposit your paycheck, leave enough money in your checking account to cover fixed expenses. Take the balance of your paycheck in cash for variable expenses. Based on your budget, divide that cash accordingly into separate envelopes for groceries, gas, entertainment, and other anticipated expenses, such as allowances for each family member. This system limits your spending to whatever cash you have on hand. If you run out of money for one expense category, you can borrow from another envelope, but in the end, there's only so much money you have to spend.

Whatever system you use, be sure to balance your checking account each month as soon as the statement arrives. One little mistake in addition or subtraction can end up costing you a fortune in overdraft and bounced check fees. And banks can make mistakes, too; you'll want to catch and address such errors promptly.

Organizing Financial Records

Most of us save more paperwork than is necessary, and we do it because we think we have to or because we've always saved everything. But really, how often do you refer back to your cable bill? If there's no need to save paid bills, filing them is a waste of time and energy, not to mention a waste of filing space.

Following is a guide to help you determine what papers you should save and which ones you can toss. This is only a guide. For complete and current guidelines for keeping tax-related papers, refer to Internal Revenue Service (IRS) publication 552, "Recordkeeping for Individuals," at www.irs.gov/.

- **Paycheck stubs**. Check each one for accuracy. Then toss them. Save only the most recent stub, which may be requested as proof of income or employment if you decide to apply for a loan.
- **Deposit slips, ATM withdrawal slips, and debit charge receipts.** Save them to verify amounts on your next bank statement, and then toss. Save debit charge receipts only if they represent a tax-deductible expense or will provide proof for a warranty claim.
- **Bank statements, canceled checks, and check registers.** Save bank statements for three full tax years. You may need them for a tax audit or to prove that you paid a bill if you don't have the receipt. You'll also need to produce bank statements if you apply for a mortgage loan to prove that the money you intend to use for the down payment is not borrowed money. After three years, you can shred or burn statements. Save canceled checks for one year, then destroy all but the ones that support tax-deductible expenses. Keep canceled checks in the envelope with the bank statement, label the outside of the envelope with the start and end dates of your statement period, and file in your current year's files. In an effort to reduce paper, see whether your financial institution will send your statements electronically and keep your canceled checks. Do save check registers, as these will help you to track down the canceled checks. Write start and end dates and starting and ending check numbers on the front of the register.

- **Non-tax-deductible credit card receipts.** If you use a credit or debit card to make purchases, save all receipts from these purchases to verify the amounts on your statement. You may want to save all merchandise receipts for thirty days as proof of purchase should you decide to return an item for a refund or exchange. If an item comes with a warranty, staple it to the warranty certificate or product guide. It's also a good idea to save receipts for expensive articles of clothing, so that you have documentation of their value if an item gets lost or ruined by the dry cleaner. You may want to save receipts for furniture and other large-ticket items (anything over $100, for example) in a safe deposit box or fireproof file cabinet, along with photos and a household inventory list to document replacement value. Toss receipts for items you no longer own.
- **Tax-deductible credit card receipts.** Verify amounts against your next statement, record in your bookkeeping system, and file

with other tax records, which you should save for up to three full tax years. After three years, the government cannot ask for supporting documentation.

• **Credit card statements.** Check to be sure that your last payment was received and verify any new charges. When paying the bill, write the amount and date paid and check number on your statement. Save statements for credit cards that are used for tax-deductible expenses. Otherwise, you can toss last month's statement and keep only the most recent one.

• **Utility bills.** When the next bill arrives, check to make sure your account was credited for the correct amount, and toss the old bill.

• **Insurance policies and bills**. Save insurance policies for the period in which they are in effect. Save each monthly bill until the next one is received to check that your account was properly credited. Toss canceled insurance policies and related statements.

• **Tax returns.** The IRS has three years to audit your return, so keep tax returns for three consecutive full tax years. If you underreport your income by 25 percent or more, the IRS has six years to audit your return. And if you don't file returns at all or file a fraudulent claim, the IRS can audit at any time. All tax deductions must be backed up by receipts. Store tax returns and receipts in large manila envelopes. Label each envelope "Tax Return — 20XX." File it with previous years' returns in a cardboard storage box with lid and label the box. If you decide to destroy tax returns that

For Safety's Sake

Storing important documents. Rent a safe deposit box from your financial institution, or buy a fireproof safe for storing important financial and legal documents and any other information or items that cannot be replaced. Following is a list of documents that require safe keeping.*

• Marriage, birth, and death certificates
• Settlement and divorce papers
• Adoption, custody, and citizenship papers
• Trust papers, living will, and powers of attorney
• Property deeds
• Motor vehicle titles
• Stock and bond certificates
• U.S. Savings Bonds
• All contracts, including mortgage and land contracts, promissory notes, and other legally binding agreements
• Military papers
• Patents and copyrights
• Important diskettes
• Home inventory list, photos, and receipts

If you decide to store your will in a safe deposit box in your name only, be aware that the box will be sealed on your death, which could delay the transfer of your assets.

are older than six tax years, it's best to shred or burn them. Before destroying, be sure that your income for that year is reflected on your most current Social Security benefits statement.

- **Investment records.** Save all investment records and bank statements related to investments. If investment summaries are cumulative, you need to save only the most current one. It is not necessary to keep the prospectus from year to year. Keep savings certificates, stocks, bonds, and other securities in a safe deposit box or fireproof file cabinet.

- **Property records.** Keep real estate records for the duration of ownership or longer if needed for tax purposes. Real estate records include real property deeds, title papers, abstracts, mortgage and other lien documents, burial lot deed, tax assessment notices, purchase contracts, records of capital improvements (including rental property), motor vehicle titles, and purchase receipts.

- **Other.** If you have had a history of bad credit, or if your bank or credit company has made mistakes on your billing, keep those bills and any correspondence you have sent or received, especially correspondence that confirms a satisfactory outcome.

In most households, one person is responsible for managing the files. Would your partner or children know where to look for important legal or financial information they may need in the event that you cannot tell them? It's a good idea to set up a folder in your filing system labeled "In Case of Emergency." Give the hanging folder a red or yellow plastic tab that makes it stand out in the drawer. In this folder, include bank account numbers and passwords; phone numbers for your attorney, accountant, financial planner, and investment broker; the location of important documents, such as insurance policies, will, and power of attorney, and the location of the key to your safe deposit box or combination to your lockbox. Let your partner, adult children, or a trusted friend know that you have created this folder and where to look for it if necessary. Update the file periodically.

Preparing for Tax Time

The simplest way to be ready for tax time is to prepare throughout the year. Keep good records and store all your tax-related documents and records in one place so that you can find them when it's time to prepare your returns. If you did not do this last year and the deadline for filing your tax return is fast approaching, refer to the Tax Preparation Checklist on page 129 for a list of the records, documents, and information required to prepare your return.

You don't have to have a fancy filing system. The important thing is to create *some* kind of system for recording income and expenses and storing corresponding paperwork throughout the year. Your record book could be as simple as a spiral notebook in which you note the date, item, and who it was paid to or received from. Your filing system might be as simple as a file folder, envelope, or even a shoe box labeled "Taxes 20XX." File all receipts immediately so you don't lose them. Separating receipts by month or by type of expense such as postage or utilities will make it easier to track down a particular receipt in the event you are audited. Also file all documents marked "Important Tax Information."

Avoid mixing business with pleasure. Deposit all business income into a business checking account and use this account to pay business bills. If you use a credit card for business expenses, use that card for business expenses only. Keep your bank and credit card statements with your tax records along with canceled checks. Refer to page 125 for details about how long to save financial records.

The Honorable Learned Hand, former U.S. Appeals Court justice, once said, "There are two systems of taxation in our country: one for the informed and one for the uninformed." Unless your tax income returns are extremely simple, it's almost always worth paying a professional tax preparer to do them for you. You may be very good at math and enjoy working with numbers, but do you know and understand all of the most recent changes in tax law that could affect your tax liability? The extra you may unknowingly pay in taxes can easily offset the cost of hiring a good tax preparer. And it's a tax-deductible expense!

Ask your friends, family members, and business colleagues to recommend a tax preparer or certified public accountant (CPA). The best way to determine how much it will cost to prepare your tax returns is to bring copies to your prospective preparer. Keep in mind that the cost of preparing your return is one thing.

If you bring your shoe box full of receipts expecting your tax preparer to sort through it all, you will have to pay extra for that service. On the other hand, you may be able to save money on the cost of tax preparation by using a computer program for record keeping if the preparer is able to use your data files.

Be sure to inform your tax preparer of any major life events that occurred throughout the year. Life events that might change your tax status include:

- Adopting a child
- Birth of a child
- Going back to school
- Sending a child off to college
- Getting married or divorced or becoming widowed
- Buying or selling real estate
- Moving
- Starting your first job
- Changing jobs or being laid off
- Retiring

When you think about preparing your taxes, think about what you can do now to reduce your tax liability next year. For example, if you are expecting a baby by the end of the year, you can expect an additional tax deduction. So, if you wanted to, you could decrease the amount of tax withheld from your check so that you don't end up overpaying. Or, if you receive a windfall, you may want to increase the amount of your withholding to offset the amount of additional tax owing at the end of the year.

tax preparation checklist

Whether you meet with a tax preparer or do your own taxes, the first step is to gather all tax-related documents and information for the entire year including the following.

- Social security numbers for you, your spouse, and your dependents
- Current residential address and other residential addresses during the tax year

Income Records and Documentation

- Employment (W-2 forms)
- Trust, partnership, or S Corporation income (Schedules K-1)
- Unemployment compensation (1099-G forms)
- Miscellaneous income (1099-MISC forms and/or bookkeeping records)
- Retirement plan distribution, pensions, and annuities (1099-R forms)
- Social security benefits (RRB-1099 forms)
- State and local income tax refunds (1099-G forms)
- Sale of your home or other real estate (1099-S forms)
- Interest income statements (1099-INT and 1099-OID forms)
- Dividend income statements (1099-DIV forms)
- Proceeds from broker transactions (1099-B forms)
- Records for any other income that may be taxable or reportable including alimony, jury duty pay, gambling or lottery winnings, prizes and awards, scholarships and fellowships

Tax-Deductible Expenses*

- Mortgage interest paid (1098 form)
- Other interest paid (second mortgage, student loan)
- Real estate taxes paid
- Moving expenses
- Auto loans and leases if vehicle used for business (need account numbers and car value) or mileage records
- Contributions to retirement plans, early withdrawal penalties on financial assets, and investment expenses
- Charity gifts and donations
- Unreimbursed expenses related to volunteer work such as mileage
- Unreimbursed expenses related to your job including travel expenses, uniforms, union dues, subscriptions, office supplies
- Job-hunting and job-related education expenses
- Child care expenses (need name, address, and tax ID or social security number for payee)
- Medical savings accounts
- Alimony paid (requires social security number for payee)
- Tax return preparation fees
- Self-employment business expenses, including health insurance premiums and estimated income tax paid (requires documentation)

*Consult your tax preparer about allowable deductions in your situation.

One Challenge . . .

Every year, I find myself scrambling around trying to pull together all of the information I need to prepare my taxes. Last year, I was audited and it took me hours to find receipts for those tax-deductible expenses I had claimed in the previous year. Is there a simple way to keep track of my expenses that will also allow me to find whatever receipts I may need to produce in the future?

Three Solutions

1 FROM PAT S. MOORE, THE QUEEN OF CLUTTER: I like to keep things as simple as possible, especially when it comes to setting up something like a bill-paying center. I recommend having a separate spot for all unpaid bills — even a special napkin holder — to separate bills from other papers. I jot the due date on the envelope where the stamp goes and keep the bills in order of payment. When the bill is paid, the receipt (if you need to keep it for tax or legal purposes) goes into a file box, file drawer, or accordion file for the current year's records. At the end of the year, clean out the current year's records and archive anything tax-related to the tax file. Archive anything else you think you might need in a file out of your current box and shred everything else.

2 FROM JULIE SIGNORE, 1,2,3 SORT IT: I recommend what I call the *record book system,* which requires a sturdy, bound ledger. On the first twelve right-hand pages, enter the months of the year for the entire year. Leave the left-hand pages blank for recording all income. Under each month, enter the bills you pay regularly in that month. As you receive bills, fill in the amount due to the right of the entry and log the due date to the left. Store bills to be paid in your account book. Use the extreme left-hand column to record the date paid and use the extreme right-hand column to record the check number and amount paid. File all paid bills and receipts in manila envelopes (one for each month). If you need to find a receipt, the book will direct you to the envelope.

3 FROM JUDY WARMINGTON, WOMAN TIME MANAGEMENT: I usually recommend an eight-pocket portfolio folder for storing a year's worth of tax information. Label one pocket for each major expense category; for example, credit card statements, utilities, charitable donations, etc.). Or buy a letter-size, accordion-style folder with compartments that are preprinted with the months of the year. File all paid bills, canceled checks, and receipts in the appropriate month. Either way, you'll have all of the documentation for your taxes in one place at the end of the year.

CHAPTER 14

SPENDING AND DEBT

The more we earn, the more we spend, and the more we dig ourselves deeper in debt. There's only one way out to get out of debt. Start spending less than you earn, and make debt reduction your number one financial priority. Set some goals, keep track of your progress, and before long your debt will be history.

Debt-Reducing Strategies

You don't necessarily need to make more money to reduce your debt. Rather, you probably need to change what you do with the money you have. It's easy to fritter away money unless you realize how a buck here and a buck there adds up. Here's a good example: If you spend one dollar on a can of soda or a snack from the vending machine each day, you're spending $5 a week, or $20 a month. If you brought your own soda and snacks from home, you could apply the difference toward getting rid of your debt that much quicker.

Let's say that you have a credit card balance of $1,000 at 18 percent interest and that $15 of your minimum monthly payment of $25 goes toward interest. If you continue to pay the minimum every month, it will take you 12.75

years pay it off, and the total amount you will end up paying is $2,115.41.

The trick to reducing credit card debt is to pay back more than the minimum each month. If you make a fixed payment of $40 each month toward that same $1,000 debt, it will be paid in 2.67 years and the total amount paid will be $1,262.79. You might think that you can only afford to make the minimum payment, but as you can see from this example, paying the minimum ends up costing you more in the long run. Don't leave yourself short on cash for regularly occurring expenses, but do pay as much as you can each month on your debt. If it means going without a little luxury or two, that's probably appropriate.

If you can't pay more than minimum amounts due, just keep paying the *current* minimum amount due on each one of your card accounts. As your credit card balance goes down (because you're no longer charging things, right?), your minimum monthly payment will also go down, which actually lengthens the amount of time it will take to pay off your debt and puts more money in the bank's pocket. Look up the amounts you paid last month, and pay those same amounts every month.

Be sure to make credit card payments on time every month. If you make even one late payment or skip a payment one month, many credit card companies will increase your interest rate dramatically, making it take even longer to pay off your debt.

Work on paying off your debts one by one. List your debts in order of the lowest to highest amounts owed. Use whatever money you have freed up in your budgeting process to pay extra toward the first debt on your list. Pay the current minimum amount due on the other debts. Continue to do this each month until the first debt on your list is paid. Now, here's where you really start making progress. Combine the amount you've been paying on the first debt to the minimum monthly amount due on the next debt until it too is paid. Continue this process until all debt is paid. Then begin to apply your total debt reduction payment each month to savings and investments.

financial trouble?

In the last three to six months, have you:

- Paid only minimum payments on credit cards? **Yes/No**
- Had to borrow or take an advance to pay basic living expenses? **Yes/No**
- Consolidated debts by borrowing at a higher rate of interest? **Yes/No**
- Taken a cash advance on one credit card to pay another? **Yes/No**
- Missed one or more payments on charge accounts? **Yes/No**
- Paid your rent or mortgage late? **Yes/No**
- Received a collection notice or call? **Yes/No**
- Invested nothing in savings or retirement accounts? **Yes/No**
- Wondered how you would make it to the next paycheck? **Yes/No**
- Lost your spouse, been laid off, or unable to work due to illness? **Yes/No**

- Relied on credit cards to make ends meet? **Yes/No**
- Been afraid to open the mail or add up how much you owe? **Yes/No**

Scoring: Tally up the number of "yes" responses, then read below.
1–3 Take steps to protect your financial future by establishing a budget that includes debt reduction or regular contributions to savings.
4–7 Your "yes" responses are warning signs that you need to pay more attention to your finances. You may not feel like you're in trouble, but unless you learn to manage your money better, you are definitely headed for harder times.
8–14 You really didn't need to take this quiz because you know you're in trouble. Don't give up hope on your financial future. Seek the advice of a debt counseling service.

Keep in mind that banks want you to owe them because that's how they make money. From time to time, you may receive credit checks with an advertisement enticing you to use them to go on a well-deserved vacation, install a backyard pool, or get some other nice treat. Don't do it — it's a debt trap. Shred or rip up the checks (so that no one else can use them) and throw them away immediately.

Until you can pay off the entire balance every month, stop using your credit cards. Better yet, cut them up and throw them away. If you can't bring yourself to do that, put your credit cards in a small plastic tub filled with water and place the tub in the freezer. Freezing your credit cards will curb impulse credit card shopping by helping you make a conscious choice about what and when you will buy on credit. Once you get used to buying on cash (and you see your credit card balances going down), you may relish cutting up those credit cards.

Close unused credit accounts. It's a good idea to cancel credit cards that are paid in full for two reasons. First, it will keep you from getting sucked back into charging. Second, having too much open credit could result in a loan denial for a major purchase such as a home or car. When you cancel accounts you aren't using, the credit card companies will notify the credit reporting agencies that will update your credit file.

Trade credit cards for debit cards. A debit card combines the convenience of a credit card with the sensibility of paying cash. Debit cards are different from credit cards as they are tied to cash in a bank account. They are particularly useful for making airline, hotel, or car rental reservations over the telephone.

You can take steps to reduce your mortgage debt too. Pay extra monthly, annually, or whenever you can toward the principal in your mortgage. As little as $25 extra per month can add up to tens of thousands of dollars in savings in interest. It doesn't matter whether you pay this extra money monthly or in one lump sum at the end of the year. If you get a tax refund, consider applying it to your mortgage loan. When you are shopping for a mortgage or refinancing a home, consider a fifteen-year versus a thirty-year mortgage. The monthly payments will be slightly higher, but you'll own your house free and clear in half the time and save money in the long run.

Lowering Monthly Bills

One way to find more money for reducing debt or increasing your savings is to lower your monthly bills. Start first by looking at your largest expense — your home. We all need shelter, but your mortgage or rent payment may be eating up too much of your budget. One option for homeowners is to look into refinancing your mortgage. If interest rates have dropped since you financed your current loan, you may be able to reduce your mortgage payment. If you rent, look for a less expensive apartment or house.

Consider raising the deductibles on your insurance policies. Changing the deductible from $250 to $500 on your automobile could result in significant monthly savings. For self-employed individuals, choosing a higher deductible can make a huge difference in health insurance premiums. If you decide to raise your deductibles, be sure to have enough money in your emergency fund to pay the deductible without putting strain on your budget.

You may be able to reduce your telephone bill. Ask your telephone service provider whether you have the most economical plan for local calls based on your actual use. Ask your long-distance carrier for their best deal. Compare both plans with those of other providers and switch if it will result in savings. Make regional and long-distance calls during

off-peak hours. Look up telephone numbers in the phone book instead of calling information. If you are paying for optional services that you aren't using or really don't need, cancel them. Also shop around for the best cellular phone plan. There's no sense in paying for time and features that you are not using.

Take some simple steps to reduce heating and cooling costs. Consider installing energy-saving shades, especially if you live in a region with very hot summers or very cold winters. At the very least, lower your shades to keep the sun out on hot summer days and to keep heat in on cold winter nights. Turn lights off when not is use. A single light bulb left on twenty-four hours a day can cost you as much as $75 over the course of the year. In winter, turn your thermostat down at night and when you go to work. For every degree you lower your heat, you will save 2 percent on your total heating bill. You can safely lower your thermostat to 55°F if you will be away for an extended period of time. Ask your local electric utility company whether they offer a free home checkup and tips for reducing your energy use.

One way to save on your electric bill is to keep appliances operating at peak energy efficiency. Clean your dryer lint trap after every use, drain your hot water heater periodically, and vacuum refrigerator cooling coils twice a year. When purchasing new appliances, look for products that carry the Energy Star logo. (Energy Star is a program administered by the U.S. Environmental Protection Agency that offers energy-efficient solutions to consumers and businesses.)

Using Credit Cards Wisely

When you limit the number of credit cards you use, you reduce the number of bills you have to pay — and the time it takes to pay them each month.

If you are carrying debt on your credit cards, you can decrease the total amount you have to pay in interest by reducing the interest rate. To find the best rates available, go to Cardweb.com or Bankrate.com. If your credit history is good, you may be able to transfer balances from higher-rate cards to one lower-rate card. Be sure to read all the fine print that goes along with that great introductory offer. You may also be able to consolidate your credit card debt with a home equity loan. However, you could lose your house if you cannot pay back the loan.

At department stores, cashiers will often offer a discount on your purchases if you apply for the store's credit card on the spot. Your safest bet is to decline the offer. Take the offer only if you can *definitely* (not probably) pay off the entire balance when the bill arrives. Then cancel the account and cut up the card. Store credit cards generally have very high interest rates.

Consider choosing credit cards with a payback. Some cards offer frequent flyer miles or membership rewards. If you use it for everything (groceries, gas, restaurants, travel, and so on), you get back a little something. The Discover card offers 1 percent cash back on total annual purchases; you could invest this refund in savings or investments. You must pay off your balance every month, however,

For Safety's Sake

Guard against fraud. Sign new credit cards immediately and protect cards like you would cash. Destroy or file credit card receipts or any document that lists your account number. And never give out your credit card information over the telephone unless you are the one placing the call and you are confident that you are dealing with a reputable company.

otherwise the interest you pay will far outweigh the cash you get back. And be sure to choose a card that doesn't charge an annual fee, definitely an unnecessary expense.

Charge big-ticket items as soon as possible after your credit card's billing cycle closes. Look at a recent credit card statement to determine when that date is. By timing your purchases, you'll be able to use and enjoy them for one whole month before having to pay for them. But do this only if you are going to pay off your entire balance at the end of the month. Otherwise, you'll end up paying more in interest.

Kick the Shopping Habit

Most of us go shopping with nothing particular in mind. But we always come home with something. According to the American Consumer Credit Counseling Service, half of all purchases are made on impulse. Unfortunately, these are the things that end up cluttering our homes!

Before you make the decision to buy a particular item, ask yourself if it is something you *need* or something you *want.* If you think you need it, ask yourself: Do I already have one or more of these? Is it going to improve the quality of my life in any way? Do I really need it, or would I rather put the money I would have spent into my savings account? If it's a luxury item and you really "must" have it, save up for it.

Go shopping only when you need something. Go with a list and stick to it. To minimize impulse buying, leave your credit card at home. When you shop with cash, you tend to think twice about your purchases. If you really want to buy something, walk away from it. Go to a different store, get a drink, or use the restroom. Then decide whether it's worth the walk back. Better yet, go home and think about it for a few days.

Resist the urge to splurge. If you are trying to reduce your spending so that you can pay down debt or increase your savings, remind yourself that waiting has its reward. Work on changing your mindset from "I want it now" to "I can have this and more if I wait until I reach my goal."

PAY DAY

Request a change in your credit card billing date if you have a bill that comes due at an awkward time of the month for you. Banks are usually willing to accommodate you.

—Lynne Crew, Affairs in Order

Consider the real cost of your purchases. Every dollar you spend represents the time and energy you gave to earn it. Think in terms of how many hours you need to work to pay for each item you want to buy. For example, if you earn $15 an hour and an item costs $120, ask yourself whether you would be willing to work eight hours without compensation to have that item. Don't buy something just because it's cheap or on sale. Buy it because you need it or love it.

Buy clothes and accessories in coordinating shades. By doing so, you'll need fewer shoes and accessories to go with your outfits if you stick to the basics. Develop a wardrobe of classic styles — things you can wear year after year and always look fashionable. You can update your wardrobe each season with a few less expensive tops, shoes, and accessories. But remember the cardinal rule of maintaining a clutter-free home: For every item you add, one must go.

Need Help?

According to the American Consumer Credit Counseling agency, almost half the households in America report having difficulty paying their minimum monthly payments on credit cards. If you feel like you are in over your head, help is available. Several nonprofit credit counseling services will help consumers to work out their debt problems. These organizations can help you devise a debt repayment plan and learn practical budgeting skills so you stay out of debt. They typically negotiate with your creditors to do the following:

- Eliminate or reduce interest rates
- Eliminate late fees
- Lower monthly payments
- Consolidate multiple debts into one payment
- Improve your credit rating

In return, you will be asked not to use or apply for any credit for a specific length of time or until your current debts are repaid. To find a credit counseling service in your area, check the Yellow Pages under "Credit Counseling" or contact one of the companies listed in the Resources (see page 282).

Don't try to duck creditors. If you're getting calls at home or letters from creditors demanding payment, don't ignore them. You'll buy yourself more time (before they file a lien against you, garnish your wages, come to repossess, or sue for payment) if you show that you are willing to repay your debt. Contact your creditors. Settle on an amount that you can pay now or by a certain date, and then follow through on your promise.

Use bankruptcy as a last resort. Filing for bankruptcy may seem like an easy way out, but a bankruptcy remains on your credit report for ten years and will affect your ability to secure a loan for a car or home. It also may rear its ugly head in a routine employment check and cost you a job.

Achieving Your Goals

Owing money is like living your life in reverse. Every month, you are paying for things you did last month. Eliminating debt is the only way to

For Simplicity's Sake

Instead of spending money on stuff you won't use or need a year from now, spend time with a friend or family member or a good book. Or use the time you would have spent shopping to do something nice for yourself. Remind yourself that the best things in life are free.

shift your life into forward gear and get ahead. You're the driver; you can do it by taking control of your spending and better managing your resources.

- **Come up with a realistic plan.** Figure out your total credit card debt. Then decide when you want to be debt-free. Divide the amount you owe by that many months. This will give you a rough idea of the total amount you need to pay creditors each month. If you can't afford that amount, adjust your goal.

- **Stick to your plan.** It's easy to slip back into old spending habits. But if you want to pay off your debt, you've got to stop using your credit cards. It's as simple as that. This may mean going without some things for the time being. Read chapter 16, "Living on Less," for suggestions on how to live on less.

- **Track your progress.** List your current debts on today's date in a calendar. Each month, write your new balances on the calendar. Or, use a personal finance package on your personal computer to track progress toward your goal.

CHAPTER 15

SAVINGS AND INVESTMENTS

Whatever your financial goals, budgeting is the first step, followed by reducing debts and expenses and learning to live with less. But thanks to the magic of compounding interest, saving and investing your money is the way to reach the ultimate goal of many Americans: financial freedom. All it takes is a little planning to get started and some discipline and patience to see it through.

Getting Started

If you're like many Americans, you're probably spending money as fast as you earn it. But if you overspend today, you will have nothing for tomorrow. The good news is that it's never too late to start saving. The sooner you start, the more you will have when you need it, whether you want to buy a home, finance your children's college education, or retire comfortably. So how do you get started?

• **Start by setting goals.** What do you want to save for? A new car? Vacation? New home? Remodeling the kitchen? College for your children? Retirement? Write down your goals, along with an estimate of the amount you need. Use a savings calculator, such as that

available at Bankrate.com (see Resources, page 282), to compute how much you have to save to reach your goal at various interest rates and how much you need to save every month. Or meet with a financial adviser.

• **Pay yourself first.** Take 5 to 10 percent (or whatever figure you came up with in the previous step) out of every paycheck and make a payment to your savings account or retirement plan. Then pay the rest of your bills. Learn to live on what's left rather than overspending and finding yourself unable to make regular contributions.

• **Break down your goals.** If your goal seems unobtainable, break it down into smaller goals. Let's say you want to save $10,000 for a down payment on a house over the next five years. To reach that goal, you need to save $2,000 each year. That works out to $5.48 a day. Now look at your daily expenses. Where might you be able to cut back by $5.48 each day? Start putting away that amount, in cash, every day, just as if you were spending it. Use a shoebox or coffee can. By the end of the week, you should have saved $38.36. Take it the bank and deposit it your savings account. If you do this every day for the next five years, you have saved $10,000. Actually, you'll have more than that because you will be earning interest along the way, which might just pay for closing costs or a mover. When you have enough in your savings account, open a money-market account or buy a certificate of deposit (CD) to maximize earnings with higher interest.

• **Contribute regularly to your savings.** Make it a habit to save something each month, even if it's only $10. Increase that amount as you pay off debts or get pay raises. Create a lifestyle around what you earn now, not what you hope to earn someday. When you do get a raise, continue to live on your current income and invest the extra income every month.

Strategies for Saving

Most financial planners will advise clients to save 5 to 10 percent of their pretax earnings. If that doesn't seem possible, pick an amount that you feel comfortable with and start saving that amount on a regular basis. Then gradually increase that amount. Remember that it's not how much you earn, but how much you save, that will determine your financial future.

Once you get started, you will probably find that saving money is not so hard after all. It might hurt a little in the beginning as you adjust to spending less. But the satisfaction and sense of achievement that come from having money in the bank will more than make up for any initial discomfort. Following are some painless ways to save.

• **Arrange for automatic contributions to your savings account.** Have your savings deducted automatically from your paycheck, or set up an automatic transfer from your checking account to an investment or savings account. It's easier to save when you do it automatically because you don't have to make a choice about what to do with your money each month. Think of that automatic payment as a down payment on your financial security.

• **Keep the change.** Get in the habit of putting all loose change into a jar or bowl every day. At the end of that week or month, deposit that money into your savings account.

FOLLOW THE RULES

Live within your means by using the 70-20-10 rule. Use 70 percent of your take-home pay for regular monthly bills plus other regular expenses, such as groceries, gas, and clothing. Set aside 20 percent for large-ticket items, such as a car or home. Save the remaining 10 percent for retirement.

You'll be surprised how quickly pennies, nickels, dimes, and quarters add up. You might even go so far as to never spend change from your purse or pocket. Break a dollar bill instead and save the change.

• **Invest all "found" savings.** Use coupons during grocery store shopping and deposit the amount of your savings into your savings account. Find a free parking area, take the bus or walk to work from there, and invest the savings. Make it a point to use your own bank's automatic teller machine to save processing fees. Any time you save money or make a decision *not* to spend money, make a conscious decision to invest it. Keep a running total in a small spiral notebook and write a check to yourself at the end of the week or month. Or keep the cash you didn't spend in a bank deposit envelope that you can hand to the teller next time you're at the bank.

• **Invest all extra income.** Whether you get a nice tax refund or win the lottery, plan to invest any extra cash that comes your way rather than spend it. This goes for those extra paychecks you get several times each year when there are five weeks in the month instead of four.

• **Consider adjusting the amount of tax being withheld from your paycheck for the purpose of investing the additional upfront earnings.** If you always end up getting a tax refund, that's nice, but it was your money to begin with. If you had invested it as you earned it throughout the year, you would have that amount plus interest. Divide the amount of your last tax refund by 12. That's about how much you could be investing each month without changing your lifestyle one bit. Use tax tables available through your employer or accountant to figure out how much tax to withhold so that you break even at the end of the year. If you are self-employed, work with an accountant to determine the amount of tax you should be paying quarterly to the state and federal governments.

• **Join a credit union through work or through a family member.** Credit unions generally offer higher interest on savings accounts than banks do. In addition, you can usually get lower interest rates on loans, which could give you some extra money for your savings and investments each month.

• **Involve the whole family in saving.** Ask your partner and children to think of ways they can save money each week. Keep a chart of the money saved so that you can monitor your progress. Set goals for your savings, such as paying off debts so that Dad doesn't have to work overtime or taking a family vacation.

• **Make and take food and beverages from home.** Eating breakfast or lunch out every day adds up fast, and so will your savings when you choose to eat breakfast at home and bring your lunch to work. Keep track of what you spend on coffee, breakfast, and lunch plus snacks and beverages from the vending machine every week. Add it up and multiply by four. That's how much cash you could be putting into your savings account every month, less whatever you spend at the supermarket buying these items. You could probably treat yourself to gourmet coffee beans and a coffee grinder and still save much more money than if you continued to buy coffee on your way to work.

- **Save on taxes.** When preparing your tax returns, be sure to take every deduction allowed by law. Because tax laws change frequently, hiring a professional tax preparer could result in big savings — and you can deduct the expense. If you are self-employed, save every little receipt as well as the big ones.

- **Shop smarter.** Before buying anything, ask yourself, "Do I really need this?" Always try to negotiate a better deal wherever you shop. (It can't hurt to try!) And never pay full price for anything. Shop around for car and home insurance before renewing if insurance rates are not dictated by state regulations. When you make hotel reservations, ask for their best rate. If you shop from catalogs and on-line stores that do not have a store in your state, you won't have to pay sales tax on your purchases. If you do your holiday shopping this way, minimize the cost of delivery by ordering multiple items from just one or two catalogs. Always save all shopping receipts for at least thirty days in case you need to return or exchange an item.

When shopping for a car, consider buying a good used car instead of a new car. Use the money you save by having a lower car payment to reduce your debt or increase your savings and investments each month. Better yet, shop for a car at a government auction of automobiles repossessed by the Internal Revenue Service or confiscated from criminals.

- **Take advantage of membership discounts.** Organizations and associations frequently offer member discounts on various products and services, but most people don't use them because they forget that they are available. Write down on a slip of paper the discounts available to you and carry it in your wallet or purse as a reminder. Then get in the habit of shopping where you can get additional discounts.

- **Save as you spend.** You can save thousands of dollars toward college tuition through Upromise (see Resources, page 282), a free program designed to help families reach their college savings goals. Contributing companies, such as AT&T, General Motors, and McDonald's, give you back part of your spending as college savings. In addition, relatives and friends can contribute toward your child's education, or you can contribute toward theirs. Upromise also allows you to invest your savings in a tax-deferred college investing account managed by some of the world's leading financial services firms. Their Web site has a calculator for projecting your college savings based on current and anticipated spending with contributing companies.

Short-Term Savings. Once you start saving money, where should you put it? That depends on what your goals are, how fast you want to reach those goals, and how much risk you are willing to take. Generally speaking, the higher the yield, the higher the risk. Savings accounts and other cash accounts, such as CDs and money market funds, are recommended for building emergency reserves and saving for short-term needs.

Here's what *not* to do with your savings. Don't keep them under your mattress or in a non-interest-bearing account. Don't keep them in your checking account either, because it's too tempting to spend your savings when you have easy access to it. It's also difficult to keep track of how much is savings and how much is for expenses, which may lead to accidental spending.

If you are just getting started with a savings plan, you may want to put your money in a regular savings account. After three months, or when you are able to meet the minimum deposit requirement, you might consider putting some savings into a CD. A CD allows you to deposit a certain amount of money as an investment for a fixed length of time ranging from three months to five years. CDs are federally insured and pay higher rates of return, sometimes double the interest rate paid on savings accounts. They're a great way to save for large expenditures with a definite purchase date, such as a family vacation or holiday gifts.

The benefit of a CD is that it keeps your savings out of reach for a specified term. The down side is that you might have to pay a penalty if you need to withdraw the money before the end of your contract period. But some financial institutions allow customers to cash in CDs with no penalty, and variable-rate CDs allow you to make additional deposits during the specified term and sometimes a limited number of withdrawals. This might be a good way to save for a down payment on a house.

A money market account is another option for short-term savings. It's basically an interest-bearing checking account with limited check-writing privileges. A money market account also may require a minimum balance and may be charged a monthly service fee if that balance is not maintained. The money market account is a good choice for your emergency fund because you can access your money at any time with no penalties, but the restrictions may keep you from raiding it.

Savings accounts, CDs, and money market accounts are all generally safe investments because they are insured up to a certain amount by the Federal Deposit Insurance Company. Another fairly safe savings product is a bond, through which you are lending your money to the government or a corporation. In

For Simplicity's Sake

Use the rule of 72 to figure out how many years it will take for your investment to double. Simply divide 72 by the rate of return on your investment. For example, if you currently have $10,000 invested in a fund that averages a 10 percent return, it will take 7.2 years to grow to $20,000. Keep in mind that the rule of 72 does not account for inflation.

return, you get paid a specified interest rate at intervals during the life of the bond or when it matures.

Long-Term Investments. It's easy to put off saving for the future when there are so many pressing needs and wants in the present. But the sooner you start putting money away, the more time your money has to make money for you through interest, dividends, and capital gains. If you have access to the Internet, use a search engine and enter the keywords "compounding interest" to find Web sites with calculators that demonstrate the power of compounding interest. Even if you are paying off high-interest credit cards and other debts, it makes sense to start saving for long-term goals now.

There are many different types of investment vehicles, some of which are designed for specific purposes, such as saving for college tuition or retirement. Do a little research to familiarize yourself with some of the options. Then seek the advice of a financial planning professional. When organizing your long-term investments, remember these three things:

1. **Hold a steady course.** Once you decide where to invest your money for long-term growth, be prepared to ride out the ups and downs of the market.
2. **Diversify your investments.** As your savings grow, don't keep them all in one place. Balance higher-risk investments, such as stocks, with safer investments, such as CDs and bonds.

3. **Invest comfortably.** Choose investments that suit your personality. If you are not a risk-taker, putting even a small chunk of your savings into a high-risk investment might keep you awake at night.

If your goal is saving for retirement, most financial planners will advise you to fund your 401(k) or 403(b) account to the maximum. Automatic deductions from your paycheck make saving for retirement painless. Many companies allow employees to invest up to 15 percent of their annual income (or up to $10,000). You don't have to pay tax on that money until you begin to withdraw it. Some companies even offer to match part of your contribution, which helps your balance grow quickly. And there's a plan for everyone. Self-employed individuals have similar plans through which they can save for retirement, including the Simplified Employee Pension, SIMPLE plan, and Keogh plan.

Make a contribution every year to an individual retirement account (IRA). Contributions to a regular IRA are tax deductible up to the maximum amount allowable. Your investment will then grow tax-deferred until you begin to withdraw it at retirement. Another option is the Roth IRA. Your contribution isn't tax-deductible, but your earnings grow tax-free until distributions are made. Check with your tax specialist for restrictions and eligibility requirements.

Invest regularly. Once you start contributing to an IRA, contribute every year whether you need the tax deduction or not. The amount you save on your taxes cannot begin to compare with the effect of compounding over time. One way to invest regularly is to set up an automatic withdrawal each month from your checking account to fund your investments. This is an easy way to get into the investment habit.

Saving for college tuition? You may be able to borrow against your retirement account or withdraw college expenses from your IRA with no penalty. You can also set up a 529 plan, which allows families to save for higher education without having to pay taxes on the earnings. And savings can be withdrawn tax-free when used at any accredited college, university, graduate school, trade school, or vocational school to pay for tuition, room, board, fees, books, and supplies. Another benefit is that you can change your designated future college student to another eligible college-bound family member. When saving for college, keep the money in your name, not your child's name, to increase your child's chances of receiving need-based financial aid.

Games People Play. The right attitude toward saving can go a long way toward helping you reach your goals. It's not about pinching pennies or denying yourself; it's about building wealth. And the more fun you have with it, the more likely it is that you will achieve your savings and investment goals.

• **Make it a contest.** Set an annual savings goal. Then come up with a reward that you will give yourself when you reach that goal.

• **Write checks to yourself.** You could simply transfer money each month from your checking account to your savings or investment account, but in the beginning at least, you may find it more rewarding and fun to write a check to yourself.

• **Make saving a social activity.** Join an investment club, a group of people who come together for fun and profit. Ask friends, family members, and business colleagues if they know of any local investment clubs.

• **Educate yourself.** The more you learn about investing, the quicker you will be able to achieve your financial goals because you will be motivated to do so. Read books, look for education information on-line, and attend lectures and workshops.

For Simplicity's Sake

Learn to be content with what you have. When you stop spending on useless or unneeded "stuff," you instantly have more money to invest. Remind yourself daily that the most important things in life are not things that can be purchased. Look for value in the things that no amount of money can buy. A smile on the face of your partner or child; a strong, healthy body; and the wonders of nature can be "bought" without spending a penny. Adding these "investments" to your portfolio will surely enrich your life.

CHAPTER 16

LIVING ON LESS

What are your beliefs about money? How much is enough? Many people are discovering that less is more. The less you spend, the less you may need to work, giving you more time for the things that really matter. You can reclaim control over your finances, and your life, by choosing to consume less. Though contrary to the trends of our consumer culture, it is the most direct path to a simpler life.

How Much Is Enough?

Learning to live with less requires knowing the difference between wants and needs. We *need* food, water, shelter, and clothing. We *want* things like gourmet meals, big houses, fancy cars, and stylish apparel. Do you really need twenty-three pairs of shoes? Or five sets of sheets for your bed? Or that gadget you just saw advertised on television? How many things do you own that are not being used?

Acquiring things has become such a habit that we often don't think about the cost of acquisition. Think about the cost of owning. On a practical level, your belongings cost you storage space as well as the time it takes to care for them. The more you own, the more you have to care for. If you're charging purchases and carry-ing balances on your credit cards, you're paying a lot more than the item is worth, even if you buy it on sale. Which is more painful: not having the latest widget, or looking at your credit card bill every month? You also pay the price of time spent shopping. You can always buy more things, but you can't buy more time.

Much of what we own was bought, consciously or subconsciously, to project an image of success. We tend to let our expenditures speak for our competence. Wouldn't you rather be recognized for who you are and what you have accomplished instead of what you own? No matter how much you acquire, you will never have it all. It's better to have a few possessions that you love and use than a thousand that weigh you down.

Simple Everyday Strategies

The key to living on less is being content with what you have. Look at the many things you own. Do you wear all of your jewelry and clothes? Do you use all the gadgets in your kitchen or workshop? Do you have everything you *need*? Be thankful for the abundance in your life and learn to appreciate the value of things that can't be purchased at any price — time to pursue whatever makes you happy, nature in its glory, a smile on the face of someone you love. Here are some strategies to help you.

- **Tune out commercial messages.** Advertising creates desire. Commercial messages are designed to make you and your kids feel compelled to buy this, that, and the other thing. Use television commercial breaks to get up and stretch, do quick household chores, or turn down the volume and talk to other members in your household. Consider watching less television in general.

- **Buy only to replace something that is used up, worn out, or broken beyond repair.** Also get in the habit of taking care of what you own. When you do buy items, shop around to compare prices, but don't go cheap, especially for things that will get daily use, such as mattresses or carpeting. High-quality, high-efficiency, durable goods will last longer and save you money in the long run. If your budget won't permit buying new items, look for high-quality items in good condition from second-hand stores, consignment shops, and thrift shops.

- **Borrow or rent things you use infrequently or will eventually replace anyway.** Borrow video and music tapes, and books from the library for free. Some libraries even lend framed paintings! Or rent movies instead of buying them. If you have one car that is not driven every day, compare the cost of owning it with the cost of renting a car or taking a cab on the occasions when you need a vehicle.

- **Learn to be a do-it-yourselfer.** If you can do some of your own repairs or make things you might normally buy, you can save a lot of money. See if you can find someone who is willing to teach you what you need to learn. Your local high school may offer continuing education classes. Or teach yourself by using books from the library. You can also save a bundle by making your own meals and gifts.

- **Maximize your spending power.** Train yourself to buy things like clothing, outerwear, and sporting goods out of season or during clearance sales, when you can get the most for your money. Shop for holiday cards and seasonal decorations right after the holidays and save 50 to 80 percent off the regular price. Consider buying holiday candy after the holiday at a fraction of the regular price and freezing it until the following year. There are also traditional annual sale dates for certain items, including new and used automobiles (December and January), tires (May), jewelry (January), lawnmowers and yard tools (August), mattresses (February), paint (April), and linens and towels (January and July).

- **Trade or barter services.** Think of goods and services you could provide in exchange for goods and services you need. You may be able to barter with produce from your garden, babysitting, baking, sewing, or professional expertise. If you and your partner would like to have the house to yourself for the night (a priceless treat!), make arrangements ahead of time to have your children spend the night with friends or family members with the understanding that you will take in their children another night.

- **Make the most of your children's clothing budget.** Purchase clothing in primary colors that can be mixed and matched and worn by either sex, now and as hand-me-downs.

Reducing Your Grocery Bill

One of the best ways to save money on groceries is to plan your weekly menu around specials at the supermarket. Get what you need for the week and then stock up on sale items to the extent that your budget and storage capacity allow. Some supermarkets offer "two for one" deals on perishable items. If you shop for yourself or a small family, you can still take advantage of these great deals: Split the goods — and the cost — with a family member or friend. Here are a few more simple ways to cut your grocery bill:

- **Eat vegetarian more often.** Replace one or more meat dishes each week with main dishes that feature less pricey protein sources such as eggs, beans, cheese, and tofu.
- **Avoid buying convenience items.** Single-serving packages, precooked or marinated meats, bagged salads, cookie dough, and shredded cheese invariably cost more.
- **Substitute the real thing for paper goods.** Use dish rags instead of paper towels for more economical kitchen cleanup. Use newspaper to clean windows with less streaking.

PRIORITIZING WANTS

Make a list of your wants and needs. Try to be brutally honest about which category they fall into. Then, take a look at the items on your want list. Ask yourself how much each purchase will improve your quality of life. Rate each item with an "A" for a large improvement down to "C" for negligible improvement. If an item will actively detract from your quality of life in some way, don't rate it — just cross it off your list. Now take a look at your "A" list and think about how you can balance these high-priority wants with your budget. What are you willing to give up? Where can you compromise? Perhaps you can forgo a cup of coffee and a newspaper each morning to pay for a European vacation. Or buy your designer clothes at a consignment store so that you'll have enough left over for those skis. If you make these decisions based on how the purchase will improve your life — based on your own priorities, and not someone else's — you shouldn't go wrong.

—*Ramona Creel, OnlineOrganizing.com*

Opt for cloth napkins instead of paper napkins. And if you're a new parent consider buying cloth diapers instead of store-bought diapers to save money and reduce waste.

- **Get a savings card.** If your supermarket offers an automatic savings card, get one and use it. If you don't have a savings card or forget to bring yours, ask if the cashier can swipe the manager's card so you can get the savings.

Clip Coupons. Coupons are a great way to save on groceries if you use them and you remember to bring them to the supermarket. If you clip coupons, organize them so you can find the ones you want when you need them. One method is to file them in a recipe or card file box or accordion-style canceled check file with alphabetical dividers. You could also file them by expiration date or by food category. Double your savings by shopping at supermarkets that offer double-coupon days.

TIME-SAVER

Don't bother clipping coupons for products you don't use regularly. Have your children go through your collection of coupons and throw out the expired ones. If you take the kids shopping with you, have them locate the coupon item for you. You might even offer them cash for the value of the coupons in return for helping to do the shopping, loading and unloading the car, and putting food away.

Some people believe that the best place to keep your coupon organizer is in the glove compartment of your car. That may work if you tend to make lots of trips to the supermarket or if you don't mind spending time at the store searching through coupons to see what you have. A more efficient way to shop with coupons is to make them a part of the planning process rather than the shopping process. Store your coupon organizer in the room where you clip coupons and write your grocery list. Pull the coupons you need for your shopping trip based on your list. While you compile your list, look for and discard expired coupons. Put your list and coupons together in an envelope that you bring to the store. You might also want to put a pen in the envelope so that you can cross items off your list as you pick them up. Also, bring a clothespin with you and, as you find the coupon items, clip those coupons to your shopping cart. Keep unused coupons in the envelope.

Coupons can save you money, but it takes time to clip, file, retrieve, and use them. Is it worth it? To answer that question, you have to weigh the cost of your time against the savings. You may even be able to save as much money, or more, simply by comparing unit prices or planning your meals around supermarket sales. Keep in mind that even with the savings, a coupon item may cost more than a comparable item with a different brand name or a store-brand item.

If you enjoy saving money but don't like clipping and sorting through coupons, there's a Web site you might want to check out. At www.valupage.com, enter your zip code and you will get a list of current offers from your local supermarket. Print this page and take it to your supermarket. Purchase one or more of the offers listed, go to the checkout, and hand the cashier your page of offers (which includes a barcode for scanning). Along with your receipt, you will receive cash-like coupons called *Web Bucks.* These are "good as cash" coupons you can use to pay for groceries on your next shopping trip to that store (with the exception of items prohibited by law such as liquor and tobacco).

Buy in Bulk. Buying in bulk is another way to save, but only if you will use everything you buy and have a place to store it. If it goes bad before you use it, you've wasted your money. Also, it sometimes costs less to buy a smaller container on sale than it does to buy a larger container. Always check the unit price. If you prefer brand-name items, you can save by shopping at a warehouse store for food, pet food, paper goods, laundry detergent, and more. Keep in mind, though, that many supermarket brands are made by the name-brand manufacturers and are of similar quality. This is especially true with such items as bottled water, pastas and rices, and canned foods. Experiment to see where you can cut costs without sacrificing quality.

Cheap Eats

Eating meals out regularly can quickly get expensive. If, for example, you spend an average of $6 per day for lunch five days a week,

that's $30 per week or $120 per month. You can make and take your lunch from home for a fraction of the cost. So why don't more people do this? Because making meals requires planning. You can't make a sandwich if you don't have sandwich fillings in the house. And if you don't stock your pantry with "quick and easy" meal fixings, you're more likely to take the family out for a fast-food meal or order a pizza. If you haven't already, you might want to read "More Organized Mornings," page 186, and "Meal Planning," page 210.

If all you really want from a restaurant is the food and not the ambiance that goes with it, place an order to bring home. When you eat out, you have to add an extra 15 to 20 percent to the bill for service, and you'll pay a hefty price for beverages. Ordering takeout allows you to save on the added costs of eating out while still enjoying your favorite restaurant food. Following are more simple strategies for eating out on the cheap.

* **Eat earlier in the day.** Go out for brunch or lunch instead of dinner, and get a comparable meal for up to half the price.
* **Eat earlier in the evening.** Take advantage of early-bird dinner specials, which are generally offered between 4 P.M. and 6 P.M. to get great meals for less.
* **Watch for special offers.** Restaurants will sometimes offer "buy one, get one free" dinner specials to bring in midweek traffic. Look for restaurant promotions in your local newspaper, or ask at your favorite restaurant if they offer any midweek specials.

- **Reserve eating out for special occasions.** Some restaurants offer a free meal on your birthday. Go there to celebrate family birthdays. Just be sure to bring some identification as proof.
- **Schedule and budget for going out to eat.** Avoid eating out on impulse. Schedule it as a treat.
- **Share appetizers, desserts, and entrees.** Restaurant serving sizes are often the equivalent of two or three standard servings. Sharing will save money, and calories!
- **Take home leftovers.** Bring leftovers to work for lunch the following day, or incorporate them into your next main meal. You might, for example, be able to slice and reheat steak and serve with eggs for breakfast or add gravy and serve with a baked potato for dinner.

Affordable Entertainment

In many areas throughout the United States, you can buy an "entertainment book" that offers hundreds of money-saving coupons for restaurants, movie tickets, attractions, retail stores, and services, such as dry cleaning and oil changes. Usually sold as a fundraiser for schools, churches, and community groups, the book can quickly pay for itself just in discounts. All the other discounts are then a bonus.

Take advantage of off-peak freebies, discounts, and season passes. Some museums offer free admittance on certain days of the week or at certain times of the year. Some tourist attractions offer "locals" a discounted price. Plan to attend a movie matinee instead of a prime-time show, or buy movie tickets in bulk. Many movie theater chains offer tickets by mail that save you about 40 percent off the regular price. Go to plays on weeknights instead of weekends, or catch the preview performance. If you regularly frequent a local tourist attraction or other entertainment venue, it may be cheaper to buy a season pass.

See plays and concerts for free. Many theaters and concert halls recruit volunteer ushers, who get to enjoy the performance once everyone is seated and may even get to meet the performers.

Take a "learn to" class. Many local high schools offer inexpensive continuing education classes on topics ranging from starting your own business to writing poetry to learning to swim. Arts and crafts stores sometimes offer free or low-cost classes for adults and children.

Join an outing or special-interest group. Nearly every community has groups that get together on a regular basis to go walking, hiking, or bicycling. You might also look for a writer's group or book club, or start your own with friends.

Visit your local library. Larger public libraries offer programs and services that are free and open to the public, such as the following:

- Free Internet access
- Community magazine swaps (bring one, take one)
- Writing workshops for children and adults
- How-to demonstrations and talks
- Mini-seminars on current topics
- Book and poetry readings
- Book discussions and discussion groups

- Current magazines and newspapers for browsing
- Special interest exhibits
- Free movie and audiocassette or CD loans

Check out what's happening at bookstores. Many bookstores, especially those with cafés, offer a regular schedule of free events and activities, including: book and poetry readings, writer's groups, book discussion groups (with discounts on books for members), live music (usually on Friday and Saturday nights), and special interest discussions.

If you enjoy entertaining but want to keep the cost of entertaining down, throw potluck dinner parties. Ask your friends to bring their favorite dish (and a canned good for a local relief kitchen if you wish). You can request specific courses or just see what kind of dinner develops.

Frugal Family Fun

You don't have to spend a lot of money for kids to have fun. Check your local newspaper for upcoming events and activities — free festivals, fairs, and other forms of entertainment — that offer frugal fun for the whole family. Here are some further suggestions.

- **Give yourself a visitor's tour of nearby towns.** This is a great way to spend an afternoon or day, alone or with friends or family. Go to the local chamber of commerce or visitor's center. Pick up some local interest brochures and maps, and ask about fun things to do that are inexpensive or free. Choose places and activities that are new to you. Repeat often.

For Simplicity's Sake

Chances are good that the pace of life for your kids is far more hectic than it was for you when you were their age. Following are some ideas for slowing down the pace with some simple, old-fashioned fun.

- Pick your own apples or berries
- Bake cookies or cupcakes
- Play board games
- Go fly a kite
- Build a fort, indoors or outdoors
- Send the kids out with a bucket of chalk, or organize a neighborhood sidewalk drawing contest
- Take a family bike ride
- Bring a picnic lunch to the beach
- Rent a rowboat on a nearby lake
- Schedule a family reading hour
- Put on a play or skit

- **Plan a picnic.** Pack a basket, knapsack, or cooler with the makings of brunch, lunch, or dinner, complete with the beverages of your choice. Be sure to include plates, cups, and utensils. You can use paper and plastic, or make it extra special with silverware, glasses, and dinnerware. Don't forget to bring along a blanket or cloth to spread on the ground. Choose a picnic spot in advance, or simply head out for a leisurely walk or drive and "discover" the perfect place to picnic along the way.

- **Plant a vegetable garden.** Kids love to watch things grow, especially if they have a hand in planting and caring for them. And once those veggies are ready to pick, you save on produce.

- **Take a walk, and talk.** The exercise will do you good, but the most important benefit of going for a walk is that it allows you to give your partner, kids, or friends what they want most from you — your attention. Let them talk about whatever is on their minds.

- **Allow kids to become bored.** When kids get bored, their imaginations kick in and they come up with creative ways to entertain themselves. It's a wonderful way to help children develop and enhance creativity, imagination, and resourcefulness.

- **Visit your library.** Many libraries offer free activities for children of all ages, including weekly storytelling hours, summer reading clubs, and writing workshops.

- **See what's happening at bookstores.** Like libraries, many bookstores offer free activities for children, including video release parties, storytelling times, and young readers' clubs.

- **Get tips and ideas on-line.** Whether you're looking for indoor or outdoor activities, arts and crafts ideas, or fun learning activities, you'll find hundreds of tips and ideas on-line. Enter the keywords "family activities, "family fun," or "family education" in any search engine to locate helpful Web sites.

- **Vacation at home.** It's simpler, less expensive, and can be far more relaxing than jetting (or driving) to and from a vacation destination. Create an itinerary just as you would for a regular vacation. Plan to see the sights that visitors come to see. Try out a new restaurant or two. Order takeout food, and have it delivered on some nights. Stock up on your favorite breakfast foods, snacks, and beverages. Unplug the telephone, television, and computer. Leave housework and yard work for when you "get back."

- **Take a camping trip.** Hotel stays and eating out make up the bulk of expenses on vacation. Camping and cookouts minimize those expenses, add fun and adventure to your trip, and create lasting memories. Choose your destination and look for a family campground. If you've never tried camping before, borrow a tent, sleeping bags, and other gear before you invest in your own equipment.

- **Bring your own snacks and drinks to amusement parks.** Why waste your hard-earned money on overpriced food and beverages when you can bring your own for a fraction of the cost? Load a child's wagon with a small cooler and tow it along with you. If there's enough room, young children can ride in the wagon when they get tired.

PART IV

Organizing Time

Do you wish that time would stop so that you could catch up? Instead, maybe you should slow down. When you're traveling at warp speed, as so many of us do (and on autopilot, no less), it's easy to get caught up in the "busy-ness" of living. And it's easy to forget that you are the master of your time. How much of what you do every day are you doing because you feel that you "have to" do it? Would anyone care if you didn't do something on your list? Are there things you could delegate? What do you wish you could do with your time? By making a conscious choice to organize your time around the people and things that are most meaningful to you, you can regain control of your life, at home and at work.

CHAPTER 17

MANAGING YOURSELF

We can't really manage time because we have no control over time. We do, however, have control over how we choose to spend our time — and how we choose *not* to spend it. Managing time is really about managing ourselves from day to day and moment to moment and making choices based on our values and goals.

Organizing Things to Do

We all have "things to do." Have you ever noticed that the mundane stuff always seems to get done? You don't have to put "empty the kitchen trash" on your list of things to do, because there will come a point when the trash can can hold no more. The urgent stuff also seems to get done, regardless of whether it's on your list. But what about all of those things that are important and not urgent? How many of the important things we accomplish in a lifetime, or even on any given day, depends to a large extent on how well we organize our priorities.

• **Watch your every move.** Over the next week, before you do anything, ask yourself why you are doing it. Is it important? Is it important enough to do right now? A ringing

telephone is a perfect example. Most people automatically answer the phone rather than *decide* to answer it. It's there for our convenience, but it's easy to become enslaved by it. Pay closer attention to what you are doing so that you can make more conscious choices about how you spend your time.

• **Create a list of goals you would like to accomplish over the next one to five years.** Each day, add something from your list of goals to your daily "To Do" list and make it the first thing you do. It could be as simple as making a phone call to get information or a stop at the library to do some research. Working toward your goals every day brings you one step closer to achieving them. Cross off your list any goals that were imposed on you by someone else.

● **Keep your daily "To Do" list manageable.** Some people like to write down every little thing because they enjoy crossing them off the list throughout the day. Others prefer to just write down the three most important things to do. Whichever person you are, include on your daily list only the tasks that you can reasonably expect to complete today. Next to each task, write how long you think it will take you to complete that task — then double that figure.

Many people (especially optimists) have trouble managing their time because they underestimate how long it takes to do certain things. If you are always late for work, try timing your drive tomorrow. You might find that it's a longer drive than you thought and that you haven't been allowing yourself enough time to get there. To start developing more realistic estimates, write down what you do each day and how long it takes, including breaks and interruptions. Do this for at least one week.

● **Prioritize your day.** Write the number one next to the task or activity that is the most critical or urgent. Which is the next most important task? Make that your number two priority. Continue prioritizing until you have a number next to each item on your list.

● **Keep track of action items with a tickler or reminder file.** Make one folder for each month of the year (January through December) and one file for each day of the

month (1 through 31). Place these two groups of files together in hanging files folders in your desk drawer or rolling file cart. Use the monthly folders to file reminders to yourself and any paperwork you will need in the coming months, such as birthday cards to send, airline tickets, registration forms, and meeting agendas. If you will need something later this month, such as directions to a client meeting, file it in the appropriate day-of-the-month folder. Get into the habit of checking your tickler file every day to see what is in the current day's folder. Take care of everything in that day's folder and put it back in the file behind the other day folders. At the end of each month, take everything out of the next month's folder and file in the appropriate day-of-the-month folders. Once you start using a tickler file, you'll wonder how you ever managed without it.

TOOLS TO GOALS

Before you can decide how best to spend your time, you first have to decide what you want. Think about what's truly important in your life. These are your values. What do you want to see happen in your life? These are your goals. Once you acknowledge your values and goals, you can use time-management tools to help you achieve your goals and, ultimately, those things that are truly important.

— *Sheila Delson, FREEDomain Concepts*

REWARD MONEY

To get started using the tickler file (see page 157), throw two $20 bills in, one ten days from now and one twenty days from now. When you find them, spend them on yourself!

—*Paulette Ensign, Tips Products International*

Planning Your Day

Time spent planning and organizing your day is time well spent. Take whatever time you need to plan and organize your day by using whatever method works for you. It's helpful to have a planning tool that you can use to manage your time each day. There's nothing wrong with using the back of an envelope, as long as you don't misplace it. But most people find that they can make better use of their time if they have a calendar-type tool that lets them combine things to do.

The classic planning tool is what's known simply as a planner. Choose from daily, weekly, and monthly formats depending on how much room you need to record information. Most daily and weekly planners have a monthly planning guide that lets you see the month at a glance. If you spend a lot of time at your computer, you may choose to use a scheduling program to plan your day. If you decide to use a computerized planning tool, be sure to back up your data regularly.

Use your paper or electronic calendar to keep track of scheduled appointments as well as things on your "To Do" list. Block out time for daily routine tasks too. You might, for example, block out 8 to 9 A.M. every day to do long-range planning or 4:30 to 5:00 P.M. to do filing, return phone calls, or handle incoming mail. Schedule cyclical tasks, such as paying bills and doing laundry, for certain days of the week or month. Also schedule appointments with yourself to do things you enjoy, such as taking a walk or catching up on your reading.

Keep your schedule flexible. When looking at how much time you have in a day and what you want to do, create a buffer zone around each activity that allows more time than your estimate to accommodate unexpected delays. Give yourself a little breathing time between appointments. When you write appointments on your calendar, include a phone number to call in case you're running late or need to reschedule.

Whether it's first thing in the morning or late at night, you're generally most productive at a particular time of day. Use this time to accomplish the things that require the most energy or brainpower. Save your least productive time of day for doing routine tasks, such as filing.

At the end of the day, look back on your uncompleted tasks. Why were they left uncompleted? What held you up? How can you make sure they get done the next day? If you want to know where your time goes each day, use your planner to keep a record of what you actually did so that you can compare it to your plan.

Planning in Circles. According to Nancy Black of Organization Plus, people typically think in abstract rather than linear terms. So instead of keeping lists of things to do, she recommends a technique called *mind-mapping*. Orient a sheet of paper horizontally, and draw a small circle in the middle. Write today's date and the words "To Do" in the center of the circle. From that circle, draw lines (or rays) out toward the edges of the paper; draw one line for each task. Write one task on each line. Break down the task into steps, drawing additional lines for each step and noting what must be done.

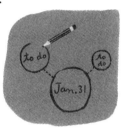

Planning this way allows you to see that many tasks involve multiple steps. It's a good reality check. When you're done, ask, "Can I really do all this in a day?" The next step is to prioritize. Choose the three most important tasks and get started. Mind-mapping is also an effective planning tool for kids.

Everyday Shortcuts

Have you ever thought to yourself, "There must be an easier way?" Often, we keep doing things the hard way because that's the way we've always done it. But if you took time to look at what you're doing, you could probably find ways to save time and energy every day, especially on routine tasks. Take cleaning the shower, for example. Why scrub soap scum when you can simply spray your shower after each use with a product that keeps soap scum from forming in the first place?

One way to simplify routine tasks and save time is to group similar tasks together and do them all at once, whether it's daily, weekly, monthly, or annually. For example, instead of filing each piece of paper as you are finished with it, put it in a "To File" folder and do all of your filing at one time. Check and respond to e-mail once or twice a day instead of many times throughout the day.

Group activities together as much as possible. If you're going to the bank, look at your master list of things to do and see if there's another errand you can do while you're in that area. Schedule routine office visits to the dentist and doctor on the same day. If you have children, plan to take them all for haircuts at the same time. Instead of shopping for cards one at a time, buy all the cards you'll need for several months or a whole year and file them in your tickler file. Saving just a few minutes here and there on routine tasks frees up time for more important things.

LISTEN UP!

Whether you use a calendar or a hand-held organizer, begin to regard that planner as a highly paid assistant who is continually reminding you about your appointments and things to do. The more attention you pay to that assistant, the better service you will get from it.

—Donna Cowan, Cowan & Company Professional Organizing

Limit the number of choices you have to make on a daily basis. Plan weekly meals in advance and post the plan on the refrigerator so that you don't have to think about what's for dinner. Pare down your wardrobe to your favorite outfits to make it easier to decide what to wear each day. Limit how much you have to remember by writing everything down or using reminder systems such as those described in chapter 4, "Staying Organized."

Get into "wash and wear." Go through your closets and drawers and consider getting rid of clothing that requires special care, such as dry cleaning or ironing. When you buy new clothes, choose clothes that are machine washable and do not need to be ironed.

Get your hair styled in a way that is natural. If you have straight hair, get a good cut that accentuates the straightness. If you have curly hair, wear it curly. Try a new cut or styling product designed for your hair type. Going natural saves time and energy. If you've been thinking about getting a really short hair cut, do it. Most short cuts look great with little or no blow-drying or fuss.

Always fill your gas tank when it gets down to one-quarter full. The last thing you want to do when you're running late for work or an appointment is discover that your car is nearly out of gas.

You have to take time to make time.

—Judy Warmington, Woman Time Management

MAKE YOUR MOVE

When the lines at a cash register are equal, choose the line that's next to an unopened register. If it opens, you might be able to move from last to first in line.

—*Mitzi Weinman, TimeFinder*

Freeing Up Time

Research shows that Americans (with the exception of parents with young children) have about forty hours more of free time each week than previous generations. According to Geoff Godbey, a professor of leisure studies at Pennsylvania State University and co-author of *Time for Life,* about twenty-five hours of free time come during weekdays, usually in thirty- to forty-five-minute increments. But the typical American estimates his or her weekly amount of free time at nineteen hours. Perhaps that is because we watch an average of sixteen to twenty-one hours of television each week.

The number-one tip for freeing up time is, you guessed it, turn off the television. How often do you sit down to watch one show and end up watching several hours of television? Try turning the television on thirty minutes later than usual or turning it off thirty minutes earlier. Then take that time to do something you've been wanting to do. Alternatively, don't turn the television on unless there is a specific show you want to see, and turn it off when that show is over. Or tape your favorite shows and watch them when it is most convenient for you. This also allows you to fast-forward through all those commercials — a big time-saver.

Another way to save a substantial amount of time is to delegate. Spend your time doing things only you can do, and let go of the rest. If you can afford it, get a professional to clean your house or mow your lawn. Let a travel agent make travel arrangements. Teach your kids how to do laundry. Hire an assistant to handle routine office tasks, such as filing or scheduling appointments, or give more responsibility to your current assistant. It may help to remind yourself that you don't *lose* control when you delegate; you *gain* control of your time and life.

Fighting Procrastination

Do you tend to procrastinate? Do you know why? Most people think that we procrastinate because we're lazy, but that's not necessarily true. There are some valid reasons for procrastination, and some simple solutions to overcoming it.

One reason why we procrastinate, particularly when faced with a large project, is because we're so overwhelmed that we don't know where to start. The solution is to break the project into a list of smaller tasks or steps. The first step can be as simple as making a phone call or setting up a file. Once that's done, you can move on to the next step. If you find yourself procrastinating at any step along the way, breaking it down will help you get started again.

Loneliness is another reason why people procrastinate. The solution in this case is to solicit a little help from your friends. See if you can get a family member, friend, or colleague to tackle the project with you. Alternatively, you might want to announce your goals to select friends, family, or colleagues. Let them know what you are doing and when you hope to be done. Sometimes it helps just to know that there is someone rooting for you. You might also try imagining that a very important person in your life is right there with you. What would he or she say to inspire you?

Perfectionism also causes people to procrastinate. If you're a perfectionist, you want to do everything just right or not at all, so you keep putting off what needs to be done. If this sounds like you, try to let yourself be the best imperfect person you can be. Keep in mind that no one else expects as much from you as you do from yourself.

MASTER THE MINUTES

Use small blocks of time to accomplish tasks rather than waiting for large amounts of uninterrupted time to take care of things. Consider what can be accomplished in ten minutes. You can organize a drawer, clean out your wallet, write a note, or read a story to your child. In five minutes, you can make a few phone calls, sort your mail, or empty the dishwasher. In one minute, you can review your to-do list, make your bed, or stop and smell the roses.

—Linda Samuels, Oh, So Organized!

Set the stage for success. Don't put off an important project until the last minute. Schedule a regular time each day to work on it. Decide before you begin each day how long you will work before taking a break or moving to another project. Also do a quick attitude check before you get started. It's easier to work on a project if you *choose* to spend time doing it rather than feeling like you *have* to do it. Whether you're trying to unclutter a closet or write up a report at work, make a conscious choice to stay focused for a specified length of time. Limit distractions by turning off the telephone ringer or closing your door.

STAYING ON TRACK

Lots of things can get your day off track. You can't do much about the unplanned and unexpected, but you can stop derailing yourself. Do you do any of the following?

- **Surf the Internet without clear objectives?**
- **Spend time on trivia and not enough time on priorities?**
- **Read e-mail before doing anything else?**
- **Socialize too long with colleagues?**
- **Start your day without a written plan?**
- **Do what is rightfully someone else's job?**

Take a step back and scrutinize your day. Determine your contribution to getting your day off track and make one change.

—Mitzi Weinman, TimeFinder

Slowing Down

Despite its seeming simplicity, it's not easy to "stop and smell the roses." We've trained ourselves to be constantly on the go, to always be doing something and thinking ahead. Try this exercise: Stand up and deliberately walk across the room in slow motion. Notice how making a conscious effort to slow down increases your awareness and expands time. That's what slowing down in life can do for you.

Try putting yourself in charge of the pace of your day. Think pace, not race. Have faith that everything that absolutely must get done will get done. You might think that moving faster or cramming one more thing into your already busy day is being productive, but it may be counterproductive if you make mistakes in your hurry. By living a frantic, rushed life, you may also be sabotaging your health and well-being.

Worry about right now. If you find yourself worrying about something that might happen tomorrow or some day, concentrate on today. Take it one day at a time. And if that's too much to think about, take it one hour at a time. Leave the past behind. Let the future be what it will be. Repeat to yourself as often as needed each day: Where am I? Here. What time is it? Now. Focus on the task at hand. Whether you are washing dishes, driving to the store, doing your job, or helping your children with their homework, try to focus all of your attention and energy on what you are doing.

Remind yourself every once in awhile that all you really *must* do today is breathe in and breathe out. The world won't end if you don't get everything on your list done today. Resist that urge to do just one more thing. Eliminate one activity that you do on a regular basis that provides you with little or no satisfaction and only adds to your sense of being overwhelmed.

Schedule a Vacation. Lorraine Chalicki of YouNeedMe.com Personal Systems offers the following advice for those who need a break from the "busyness" of their lives: You can begin to rediscover the art in your life and work by scheduling daily pauses or "mini-vacations" on your calendar. The word *vacation* comes from the Latin vacare, which means "to be empty." Pull out your calendar and for each day block out a fifteen-minute "vacation" designed to empty your mind. Slow your pace, shift your rhythm, turn your attention to your breathing, and give yourself time to just be. These silent breaks can promote solutions to problems and worries. With continued practice, you will discover that slowing down your pace and focusing on nothing but your breath will renew your energy. Do this daily and you might find that when your annual two-week vacation rolls around, you won't waste the first two days relearning how to gear down from your usual hectic pace! (See chapter 21, "Organizing to Go," for more tips.)

Managing Stress. Change is the chief cause of stress. Even positive changes such as buying a new home or getting a promotion can cause stress. The key to managing stress is to regain control over those things that are within your power. Following are some ways to do just that.

- **Schedule quiet time.** Turn off the radio during your commute. Get up earlier than the rest of your family and enjoy some peace and solitude. Make time to read or write. You might even try meditating for ten minutes a day.
- **Minimize the effects of stress on your body by taking care of yourself.** Get more sleep. Find a form of physical activity that you enjoy, such as walking, and do it for at least twenty to thirty minutes every other day. And drink eight to ten glasses of water to your health each day.
- **Learn to replace your automatic stress response with a relaxation response.** Take a few deep breaths or count to ten and then respond. Leave the room, if you can, to put some distance between you and your stressor. Or look for something humorous in the situation.
- **Create a support network.** Research shows that people who have family and friends to help them through stressful times stay healthier and recover faster than those who do not have a social support system. So be open to making new friends. And keep in touch with the supportive people in your life.

CHAPTER 18

ORGANIZING YOUR WORK

Good organizational skills at work can pay off in enhanced productivity, better relationships with co-workers, and greater career satisfaction. The basic time-management tips and strategies presented in the previous chapter can be applied at work. This chapter focuses on some work-specific issues, such as planning your workday, managing projects, and handling routine tasks.

Planning Your Work

It has been said that if you fail to plan, you may as well plan to fail. This is particularly true at work. Planning is the blueprint or map that helps you to achieve your goals, individually and as a team. It allows you to organize your time effectively and provides a way to measure your progress.

● **Start with the big picture.** When planning your work, start with your ultimate goals and work backward to what needs to be done today. Take a look at your major projects or goals. Make a list of all the tasks required to complete each one, such as requesting bids, setting up a kick-off meeting, or writing a memo. Every project or goal consists of

smaller, more manageable jobs that you can schedule into your workday or delegate. Give each task a deadline, and then schedule it into your calendar. It's helpful to break down goals into monthly and weekly goals as well as daily goals.

● **Be more proactive by planning ahead.** You can't always manage your time optimally; emergencies do come up, and urgent matters need to be attended to. But in general, deadlines should not fall into either category. By thinking and planning in advance — that is, by being proactive — you'll spend less time in reactive mode.

● **Schedule only 50 percent of your day.** Allow time in between appointments and projects and at the beginning and end of your day.

That way, if a project takes longer than you expected or you have to break away to handle a more urgent task, there's still a chance you can finish what you planned to do. If you have time left over at the end of the day, use it to get a head start on tomorrow's tasks.

• **Delegate tasks that do not require your expertise or interfere with the important priorities you are trying to accomplish.** When delegating, be sure to clearly communicate what you need to have done. Keep your instructions simple and concise. Allow questions at this stage and throughout the project. Give the project a reasonable deadline. Make the delegatee want to help by making him or her feel like a partner in your project. And don't forget to say "thanks."

Managing Your Day

Schedule your work and stick to your schedule. Identify the things that waste your time and resolve to eliminate them. Don't allow procrastination to stand in the way of achieving your goals. Offer yourself a reward for finishing a particularly challenging or unpleasant task. See page 161 for helpful tips on overcoming procrastination.

• **Establish a daily routine.** Figure out what you want to do when, and then block out that time for that activity. If you spend a lot of time out of the office, you might want to schedule one day in the office each week when you can attend to administrative duties, including developing a plan for the following week. If you have a staff meeting every

Wednesday at 1 P.M., you might want to spend Tuesday afternoon preparing for that meeting. Schedule routine tasks for times when you are most likely to be interrupted. Arrive at work earlier or leave later to find quiet time for important work.

• **Focus on the task at hand.** Concentrate on the one thing you are doing and forget about everything else. If you're having trouble getting started on a task, cup your hands around your eyes for thirty seconds to direct your attention to the task in front of you. Decide before you start a task how long you will work on it. When the time is up, move on to the next task. Let your answering machine or voice mail take messages when you need uninterrupted time. Keep a notebook handy to jot down stray thoughts and ideas about other projects or things to do.

• **Beware of multitasking.** Sure, you can read e-mail while you're on hold waiting to place an order or talk to a client. But trying to carry on a conversation and edit a document at the same time could result in accidentally deleting that document. The more complex

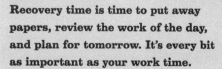

ORGANIZE YOUR DAY

Separate your work day into work time and recovery time. Recovery time is time to put away papers, review the work of the day, and plan for tomorrow. It's every bit as important as your work time.

—*Barbara Fields, PAPERCHASERS*

could you be better organized?

How organized are you at the office? Your responses will help you judge whether your organizational skills need improvement.

- Are you late for meetings and appointments more often than not? **Yes/No**
- Do you frequently need to ask for deadline extensions? **Yes/No**
- Do you routinely find the need to shift "things to do today" to tomorrow's list? **Yes/No**
- Do you feel totally overwhelmed when you think of everything you have to do at work? **Yes/No**
- Are you easily distracted from your work? **Yes/No**
- Do you have a hard time finishing what you start? **Yes/No**
- Do you frequently misplace or spend more than a few seconds looking for important papers? **Yes/No**
- Do you find it difficult to set realistic project deadlines? **Yes/No**

Scoring: One or two "yes" answers pinpoint potential problem areas for you. Three to five "yes" answers indicate room for improvement in your organizational skills. More than five "yes" answers indicates that you may not achieve your career goals unless you learn how to organize your time and work. If you had no "yes" answers, you are simply unstoppable!

the task, the more attention it requires. The cost of switching gears also grows as the complexity of the task grows. If it requires significant warm-up time to get going again, switching back and forth between complex tasks will actually slow you down.

Smart Systems

If you want to get organized, simplify your work with systems for managing projects, routine tasks, and communications. A good system is one that works for you. If you're happy with your current systems, don't change a thing. If, however, you have no systems or want to get better organized, following are some ideas for systems that you might consider implementing.

Managing Routine Tasks. Set aside specific times for routine administrative or management tasks, such as filing or writing daily reports. Perform such activities as returning telephone calls or checking e-mail at two specific times each day. Set up action folders on your desktop where you can temporarily store papers to file, read, copy, or send to other people or departments. Get in the habit of writing your daily "To Do" list at the end of each day. That way, when you come in to work, you know exactly what needs to be done and you can get to it. If you check your e-mail first thing in the morning, consider sending your "To Do" list in a message to yourself.

Work in Progress. Create and label a new folder for each new project. While you're working on the project, this folder will be your working file. These files, also known as *hot files,* are the ones that you will refer to on a daily basis. If you have to get up to retrieve your working files every time you need them, they're too far away. Keep working files within arm's reach. Staple agendas and schedules to the inside front cover for easy reference. You might also want to develop a simple "Project Status" form that allows you to keep track of projects and tasks that you delegate to co-workers or to outside agencies. Keep the most recent papers on top so that your file is in chronological order. When the project is done, transfer your working folder to your filing cabinet.

Managing Notes. One way to organize myriad pieces of information is to keep a spiral-bound, pocket-sized notebook with you at all times. Start each day by putting the date at the top of a clean page. Throughout the day, jot down anything you need to remember: people's names, things to do, ideas, notes from telephone conversations or meetings. Clip a pen to the spiral binding so that you're never without one. If appropriate, later you can transfer this information to a more permanent location

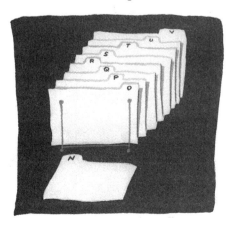

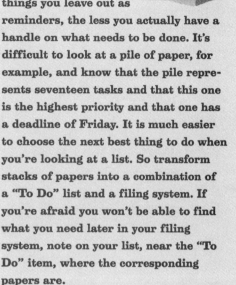

OUT OF SIGHT, OUT OF MIND?

I find that the more things you leave out as reminders, the less you actually have a handle on what needs to be done. It's difficult to look at a pile of paper, for example, and know that the pile represents seventeen tasks and that this one is the highest priority and that one has a deadline of Friday. It is much easier to choose the next best thing to do when you're looking at a list. So transform stacks of papers into a combination of a "To Do" list and a filing system. If you're afraid you won't be able to find what you need later in your filing system, note on your list, near the "To Do" item, where the corresponding papers are.

—Stephanie Denton, Denton & Company

such as a project folder or telephone directory. You can also use your computer to record notes in a contact management program.

Follow-up Systems. When you read and review memos, reports, and other documents, use a highlighter, marker, pen, or sticky flags to mark passages that you will need to refer back to so you won't have to waste time searching for the pertinent information. Respond to memos by making a handwritten note on the original memo. Note important dates and deadlines on whatever calendar system you are using. It may be helpful to also include an advance reminder to yourself: for example, "estimated taxes due next Friday." If you delegate work to an assistant or co-worker, create a folder with that person's name on it. Use it to temporarily store paperwork that you intend to pass along or notes that you need to share about the project. Make a note in your calendar of when the project or task is due back to you.

Making and Returning Phone Calls. If you need to make a lot of phone calls in a day, minimize the time you spend on each call by having an agenda in front of you and sticking to that agenda. When you leave a voice mail message, keep it as brief as possible. Be sure to say your name clearly and leave a number

One Challenge . . .

I'm always busy at work, but I don't seem to be making any progress toward my goals.

Three Solutions

❶ FROM MARIA GRACIA, GET ORGANIZED NOW!: What have you spent your time on lately? Are most of the things you're currently doing contributing to your life goals and dreams? If not, it's time to re-evaluate and re-establish your priorities. Make a list of the things you're spending your time on. Label each item A (highly contributes to my goals and dreams), B (somewhat contributes to my goals and dreams), or C (doesn't contribute to my goals and dreams at all). To achieve your goals and dreams, you must eliminate the Cs.

❷ FROM ALLISON VAN NORMAN, ORGANIZING SOLUTIONS: Decide what your top three tasks are each day, and do them first. If you have a lot of trouble prioritizing, try this method. Number the tasks as they appear on your list. Compare task one to task two and decide which has a higher priority. Give that task one point. Then compare one to three, one to four, and so on. When you've finished, compare task two to task three, task four, and so on, until you've gone through your entire list. The tasks with the most points are your highest priorities. You might be surprised.

❸ FROM CYNDI SEIDLER, HandyGirl PROFESSIONAL ORGANIZING: Make a catch-up list of tasks you have avoided or put on the back burner, and rank them from the most important to the least important. Resolve to do at least one task from this list each day.

where you can be reached. Say the number slowly. If you don't require a return call, say so. If all you really want to do is leave a message and you want to avoid getting into a conversation, make the call at a time when you don't expect that person to be there. Use the telephone when you want to establish a personal connection, need an immediate response, or require two-way communication. Otherwise, send an e-mail, fax, or memo.

Working at Home

Working at home has distinct challenges. There's the challenge of working alone. And then there's the challenge of distractions ranging from the dog barking to kids screaming and the refrigerator "calling" your name. Good time management and organizational skills are even more important for those who work at home.

Working alone doesn't have to be lonely. Plan to get out every day, whether it's to run a few errands, go to the gym, or go for a walk. Stay in contact with business colleagues by phone and e-mail. Get involved with a professional association or community group. This is also a good way to network with potential clients and other entrepreneurs. Meet up with a friend for lunch occasionally, or take a client to lunch.

The biggest challenge most home-based entrepreneurs and employees face is keeping home and office separate, physically and mentally. Start by keeping personal and business papers separate. If you have to use the same filing cabinet, at least use separate drawers. Make a point to confine all office-related paper

POWER ORGANIZING

Make your computer the central hub for all of your phone contacts, fax and letter correspondence, "To Do" lists, addresses, reminders, and calendar information. With personal information manager (PIM) software, such as Outlook, Act, Entourage, and Goldmine, you can do all that and even keep track of your e-mail. And the great thing is you only have to enter contacts once. The information in your contact database links to your PIM e-mail, calendar, and correspondence features. Have your PIM launch automatically by placing it in your start-up folder. If you're on the road a lot, download your information to your personal digital assistant (PDA) and take it with you. Using a PIM is a great way to stay organized and can help make possible the illusive paperless office.

—*Do'reen A. Hein, Artistic Designs*

and paraphernalia to your office. Make that space the most efficient, functional office you've ever had the pleasure to work in. Close the door to minimize distractions and let other family members know that you are not to be disturbed.

Set beginning and ending hours for work and be there — working — during those hours. At the end of the day, turn off your computer and close the door. Don't answer your business phone after hours. Don't respond to business e-mails. You don't have to provide service around the clock just because you work at home.

Hire help if you need it. Working at home requires you to wear many hats, from bookkeeper to chief garbage collector. Many tasks, such as bookkeeping, cleaning, filing, and other administrative work, are best hired out so that you can concentrate on doing what you do best. You can even hire a virtual assistant to do things like send out mailings and respond to voice and e-mail messages when you are on vacation. If finances are limited, look for a college student who wants a part-time job, or pay one of your children to help out with some of the simpler tasks.

Be sure that your home-based business projects a professional image. If clients come to your home office, keep it neat and organized. If you don't have a suitable space in your home, consider meeting clients off-site. If you spend a lot of time online reading e-mail or doing research, subscribe to a voice mail messaging service or get a second line so that your

For Simplicity's Sake

To avoid getting overwhelmed with new technology, focus on learning one function at a time. Look at the things you do over and over again, such as entering frequently called numbers into your fax machine or sending e-mail to the same groups of people. Open your manual to the appropriate section and learn how to do that one thing. Don't worry about all the other features. Just focus on what you need to know to make technology work for you.

—*Debbie Gilster, Organize & Computerize*

clients don't get a busy signal. When you answer the phone, answer it with a professional greeting. State your company name and ask "How may I help you?" At the very least, state your name.

For tips on setting up a home office, see page 92.

Working on the Road

Business travel presents an additional set of challenges to organizing your work. The biggest challenges include staying in touch with the office and other business colleagues while on the road, making the best use of downtime when traveling, and organizing paperwork and getting work accomplished when you're on the go.

Staying Connected. There are so many high-tech options that make it easy to stay connected wherever you go. But do yourself a favor: Before going away, ask yourself how connected you need to be. Decide which method or methods of communication would be most efficient for each trip. For example, is it worth lugging your laptop just to check e-mail each day or will you be staying in a hotel that offers Internet access?

For many office workers, keeping up with the daily volume of communications is difficult enough, and being on the road makes it even more difficult. Fortunately, there are several simple ways to reduce the number of communications that require your immediate attention when you are out of the office.

• **Change the outgoing message on your voice mail or answering machine.** Let callers know that you are away and what date you will be back in the office. If possible, give callers an option for getting immediate assistance from another staff member in your absence.

• **Forward your calls to an assistant.** Or have your assistant check your voice mail periodically so that you don't have to. If there is a matter that requires your immediate attention, your assistant can call you. Your assistant can also respond to less urgent matters on your behalf. If you don't have an assistant, consider hiring a virtual office assistant. Refer to page 279 for a few options.

• **Set the "out-of-office" automatic reply to incoming e-mail messages.** If you have this option, you won't have to worry about check-ing e-mail at all. Or, if you do check it, you can respond to just those messages that are most urgent and get back to everyone else when you return to the office.

• **Let current contacts know that you will be away.** In the days or weeks preceding your trip, make a point to let those people you are working with on a daily basis know that you will be out of the office, who will be covering for you, and how to reach you if necessary.

Managing Time Away. The secret to managing time and getting things done comes down to being realistic about what you can and cannot accomplish in any given situation. So plan your time and your work wisely. For example, if you need to work on your laptop while at a hotel, make sure that your room is equipped with a desk and dataport. Find out in advance what business services are available and at what cost. Also, be sure that your hotel is conveniently located so that you don't waste work time.

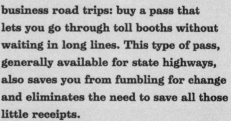

DO PASS GO

Here's a way to shave time off your daily commute and local business road trips: buy a pass that lets you go through toll booths without waiting in long lines. This type of pass, generally available for state highways, also saves you from fumbling for change and eliminates the need to save all those little receipts.

— *Diane Hatcher, Timesavers Services Professional Organizing*

- **Plan to use travel time as productive down-time.** Many business travelers say they do some of their best creative thinking in the air. Bring a notebook and pen to write down stray thoughts and ideas on current or upcoming projects. Or, if you are traveling by car, bring a handheld voice recorder to capture whatever jewels might spring to mind.

- **Prepare and organize in advance the work you plan to bring with you.** One type of work that lends itself well to travel is filling out forms and expense reports. Gather everything you will need for this project and put it into a folder or large envelope. If you decide to use travel time to catch up on your reading, organize the various types of reading (memos, reports, articles, newsletters, magazines) into these categories and keep them all together. If you decide that you will take advantage of uninterrupted travel time to make some headway on a particular project, you may want to download information onto a floppy disk or CD so you can access it on your laptop. If you need paper files, consider having them sent via overnight courier to your hotel so you don't have to carry them.

- **Make a list of the tools, supplies, and paperwork you need to bring with you.** Create this list on your computer so that you can add to or delete from it and print it for your next trip. Here's a list to get you started:

- Tickets and itinerary
- Laptop computer
- Maps and directions
- Cell phone
- Passport for international travel
- Notepads
- Reading materials
- Business cards
- Appointment calendar
- Address and phone directory
- Project folders
- Personal digital assistant (PDA)
- Prepaid or corporate calling card
- Pens, pencils, highlighters, markers
- Pocket calculator
- Special requirements

THREE E-MAIL TIPS

- **Use detailed subject headers when composing e-mails.** This saves time for the recipient, and it saves you time when you search for old e-mails. For example, "Question about Smith account" is a useful subject heading because when you see it two months later, you know exactly what the e-mail is about. "Question" is too general for a heading. No subject heading at all is even worse.

- **Delete unneeded e-mails.** Some e-mail messages can be deleted as soon as you've read them. Other messages you need to save for a short time but can safely delete later. Once a month, go back and delete any e-mails you no longer need, and archive those e-mails you must keep.

- **Use your in box as an extension of your "To Do" list.** If you regularly clean out your e-mail in box, all that remains there are things you have to act on. So your in box becomes a useful tool rather than a junk-filled, long-term storage area.

—Jan Jasper, Jasper Productivity Solutions

CHAPTER 19

BALANCING HOME AND WORK

Everything in moderation — that's the secret to happiness and good health, right? So why is it so difficult to maintain balance in our lives? Because it takes conscious effort and attention. How do you know when your life is in balance? When you function almost as well when things are going badly as when things are going well and your overall satisfaction with life remains the same.

What's Important to You?

Knowing what's important to you is the first step toward creating more balance in your life. Imagine that you had only one month to live. How would you spend your time differently? How would your priorities change? What would become more (or less) important to you? To assess your priorities, ask yourself the following questions.

• What makes me happy?
• What is the one thing I most want to accomplish?
• What do I value most?
• What do I want to be remembered for?

Then develop a strategy based on your answers.

• **Keep focused on your values.** Take five minutes at the end of each day to reflect on how you aligned your expenditures of time, energy, and money with your values throughout the day. You might want to keep a journal to chart your progress. As you plan your day, know what is most important to you today. The more time you spend thinking about your values, the more likely you are to express your values through your actions.

• **Don't be afraid to let the world see who you really are.** When you are being yourself, you give others permission to do the same. With no false fronts to keep up, life is much simpler and more satisfying.

• **Pare down your commitments.** Assess your involvement with various committees, boards, and clubs. Is the time you are spending on each of these commitments aligned with your values? Are you getting a sense of satisfaction or fulfillment from your involvement? When you volunteer your time, know why you are doing it. Do you enjoy it? Does it help you meet personal goals? If not, politely excuse yourself from commitments that are creating undue stress.

Finding Your Balance

It's not easy to juggle multiple priorities, especially when it means juggling the demands of family and career along with your own needs. But that's what we do day after day. On some days, we accomplish extraordinary things and even manage to keep everyone happy. But at what cost?

No matter how valiantly we try, we can't do it all, all of the time. And we can't do some things as often or as well as we would like to do them. So we wind up feeling like we've failed somehow. We're stressed out, tired, and maybe even a little angry. Because more often than not, we sacrifice our own plans and goals to meet the needs of others. Or we don't even make plans and goals for ourselves, because we figure, "Why bother?"

Every time you say yes to something, you are saying no to something you've already said yes to.

—Mitzi Weinman, TimeFinder

TEN-MINUTE GOALS

One of the oldest phrases in the book is, "I'll do that when I have the time." Problem is, that time never seems to come. If you really want to do something, the time can generally be found pretty easily. For example, if you just won an all-expenses paid trip to the land of your dreams, you'd probably find time to fit it into your busy schedule. It's time to begin fitting in those things you want to do, and ten-minute goals can help. Schedule ten minutes a day to catch up on your reading, begin learning a foreign language, or have fun with your children.

—Maria Gracia, Get Organized Now!

- **Bring balance to your life by focusing attention where attention is needed.** The next time you feel angry, frustrated, guilty, resentful, or stressed, note whether it is about home issues, career issues, or leisure or private time. Do you frequently feel this way about this area of your life? If so, resolve to bring your attention to this area and make an effort to make some changes that will bring your life into balance.

- **Imagine life as a game in which you are juggling five balls in the air.** Name those balls work, family, health, friends, and spirit. Work is a rubber ball; if you drop it, it will bounce back. But the other four balls — family, health, friends, and spirit — are made of glass. If you drop one of these, it will be nicked, damaged, or shattered.

- **Detach yourself slightly from your environment to become more objective about your role at home and at work.** As a more objective observer, you are more likely to find ways to improve your balance. Ask yourself this: Are you a hard worker or a workaholic? The difference between the two is state of mind. Working hard to achieve a goal is admirable. Workaholics work for the sake of working in the belief that work will somehow make them worthier. If others see you differently from the way you see yourself, imagine for a moment that their perspective is the true perspective. See if you can justify their position and then try to justify your own.

- **Structure your day for balance by scheduling specific times for work, home, and play.** When you are at work, engage fully in your job. When you are with your family, give them 100 percent of your attention and energy. And when you are playing, concentrate on your enjoyment. Live each moment to the fullest.

- **Spend less time talking about your need to relax and more time doing it.** Play hooky from work. If you've been swamped with deadlines, spend a whole day with no plans. Just do what you feel like doing, when you feel like doing it. If you have to make a lot of decisions at work, give yourself a time-out from making decisions. Let someone else decide where to go, what to do, and what to eat. If your job requires constant contact with people, escape into solitude. Go for a walk in the woods or paddle a canoe on a quiet lake.

- **It's okay to stop and rest.** If your life is a whirlwind of activity seven days a week, try balancing it with some true leisure time — a time to sit and rest — without feeling the need to be productive or busy doing something. It will refresh your spirit and make you more efficient when you return to your responsibilities. If an appointment or activity is canceled at the last minute, resist the urge to fill up that time slot with another appointment or activity. If you work particularly long and hard one day or if you feel exhausted, make a conscious effort to take it a little easier the next day. Sleep later if you can. Leave work half an hour early (or at least on time). Squeeze in a nap. Put your feet up and read a book. Or do nothing at all. A change from your regular routine can be just as relaxing as a rest, and maybe even more restful if you're the type that finds it hard to sit still. Try doing something you really love to do but haven't done in a long while.

GO AHEAD . . . DROP THE BALL

Let some of the balls you are juggling intentionally drop. To do this, you may need to deal with the source of the symptoms that cause you to overcommit yourself. Do any of these fit for you?

- Trying to please everyone
- Trying to be liked by everyone
- Trying to be the star or the savior (What would they do without you?)
- Trying to do everything perfectly
- Trying to say yes to everything and everyone
- Addiction to the emotional "high" of running on adrenaline in crisis situations
- Feeling like you have no choice — there's no one else to do it

After you've identified the source of being overcommitted, take at least one action step each week to help you consciously drop some of the balls you choose not to juggle anymore. For example, if you're a perfectionist, ask yourself if perfection is required (in your housekeeping, for example) or if it truly serves you to strive for perfection. Most gold medalists in the Olympics don't get a perfect score. Unless you're a rocket scientist working on a space shuttle, perfection probably isn't required.

—*Kathy Paauw, Paauwerfully Organized*

Learn to Say No

Is it worse to say yes and feel angry, or to say no and feel guilty? The answer goes back to your values and beliefs. When you act from your values and beliefs, your decision feels right. Frustration is a signal that you are doing more than what feels comfortable.

Don't let guilt make you take on more than you can handle or take you away from what's really important to you. According to Miss Manners, the polite way to refuse is to offer an apology but no excuse. She suggests the following polite denials: "Oh, I'm terribly sorry, but I can't." "I'd love to, but I'm afraid it's impossible." "Unfortunately, I can't, but I hope you can find someone."

If you feel stressed most days, examine your schedule. Is there a commitment you can forgo? Or is there someone else who can do some of the things you are doing? Ask other members of your household which obligations they would be willing to pick up. You might find that your husband doesn't mind vacuuming or that your daughter actually enjoys ironing.

Minimize your shuttling responsibilities. A 1999 report by the Washington-based Surface Transportation Policy Project shows that American mothers with kids in school spend an average of 66 minutes each day driving. If it's safe, encourage children who are old enough to walk, cycle, or skate to school and to after-school activities, or use public transportation. If other mothers you know are in the same time bind, see if you can work out a weekly schedule of pick-ups and drop-offs that provide all of you with a little extra free time.

twenty ways to say no

Ramona Creel of OnlineOrganizing.com offers these suggestions for saying no.

- I can't right now, but I can do it later.
- I'm really not the most qualified person for the job.
- I just don't have any room in my calendar right now.
- I can't but let me give you the name of someone who can.
- I have another commitment.
- I'm in the middle of several projects and can't spare the time.
- I've had a few things come up and I need to deal with those first.
- I would rather decline than end up doing a mediocre job.
- I'm focusing more on my personal and family life right now.
- I'm focusing more on my career right now.
- I don't really enjoy that kind of work.
- I can't, but I'm happy to help out with another task.
- I've learned in the past that this isn't my strong suit.
- I'm sure you will do a wonderful job on your own.
- I don't have any experience with that, so I can't help you.
- I'm not comfortable with that.
- I hate to split my attention among too many projects.
- I'm committed to leaving some time for myself in my schedule.
- I'm not taking on any new projects.
- No.

Making Time for You

Yes, family is important. Yes, work is important. And yes, there's only so much time in a day. But if you don't take care of your own needs, who will? If you want to unclutter your life, begin by choosing to put yourself first. It's not being selfish; it's being self-caring. There's a big difference.

Caring for yourself — physically, emotionally, intellectually, socially, and spiritually — will make you happier, healthier, and better able to cope with the demands of daily living. In fact, by putting your own needs first and reserving even just a little more time and energy for yourself, you will have more to give to others.

You're in charge of your time, so go ahead and make some time for yourself. Schedule free time into every day. Block out some time in your calendar and write the word "FREE" in that time slot. Use this time for activities that you really enjoy, such as spending time with your children, visiting friends and family, or gardening. Then schedule everything else around those times. Why should it be the reverse? Allow some flexibility in your schedule, however. Don't try to plan every minute of your time. Leave some time to do whatever you feel like doing at the moment, which may be nothing at all.

Free up time by taking advantage of all that technology has to offer. Have your paycheck deposited directly into your checking account. Set up automatic payments for your bills. Shop on-line, especially if you don't like shopping. Use your computer to create a grocery list or to manage your finances. Let your answering machine take your calls during dinner or when you are trying to enjoy some quiet time. Just don't become a slave to technology. Remember, you are ultimately the master of your own time.

Try designating a night to do your own thing. If your children are old enough to fend for themselves, consider making one night a week a night when everyone is on their own. This can be your time to take a class, read, write, draw, or do whatever makes you happy.

UNCLUTTER YOUR MIND

It's hard to concentrate on work or home when your brain is overloaded with things you are trying to remember about one or the other. Here are two simple ways to clear mental clutter:

1. **Keep a small notepad or voice recorder with you to capture thoughts, ideas, or anything you want to remember.**

2. **Call home or work to leave yourself a reminder on your own voice mail system or answering machine.**

—LaNita Filer, LFJ Organizing Concepts Plus

Carve out a chunk of time that is your "do not disturb" time. Let everyone in your household know about this time and make it clear that you are to be interrupted only in case of emergency. Go through possible scenarios with them to make sure they understand what constitutes an emergency. If they see blood, smoke, or fire, that's an emergency. Everything else can wait. If one of your kids wants to go over to a friend's house and needs your permission, he'll have to wait a half hour until you are free. If your husband can't find his favorite golf shirt, he keeps looking himself, gets the kids to help him look, or wears another shirt. Hint: It's a lot easier on everyone if you spend your "do not disturb" time behind a closed door.

Make use of the free time you do have. If you have an hour for lunch, plan to spend thirty minutes eating and thirty minutes doing something that you want or need to do such as:

- Read a book
- Take a nap
- Take a walk
- Pick up a few groceries
- Make personal phone calls
- Write a letter
- Run a couple of quick errands
- Listen to music on your headphones
- Sit and think

If you can't manage a whole hour or more of time to exercise or read or whatever, start with ten minutes. Ten minutes of time for yourself is better than zero minutes. If you can, keep your hobby stuff handy so that you can

One Challenge . . .

There are so many things I would love to do, but because I work fifty hours a week, I just never seem to have the time. How can I make more time for myself?

Three Solutions

1 FROM LORRAINE CHALICKI, YOUNEEDME.COM PERSONAL SYSTEMS: Include your personal passions in your workday. If you're a shutterbug, bring your camera to work and take photographs during your lunch hours. Or schedule a five-minute "fun break" or two throughout your workday to leaf through your favorite photo magazine or catalog. If you love music, bring your favorite CDs or tapes to work and take a lunchtime break with your headphones. As you begin to build these breaks into your workday, you'll quickly discover that they provide a major boost in energy and improve the quality of your work and mental processes.

2 FROM MARIA GRACIA, GET ORGANIZED NOW!: You really can't add anything to your schedule without subtracting something else from it. Think about what things you can choose to subtract so that you can add the things you really want to do. Do away with anything that is not helping you fulfill your goals and dreams.

3 FROM JAN JASPER, JASPER PRODUCTIVITY SOLUTIONS: Schedule appointments with yourself to make time for the things you keep "not getting around to." This works for everything from taking the next step on that back-burner project to making sure you get yourself to the gym twice a week.

make good use of spare moments throughout the day and of waiting and commuting time.

Time for Family and Friends

At the beginning of each month, put "fun stuff to do" on your calendar to balance the demands and responsibilities of home and career. If you wish you had more time for your family, think about how you can make more time for them. Where there's a will, there's a way. Perhaps you can try the following techniques to see what works best for you.

- Cut back on work hours.
- Change jobs.
- Trade full-time for part-time work.
- Cut commuting time by working closer to home.
- Work at home one or more days a week.

Unite the three Fs: family, friends, and fun. One way to make more time for friends without shortchanging your family is to invite friends to join in some family fun. Choose activities that everyone, even friends without children, can enjoy.

- Attend a sporting event.
- Go to a water park.
- Take a hike.
- Fly a kite.
- Rent boats or canoes on a nearby lake.
- Go camping for a weekend.
- Go skiing or cycling.
- Have a picnic at the beach.
- Make plans to go on vacation together.
- Celebrate the holidays together.

For more ideas on organizing togetherness for your family, see page 190.

Friends help us maintain the balance between work and play. It's so easy to get caught up in doing and achieving that we often neglect to make time to be with the people we care about most. Yet research shows that people who have family and friends to help them through stressful times stay healthier and recover faster than those who do not have a social support system.

Dedicate time to friendship time. Take a few minutes to send an e-mail message or a "just thinking of you" card. Make a quick phone call, or leave a "hello" message on a friend's answering machine. Make a standing date for coffee or lunch with your best friend once or twice a month.

CUTTING BACK

Identify some specific areas where you might be able to cut back on your responsibilities. For each item on your list, ask yourself:

- How easy or hard will it be for me to let go?
- What consequence would ensue if nobody took up the slack when I let it go?
- Who is the logical choice to take up the slack in responsibility?

Now work your list. Start with the items that are the easiest for you to let go of, with the least dire consequences, and for which someone can pick up the slack. Select at least one per week to let go. Where appropriate, you'll want to inform those who will be affected that you're doing this. In some cases, that will mean training someone else in how or what is required for them to pick up the slack. And you'll need to accept their mistakes and the inevitable chaos that ensues. Ultimately, you'll reap the benefits of increased time, freedom, and a happier, more satisfying life.

—*Rose Hill, The Academy for Business Success*

PART V

Organizing Home Life

Most people will say that family and home life are their number one priority. The way to organize your home life — and maximize time with your family — is to implement schedules, simple routines, and systems that are easy to maintain. In chapter 20, "Organizing Your Family," you'll find suggestions for keeping track of who needs to be where when, as well as ideas for creating opportunities for family togetherness. Chapter 21, "Organizing to Go" offers tips for getting and staying organized before, during, and after your next vacation or business trip. Chapter 22, "Managing Your Household," outlines a plan for preparing meals and keeping your home presentable with minimal time and effort. And, in chapter 23, "Organizing for Safety," you'll learn ways to keep your family safer and more secure at home. All it takes to accomplish these things is a willingness to try something different.

CHAPTER 20

ORGANIZING YOUR FAMILY

Think of your family as a team, with you as the team's manager. Your job is to organize the team and minimize the chaos. As the manager, you need to know where all players are at all times. Players need to know the rules. You all need to work together as a team to achieve your goals, whether playing at home or away.

Managing Family Schedules

Trying to keep track of who needs to be where and when can be daunting. Try implementing a family planning system. It could be as simple as making notes on a calendar that hangs on the refrigerator. For families that are always on the go, consider a slightly more sophisticated interactive scheduling system that enables family members to make plans around each other's schedules.

A great tool for keeping track of family schedules is a large blank write-on/wipe-off wall planner with a spacious grid that provides plenty of room for writing in daily, weekly, or monthly events and activities. These boards sometimes include a separate planning area where you can note future events and activities. Assign a different color marker to each

family member for writing in appointments, meetings, practices, games, gym time, celebrations and outings, and such tasks as grocery shopping or taking garbage to the dump. Each family member should be responsible for entering his or her own schedule.

Another effective tool for family scheduling is a group practice appointment book. This is the kind of planner used in physician offices. Available for four- and eight-person groups, the group practice appointment book lets you block out the time in quarter-hour increments for each family member, so you can see everyone's schedule at a glance. Look for an undated planner that lets you make "appointments" from as early as 7 A.M. to as late as 9 P.M. Use a large, magnetic clip or two to attach the calendar to the refrigerator.

When coordinating your family's schedule, don't forget to block out time one day a week for family clutter control. During this time, everyone goes through the house picking up and putting away misplaced items that belong elsewhere. Setting up a specific time for uncluttering eliminates the need to nag, and without question the results are far more dramatic when every room gets uncluttered simultaneously. If once a week doesn't suit your family's style, try doing it for five minutes every night after dinner.

Rules and Routines

Kids need rules and routines. They may not always like the rules, but knowing what to expect — and what is expected from them — makes them feel more secure. The rewards and punishments that come with rules also teach kids that people are responsible for the consequences of their actions. But kids can't learn that lesson unless you apply rewards and punishments consistently, and that's the hard part. It may be easier to create and enforce several important rules rather than trying to enforce lots of little rules.

What is your family's daily routine? Routines help your family get organized and stay organized. They also help to reduce the stress and frustration that comes from having to nag kids about doing their homework and chores. If the idea of routines seems stifling, consider this: Having them may allow more time for fun because routines help kids, and you, manage time better. Following are some ideas for developing routines.

- **Morning routine.** In the morning, the goal is to get kids out the door on time with the least amount of whining and complaining. It might be easier to yell "Time to get up!," but why start your day yelling? Try waking your kids with a little tug on their big toes or a tickle. Or put on their favorite music, and turn the volume up. If your kids have trouble tearing themselves away from the television in the morning, try turning it off fifteen to thirty minutes before "go" time, or don't turn it on at all. Parents can get weather, news, and traffic reports from the radio and Internet. Post morning chores where kids can see them when they're getting dressed.

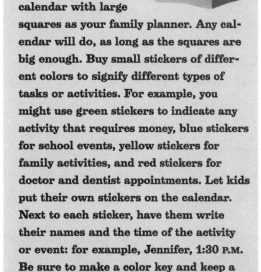

MAKE PLANNING FUN

Try using a paper calendar with large squares as your family planner. Any calendar will do, as long as the squares are big enough. Buy small stickers of different colors to signify different types of tasks or activities. For example, you might use green stickers to indicate any activity that requires money, blue stickers for school events, yellow stickers for family activities, and red stickers for doctor and dentist appointments. Let kids put their own stickers on the calendar. Next to each sticker, have them write their names and the time of the activity or event: for example, Jennifer, 1:30 P.M. Be sure to make a color key and keep a supply of stickers and a pen handy.

—Debbie Williams, Let's Get It Together

- **After-school routine.** Just like adults, kids need time to wind down after a busy day. Allow them time to have a snack, watch television, play computer games, or play outdoors with friends. Down time is important, but if homework or chores are not getting done, you may need to help kids manage their time better by setting up specific times for these activities. If you can, schedule a set "homework time" for all of your kids. This is also a good time for you to work on quiet activities, such as reading, writing, or paying bills. Get kids in the habit of putting all permission slips, forms, and notices in your "in box" when they come home. If there's something that has to go back to school, put it in your child's "in box" or directly into his or her school bag.

- **Bedtime routine.** It's important for kids (and you) to get enough sleep. Lack of sleep is one of the chief causes of daytime fatigue and is linked to poor performance in school. Get your children in the habit of going to bed each night at the same time. Reserve after dinner as time for quiet activities, such as reading, writing, working on homework or projects, and

watching television. Help young children wind down for the night with a bedtime story, singing, or some snuggle time. Establish a time for "lights out" and stick to it.

More Organized Mornings

Are weekday mornings hectic in your home? Take the madness out of mornings by getting as much as possible prepared the night before and by implementing workable routines for your family.

- **Select outfits the night before.** Have your children decide what they want to wear to school the next day, or take it one step further and get them to pick out school outfits for the whole week on Sunday. Hang the complete outfit on a single hanger in the closet or behind their bedroom door, or lay it out on a chair. Now do the same for yourself. Lay out everything you need, from underwear to shoes to jewelry, so you won't have to search for things in the morning or be forced to wear a wrinkled shirt or pantyhose with runs. Selecting outfits the night before also helps keep your bedroom neater, since you'll have plenty of time to put away any clothing you decided not to wear.

- **Prepack book bags and briefcases.** In the evening, get your children in the habit of putting their books, papers, and anything else they will need at school the next day into their book bags. Do the same with your gym bag and briefcase. If you are active on various committees or boards, consider keeping separate briefcases for each to ensure that you always have what you need for meetings. Place bags, briefcases, and anything else that should leave with you, such as library books and videos to be returned or clothing that needs to go to the dry cleaner, near the front door. If you check the weather forecast the night before, you can also select and place outerwear near the door.

• **Make breakfast before going to bed.** Put water in the coffeemaker and coffee in the filter, so all you have to do is turn it on in the morning. Have your children set the table the night before with breakfast cereals, bowls, glasses, and silverware. For a special treat on the first day back to school or for a birthday, you could make waffles the night before and reheat them in the toaster oven.

• **Make lunches ahead of time.** Consider making a week's worth of sandwiches at once. Your kids might enjoy being part of the production line. Freeze sandwiches in separate plastic bags, then place them all in a large airtight zipper bag labeled with the type of sandwich inside. Remove sandwiches from the freezer each morning, and they will defrost by lunchtime. Fillings that freeze well include peanut butter, deli meats, and tuna salad made with sour cream or salad dressing. Mayonnaise and jelly do not freeze well. Prepare and refrigerate separate sandwich bags of lettuce, sprouts, onion, or tomato to add to the sandwich once it's defrosted.

• **Develop wake-up routines.** Stagger wake-up times for better traffic control (and less fighting) in the bathroom. If this is a big issue at your house, use a kitchen timer to set limits on bathroom time and move such

NO MORE HIDE-AND-SEEK

Create a standard checklist to remind kids of what they need to bring to school on any given day, including:

• **Homework and project materials**

• **Permission slips or other school forms**

• **Band instrument**

• **Gym clothes**

• **Sports equipment**

• **After-school necessities**

• **Special items for events or activities**

• **Library books**

• **Lunch money**

You can make a note of where the kids tend to leave things, if that helps: for example, "gym clothes — check the laundry basket." The goal is to make sure that everything they need for school is in one place when it comes time to leave. That way, your children can simply grab their bags on the way out the door instead of playing hide-and-seek with their school supplies. For kids who split their time between parents, you might want to create a standard list of things the child might need while at Mom or Dad's place, and use that list when packing for the visit. Consider keeping small, inexpensive items such as school supplies, toothbrush, socks, and underwear at both houses.

—*Ramona Creel, OnlineOrganizing.com*

activities as hair drying and getting dressed into the bedroom. It's also helpful if some family members shower or bathe the night before. Another way to stay on schedule in the morning is to set a kitchen timer or alarm to go off ten minutes before it's time to head out the door.

The Message Center

A message center is a must in a busy household. Designate one area for picking up messages and mail, preferably in a central location, such as the kitchen or wherever there is a telephone and some desk or counter space.

Hang an erasable board, bulletin board, or sticky board for posting messages, or keep a small notepad and pen near the telephone for writing down messages. Secure the writing implement to the phone with a string or cord so that it doesn't "walk" away with the last person who used it. Or keep a supply of pens and pencils within reach of the telephone.

For Simplicity's Sake

Use a message pad with carbonless duplicates for recording messages and conversations. You can tear off the note and feel comfortable that there is still a record somewhere. The message form also helps train children to take complete messages.

—*Debbie Gilster, Organize & Computerize*

If you use an answering machine to take messages, consider having family members use the "memo" feature to leave messages for each other when they go out. You can also use this feature to remind yourself to do something upon your return.

Make it clear to household members that the message taker must leave the message in the designated area. The message center is also the best place to store incoming mail. Use labeled stacking trays or a vertical file sorter to separate mail for each recipient. Be sure to have a large trash can or recycling bin nearby for collecting opened envelopes, junk mail, and other paper garbage.

Keep a list of emergency and frequently called phone numbers near the phone. If your message center is in your kitchen, you might tape the list to the back side of a cabinet door. The list should include telephone numbers for police, fire, and ambulance, and Poison Control Center (800-222-1222); it may also include numbers for family dentists and physicians, veterinarian, utility companies, plumber and electrician, day care and schools, and favorite restaurants and movie theaters.

Keep a current telephone book in your message center. It makes sense to store your own personal telephone directory here, too. When you receive cards and other personal correspondence, check the return address to see if you have the most current one in your directory. Consider using a revolving card file with individual A–Z tabs. If an address or phone number changes, fill out a new card and throw out the old one.

To ensure that you get all of your telephone messages, Stephanie Denton of Denton & Company recommends subscribing to a voice mail messaging service through your local telephone company. Set up separate mail boxes to route telephone messages directly to the appropriate party. This system also works well for keeping personal messages separate from work-related messages.

Household Chores

No one wants to do household chores, but they need to be done. The fastest way to get chores done is to divide the work between household members. This will probably require a family meeting to determine who will do what.

So how do you divide chores fairly? One way is to make a list of routine chores — those that need to be done on a daily or weekly basis. Once you've got your list, break it down into categories, such as preparing for meals; cleaning up after meals; doing laundry; vacuuming, dusting, and general cleaning; yard work, garbage and recycling; and pet feeding and dog walking. Then assign one or more categories of chores to

TIME-SAVER

In your revolving address directory, attach a tiny sticky tab to the cards you search for most frequently. These stickers are available wherever office supplies are sold.

each family member for one week. At the end of the week, rotate the schedule. A variation on this strategy is to ask family members to volunteer for the chores they don't mind doing on a regular basis and rotate the chores that no one likes to do. Obviously, there are some chores that only you or your partner can do, such as paying bills, grocery shopping, or cooking.

Create a "job jar" for jobs that fall outside the daily chores. Write jobs on slips of paper and assign a wage or points for each job. Put these slips of paper in a large jar or empty coffee can. One night a week, have each family member draw a chore from the job jar. Hang a write-on/wipe-off board on the refrigerator for kids to keep track of their weekly wages or points. If you like the idea of a point system, assign a reward for various point levels. For example, twenty-five points might earn the chance to stay up one half-hour later on a weekend night or to skip one weekly chore the following week. Let kids know that they may earn additional wages or points by doing additional chores.

Make an Agreement. Be sure to give a specific time frame for daily chores. For example, whoever has laundry duty needs to check the dryer

SLOW DOWN

- **Plan at least one day during the school week with no scheduled activities.**

- **Set a limit to the number of outside activities.**

- **Schedule weekly family meetings to review the coming week's events and commitments.**

—Mitzi Weinman, TimeFinder

each day after school and fold whatever clothes are in there. Make it clear that privileges depend on response to family requests. If assigned chores don't get done on time, no privileges are awarded. Privileges may include going to a friend's house after school or overnight, going to the movies or to the mall, or engaging in other extracurricular activities.

Offer children a per-job salary or weekly allowance as incentive. Inspect each chore as it's done and give praise to help reinforce good habits and build self-esteem. Even small children can help. While one family member is vacuuming, a younger one can follow along behind cleaning baseboards with socks on his hands. If you have two or more little ones, make it a contest to see whose sock puppet gets dirtiest.

Julie Signore of 1,2,3 SORT IT suggests creating a work agreement with your kids. Be very specific because kids will find any loopholes. Decide on the instances in which a concession may be made. Can chores be traded? Who is

responsible for seeing that they are completed? List the penalties of breaking the agreement. Whatever you do, create goals that are realistic. You are aiming to keep your home organized and enhance your kids' self-esteem, not set them up for failure. Create penalties that you will stick to. Do not create consequences that will be hard for you to follow through with. Kids test adults — it's the nature of being a child. Remember, the art of discipline is also an expression of love. You are not taking away from a child's childhood by teaching responsibility and self-discipline.

Organizing Togetherness

Togetherness is the key to building a strong family. Do you set aside time to be with your children, partner, sisters, brothers, parents, and extended family? In today's busy world, it's easy for families to drift apart. But you can cultivate togetherness by making an extra effort to "be there" for your children and for other family members — not just on birthdays and holidays, but every day. For many families, just sitting down to eat dinner or breakfast together would be a major step in the right direction.

One way to ensure that you get together on a regular basis is to hold regular family meetings. This is a time when you can share upcoming schedules and any past, present, or future concerns. Having an open forum helps kids to bring up subjects they might not otherwise have the courage to broach on their own. Call special family meetings as necessary to work on special projects, make an important announcement, or to discuss a controversial issue.

Carve out some "together time." Set aside one morning, afternoon, evening, or day every week to do something fun together. Take turns making suggestions about what to do next. You might go to a movie, sporting event, play, or concert. Visit one of the kids' aunts or uncles. Or stay home, make popcorn, play board games, and talk. Let the answering machine take messages or limit phone calls to a quick "I'll have to call you back" conversation.

Find ways in which you can get some exercise together, such as walking, hiking, cycling, or in-line skating. Recent studies show that nearly two-thirds of all school-age children can't measure up to the minimum standard of fitness. A recent Surgeon General's Report on Physical Activity and Health shows that about the same proportion of adults do not engage in the recommended amount of physical activity, and 25 percent are not active at all. Exercising together is a way to bring you closer as a family while helping to improve your health and fitness.

You can even make chore time into quality one-on-one time with your children. Try asking children to take turns helping you to prepare dinner. They might balk at first but will soon begin to look forward to their turn if, during your time together, you shower them with attention. Ask about school, extracurricular activities, friends, favorite subjects, and dreams.

TEN-MINUTE CHORE BOX

Rather than spending hours organizing, and doing it all yourself, create a ten-minute chore box for yourself and one for each family member. Each person's box should contain chores or tasks that take a maximum of ten minutes to accomplish. Gear chores to abilities: For example, while older kids can help out with vacuuming, a three-year-old can pick up her toys. Write these chores or tasks on slips of paper. Each day, each person pulls one slip of paper from his or her box. When the chore is completed, that slip of paper is placed in a holding envelope until the chore box is empty. The boxes are then refilled, and the system starts over again.

This system also works well for getting tasks done at the office. Create a ten-minute chore box with individual slips of paper on which you write tasks that take ten minutes or less to do, including filing, purging files, reading articles or e-mails, doing on-line or telephone research, straightening up your desk, and dusting and watering plants.

—Maria Gracia, Get Organized Now!

Projects are another way to build unity within families. Work together to rake fall leaves, decorate the house for the holidays, or unclutter the basement to make room for a game room. Try setting some goals together as a family. You might work together to raise money for a charitable organization, volunteer your services in the community, train for and participate in a local race, or set up a family savings plan for a vacation.

One Challenge . . .

I am always having to rearrange my schedule to accommodate my family's schedule. Usually, it's because my kids leave it until the last minute to tell me that they have to be somewhere. How can we plan better together as a family?

Three Solutions

1 FROM RAMONA CREEL, ONLINEORGANIZING.COM: I suggest setting aside time once a week for a family planning session at which everyone can discuss their upcoming activities, appointments, events, and things to do. Record everything on your family calendar. Just taking time to discuss plans and making sure they gel with everyone else's plans is a huge step toward getting better organized.

2 FROM STEPHANIE DENTON, DENTON & COMPANY: Consider putting technology to work. Many families use handheld electronic organizers for keeping track of their schedules. Look for models with infrared ports that allow you to "beam" calendar entries to other family members. Being able to see everyone else's schedule at a glance helps to avoid scheduling conflicts and allows you do things like make your next doctor's appointment while at the doctor's office.

3 FROM GLORIA RITTER, PAPER MATTERS AND MORE, INC.: Keep your family calendar on the Internet so that everyone has access to it wherever they are. Yahoo! (see Resources, page 279) offers a free calendar tool that lets you share your schedules, find free times, and send appointment reminders. You can also use this tool for entering things to do along with deadlines.

CHAPTER 21

ORGANIZING TO GO

Planning a family vacation or a weekend getaway? Going abroad or out of town on business? You don't have to be a veteran traveler to organize a safe and memorable trip. But there *are* simple things everyone (even veteran travelers) can do to avoid unnecessary fuss, hassles, and expense. And, with a little know-how, anyone can learn how to pack like a professional and stay organized wherever you go.

Smart Vacation Planning

Rule number one: Plan ahead. If you're traveling for leisure, plan your trip at least one month in advance. For travel during peak periods (namely, winter holidays, spring break, and summer), you may need to book months in advance to ensure availability.

• **Be flexible.** The more flexible you can be in making your travel plans, the better deal you'll get. Virtually every vacation destination has its "off-peak" seasons when airfare, hotel rooms, and car rentals are offered at reduced rates. Consider planning your vacation around special offers from airlines that are trying to fill flights to various destinations. Go to the Web sites of the major airlines and sign up for e-mail

announcements of these reduced fares, including last-minute fares at a fraction of their regular price.

But what if the only time you can travel is when vacation demand and prices are at their peak? You may still be able to enjoy significant savings on airfare by being flexible about what days you can travel. Generally, lower airfares are offered midweek. Traveling midweek is also good because traffic is lighter. So even if your flight is delayed due to weather, you are more likely to experience only a short delay.

Adding a Saturday night stay almost always brings the cost of air travel down. Being flexible about the time of day you travel can also make a huge difference. For example, you may be able to get a cheaper flight by leaving your destination after noon on Monday or before 8 A.M. on Friday. Also, investigate the possibility of flying into and out of nearby airports that may offer lower fares. The savings can be well worth the extra drive at either end.

• **Consider electronic tickets.** Many leisure travelers prefer to have paper tickets, but electronic tickets actually provide more security and peace of mind. If you lose your paper ticket or it is stolen, you have to fill out a lost ticket claim with the airline and then purchase a new ticket. If the old ticket is not found within a certain time period, you will be reimbursed for one of the tickets. Though you will be able to get the new ticket at the original price you paid, you will need to pay a lost ticket fee, which can be quite steep. With an electronic ticket, there's nothing to lose. You simply present your photo identification (which you need anyway) to get your boarding pass.

• **Join a frequent-flyer program.** Frequent air travelers can earn free tickets and upgrades by becoming a member of one or more airline frequent flyer programs. Even if you are not a frequent air traveler on a particular airline, it doesn't hurt to "join the club" and collect frequent flyer miles. After all, there's no cost to join. With some frequent flyer programs, miles earned are valid indefinitely, so sooner or later, you might well have the requisite number of points for a free roundtrip ticket or upgrade. Overnights at selected hotels and car rentals also earn frequent flyer miles with most programs. Some programs even offer awards on qualifying foreign exchange transactions and on long-distance use with selected carriers.

• **Book to your advantage.** If you are traveling by air, book your flight first and then your hotel. You can often get a better rate on your hotel when you book it as a package with your flight. This is not true of car rentals. You can usually get a much better deal if you book your car rental separately. In both cases, don't assume that a 50 percent–off coupon you might have is always the best deal. Generally, the discount is off the regular rate, and you can get a better rate without it. If you are booking your hotel separately, be sure to compare apples to apples. For instance, one hotel might appear to be cheaper, but daily-parking costs may offset the savings. Conversely, a higher rate per night that includes breakfast might work out cheaper than staying in a hotel with a lower rate.

When booking your hotel, always ask if the rate quoted is the best rate available. Ask if any of your association memberships or credit cards entitle you to a discount; you can often save 5 to 10 percent off the best rate this way. You may be able to get a better rate on your hotel room by purchasing in advance and paying a deposit on all or part of your stay.

Also ask if the hotel has any special packages available, which may include breakfast, discount coupons to restaurants, room upgrades, or special amenities. Ask again when you arrive at the hotel if your rate is the best available, as rates do change.

- **Shop around for savings on land travel.** There are ways to save on land transportation costs as well. If you are traveling by train, Amtrak offers a discount to members of the Automobile Association of America (AAA). Riding the rails during off-peak hours — that is, before or after busy commuter hours — generally results in additional savings. Daily rates on car rentals can be pricey, but if you rent for five to seven days, you will get the weekly rate.

- **Be a savvy car renter.** Be aware that car rental companies usually quote a rate for a midsize car. If you don't need the extra room, ask for the rate on a compact-size car. A smaller car generally gets more miles to the gallon, which can add up to savings on gasoline as well, especially if you plan to do a lot of driving. Unless you expect to do very limited driving, look for a car rental that offers unlimited miles. Otherwise, the cost per mile above and beyond the free miles offered can add up quickly.

The car rental company agent will encourage you to sign up for optional insurance on the rental vehicle. Check with your automobile insurance agent beforehand to see if your policy covers a rental car; it usually does. Also, most credit card companies provide insurance coverage automatically when you use their card to charge the rental. To avoid unnecessary hassles at the car rental company, make and bring with you a photocopy of your insurance policy or your credit card agreement. Most automobile insurance policies do not cover car rentals outside the United States. In that case, you would be wise to purchase automobile insurance in that country with coverage amounts similar to your policy at home.

Before driving away in your rental car, inspect it inside and out. If you notice any dents or scratches or damage to the interior that are not noted on the rental agreement, point them out to a company representative, who should then make those notations on the agreement.

For several years now, car rental agencies have offered a "prepay" option for gas, and many travelers find this convenient, especially when they're unfamiliar with the locations of area gas stations or will be racing to catch a flight for a plane when they return the car. The prepay option is more expensive, and if you prefer to fill the tank yourself, always remember to return the car with a full tank of gas. As you leave the car rental place, look for the nearest gas station and make a note of it on your map. You do have a map of the local area, right? If not, get one from your car rental agent.

too good to be true?

If a travel offer sounds too good to be true, it probably is, especially if the mail solicitation requires you to call a 900 number or the caller wants you to make an immediate decision without anything in writing. Those travel "awards" that require you to make a payment to collect your "prize" or to disclose confidential information such as your checking account or social security number are travel scams.

- **Organize your road trip.** If you will be traveling by car, plan your route in advance to minimize the possibility of getting lost. Free mapping services are available to AAA and other automobile club members. You can also get maps and written driving directions from several mapping services on the Internet. (See page 284 for several such services.) The other option is to buy a good road map and use a highlighting pen to mark your intended route. Separate and store change for toll roads in empty film canisters with a sample coin taped to the top of each lid for easy identification. If you have some spare room in your trunk, pack food and beverages from home in a cooler and plan to have picnics along the way. Look for good picnic spots on the map.
- **Put your affairs in order.** One last word about smart vacation planning: It's a good idea to have your affairs at home in order. Leave a copy of your current will, insurance documents,

and power of attorney with your family or a friend or let them know where they can find these documents. For more information about organizing your estate, refer to chapter 27.

Smart Money Moves

There are some smart things you can do to protect yourself financially from the time you make your travel arrangements until the time you return home. You may have heard of trip insurance. That's the first thing to consider. There are also simple things you can do to keep yourself from getting ripped off while away from home.

Trip and Travel Insurance. If you have to postpone or cancel a flight due to an illness or death in your family, regularly scheduled airlines will usually give a refund with a note from a doctor or a death certificate. But you may get no refund at all on a travel package unless you have trip insurance. Take the quiz on the next page to help you decide if you should get trip insurance.

Trip cancellation and trip interruption insurances provide financial protection for nonrefundable travel expenses. Cancellation insurance reimburses you if you are unable to depart for your trip due to an unforeseen accident or illness that affects you, a close family member, or a traveling companion. Trip interruption insurance reimburses you if an injury, illness, or other event prevents you from continuing your trip.

Trip cancellation and interruption insurances are usually bundled together at a cost of pennies on the dollar. If you are booking a travel package, your travel agent will almost always ask if you want to buy this insurance. Before signing, read the insurance policies carefully to find out if there are any exclusions such as preexisting medical conditions, mountain climbing, or terrorism in the country where you are headed. Look for a policy that will waive any of the exclusions you want to have covered. Also, make sure that trip cancellation insurance covers you while you are on the way from home to your departure point, as many policies do not.

Most other types of travel insurance are usually unnecessary because they duplicate coverage you already have. Unless you are traveling to a foreign country where your medical insurance is not valid, you probably don't need to buy a separate insurance policy that reimburses you for medical or hospitalization expenses incurred while traveling. If you have accidental and death and dismemberment insurance or life insurance, you're already covered for that wherever you go. Lost baggage is usually covered under your standard renter's or homeowner's insurance. Checked and carry-on luggage may also be covered by your credit card company policy if you used that card to make your travel purchase.

Credit Cards. Using a credit card to pay for your hotel or rental car, meals, and other incidentals is a good idea because you won't need to carry as much cash. Just be sure to check your available credit before you go. Bring an envelope to keep all credit card receipts together. When you return home, check the purchase amounts on your billing statement against your sales receipts to make sure they match. This is especially important if the charges are in a foreign currency. Without the receipts, it would be difficult to verify the correct amounts. If you find any discrepancies or transactions that are not yours, contact your credit card company immediately.

While you're out and about, protect your credit cards as if they were cash. Do not leave them unattended in your hotel room or car, on the beach, in a nightclub, or anywhere else.

should you buy trip insurance?

If you answer "Yes" to any of the questions below, it may be wise to purchase trip insurance.

- Are you buying a travel package, charter flight, tour, or cruise? **Yes / No**
- Are you booking a bargain vacation with a tour operator you've never used before? **Yes / No**
- Will you be traveling with a baby or young child? **Yes / No**
- Are you or any of your traveling companions in frail health? **Yes / No**
- Do you or any of your traveling companions have a chronic medical condition that could flare up before or during the trip? **Yes / No**
- Do you plan to participate in a risky sport or activity while on vacation? **Yes / No**
- Are you traveling to a country where you might need to evacuate due to political unrest or terrorism? **Yes / No**

Report a lost or stolen card immediately. Before leaving home, make a list of the credit cards you are taking on your trip, including the account number and expiration dates. Also include the phone number to call if your credit cards are stolen. If you are traveling abroad, you won't be able to call an 800 number so be sure to get another you can call. Keep one copy of your list in your checked luggage and one copy with you. Not all credit cards are accepted everywhere, so consider bringing a different brand of card with you as a backup. Leave unneeded credit cards at home.

"Safe" Money. Traveler's checks provide a safe, secure way to carry money, especially when traveling abroad or when you prefer to spend cash instead of using credit cards. If you bring traveler's checks, make a list of your check numbers and make two copies. Keep one copy with your checked luggage, and leave one copy with someone at home. Also, in case of loss or theft keep your receipt for your traveler's checks separate from the checks. Cash checks as you need them, not all at once, and cross used check numbers off your list.

An even safer, more convenient alternative to traveler's checks is Visa TravelMoney. This is a prepaid travel card that gives you 24-hour access to your travel funds in the local currency at favorable exchange rates. You can access your Visa TravelMoney funds with a Personal Identification Number (PIN) at any Automatic Teller Machine (ATM) where Visa is honored. The value of prepaid funds with Visa TravelMoney is that the funds are stored on the Visa TravelMoney system, not on the card. So if you lose your card, you don't lose your money. Just be sure to memorize your PIN, or, if you do write it down, keep it separate from your Visa TravelMoney card. Another plus is that you can purchase additional cards for traveling companions or to keep in case your primary card is lost or stolen. Visa TravelMoney is available around the world through Travelex. See page 285 for contact information.

Of course, using your own bank ATM card is also an option as long as the ATM service you require is available where you are going. Most modern countries have ATMs that can be accessed by your local bankcard, and the exchange rates are comparable to the going rate of exchange. If you don't know for sure that ATMs are available where you are going, plan to use your ATM card as a backup rather than a primary source of funds. Again, memorize your PIN, or, if you write it down, keep it separate from your card. Using an ATM card allows you to withdraw cash as you need it rather than carrying around large amounts of cash. If you do have a sizeable sum of money with you, don't keep it all in one place.

Safeguarding Valuables. Keep in mind that in many vacation destinations would-be thieves are on the lookout for unsuspecting tourists. Leave expensive jewelry at home. If you carry a pocketbook, sling it over your head and across your body. Men should carry their wallets in a front pants pocket to deter pickpockets. If you do keep a wallet in a back pocket, wrapping rubber bands around it will make it more difficult for someone to slip it out unnoticed. In your wallet, fold larger bills inside smaller bills so as not to "flash" the larger bills when removing cash to make purchases. The safest ways to carry cash include money belts or pouches that are worn underneath clothing or hidden pockets sewn into clothing. It's also a good idea not to carry all cash and credit cards in the same place. If your hotel room has a safe, use it to store your passport, cash, credit cards, and other valuables when you go out. Never leave cash or valuables in your hotel room.

Phoning for Less. One final word about smart money moves: Be aware that making telephone calls from your hotel room can cost a small fortune, especially in countries outside the U.S. Using the card provided by your long-distance carrier can also be quite expensive with a cost per minute that may be up to five times more than you pay for calls dialed direct from your home. Plus, the company often tacks on a surcharge for calls made from a pay phone. Using your cellular telephone could also get expensive depending on where you are going and what type of plan you have. The least expensive way to make calls when you are away from home is to buy a prepaid phone card. If your hotel charges a connection fee to call 800 numbers, use the prepaid card at a pay phone. If you plan to use the card overseas, make sure before you buy that you can use it where you are going and get the access number.

Before You Go

When you're about to head off on vacation or a business trip, there always seems to be so little time, so much to do. Following is a checklist and timeline designed to speed you on your way by helping you organize things to do before you go. Jot down any other things you need to complete before going.

One week or more prior to departure:

- Start a "Don't Forget to Pack" list.
- Decide how you will get to the airport or train station; make any necessary arrangements.
- Arrange for a house sitter/pet sitter or make kennel reservations.
- Arrange to stop newspaper and mail delivery temporarily (unless you have arranged for a house sitter).
- Get traveler's checks if you plan to bring them.
- Make copies of your passport and visa(s), driver's license, credit cards, traveler's check receipt(s), and airline tickets; pack one copy with checked luggage and leave one copy with someone at home.

Up to one week prior to departure:

- Wash clothes.
- Make a list of clothes and accessories to bring.
- Gather books, magazines, and maps you plan to bring with you.
- Give a copy of your itinerary to someone at home; include names, addresses, and telephone numbers of hotels and persons you intend to visit.

24 to 48 hours prior to departure:

- Call the airline to reconfirm your flight and inquire about better seats (keep the phone number with your tickets).
- Pay all bills that will come due while away or make arrangements to have someone else pay them; leave a bank deposit slip if you are expecting a check that needs to be deposited in your absence.
- Recharge cell phone, cordless shaver, and other rechargeable items.
- Pack your suitcases; make a note of any last-minute items you still need to pack in each bag.

Day of (or night before) departure:

- Pack last-minute items.
- Turn off your pager.
- Back up your computer and shut it off.
- Synchronize your personal digital assistant (PDA) or pack your telephone and address book.
- Forward e-mail or put auto-response message on e-mail.
- Change voicemail or answering machine message (unless you will be checking in for messages frequently).
- Wash dishes.
- Water plants.
- Unplug television and other electrical appliances that consume electricity even when off and to safeguard them in the event of severe weather, power surges, or lightning strikes.
- Call the airline or go on-line to confirm flight status just before leaving home.

For Safety's Sake

Take a few moments to write down important medical information that could be used in the event that you require emergency care. Include blood type, drug allergies, heart problems, and other medical problems such as diabetes, and any prescriptions you are taking. Also list your physician's name and telephone number and your pharmacist's number. Write this information on the back of your business card or on a small piece of paper tucked into your wallet with your driver's license or into your passport.

If you are traveling with children, do the same for each one of them; also include their age and weight. Record information for each child on the back of a wallet-size school photograph and keep it with your emergency information. The photograph could also come in handy if your child gets lost.

The more you can simplify your travel preparations, the easier it will be to pack up and go anywhere at any time. If you usually hire a house sitter, pet sitter, or baby-sitter, create a form letter that includes detailed instructions as well as emergency contact numbers. Type the letter on your computer so you can update it when you need it again. Make a note to yourself on the form to attach your itinerary.

Organized Packing

The biggest mistake travelers make is packing too much. More stuff means heavier luggage, and that can be a real problem when you have to lug it on and off shuttles, through crowded terminals, and sometimes even up and down stairs. And if you can't handle it all yourself, you end up spending more for porters or for taxis at your destination rather than public transportation. Another advantage to packing light is that you have more room for whatever you might want to bring home from your travels.

The trick to packing light is to take half as much stuff and twice as much money. You might never need the extra cash, but you'll have it if you do discover that you need something you left at home. Another way to pare down what you bring is *not* to bring anything you think you *might* be able to use; you probably won't. Following are more ideas for helping you maximize suitcase space while lightening your load:

- **Shoes and socks.** Limit the number of shoes you bring to one pair for dress, one comfortable pair for walking, and one pair of sandals if appropriate. On travel days, wear the shoes that would otherwise take up the most room in your suitcase. Use the space inside shoes to stuff socks, underwear, and other small items.
- **Outerwear.** Instead of bringing one bulky coat, bring a cardigan-style sweater and light rain or wind jacket that you can wear together. Tie both around your waist rather than packing them. The sweater will come in handy if the temperature on the plane is cool. Even if you are going somewhere warm, you might need a

CREATE A PACKING LIST

Create and save standard packing lists for your carry-on bag and checked luggage. Sometimes the most obvious things are the ones you forget! A packing list also serves as a reminder for any items you need to obtain prior to your trip. Your packing list for your carry-on might include:

- Reservation confirmations, tickets, itineraries
- Passport or driver's license
- Wallet and purse
- Medical insurance cards
- Cash, credit cards, traveler's checks
- Prepaid phone card or calling card
- Keys (house and car)
- Eyeglasses and contacts plus lens cleaners
- Prescriptions and medications
- Camera and film
- Video camera and tapes
- Magazines and books
- Snacks and drinks
- Maps and directions
- Makeup and toiletries
- Jewelry
- Personal address book
- Change of clothes

Use your packing list as a checklist for your return trip so you don't accidentally leave something important behind. While away, if you think of something you wish you had brought, add it to your packing list for next time and keep the list in your suitcase. Once you get home, make a list of "things I didn't need" so that you won't take them next time.

sweater or jacket for cooler evenings or unseasonably cold days.

- **Clothing.** Bring clothes that are versatile, such as a T-shirt that can double as a nightshirt or beach cover-up, outfits that can be dressed up or down or layered, and separates that can be worn as part of more than one outfit. Weed out everything else. Avoid bringing any clothes you never wear at home; you probably won't wear them on vacation either, unless where you are going is the only place you would wear them. Keep in mind that while natural fabrics are cooler, synthetic fabrics tend to wrinkle less and often travel better.

- **Underwear.** Plan to wash lingerie and small articles of clothing in your hotel sink, especially if you will be away for more than a week. Bring a small amount of fine-fabric detergent with you in a small plastic container.

For Simplicity's Sake

Store all travel items such as a neck pillow, alarm clock, travel-size blow dryer, and jewelry pouch in your favorite overnight bag or suitcase. That way, you have everything you need right where you need it. If you travel often, prepack a toiletries bag with travel-size containers of the things you use every day including toothpaste, shampoo and conditioner, shaving cream, razor, skin care products, and cosmetics. Don't forget to include a toothbrush! Restock used-up items at the end of each trip.

- **Jewelry and accessories.** Leave all valuable jewelry at home, along with anything else you wouldn't want to lose. Limit accessories to one belt, one hat, and maybe two scarves or ties. If a scarf can double as a sash or shawl, that's even better.

- **Makeup and toiletries.** Do bring just the basics. Don't bring full-size bottles of anything (except maybe sunscreen lotion if you are going somewhere sunny). Look for sample-size toiletries at the drug store. Or transfer shampoo, conditioner, or shower gel into small, travel-size containers or even empty film canisters. Label everything. Instead of bringing perfume bottles, moisten cotton balls with perfume and store in a film canister. (Empty film canisters are also handy for carrying earrings and rings and for keeping foreign coins separated by country.)

- **Other.** If you are traveling with someone else, check with each other so that you don't bring duplicate items of things like travel alarm clocks and guidebooks. Instead of bringing an entire guidebook, use a razor blade to remove just the section you need. Find out if your hotel offers amenities such as a hair dryer and iron. If not, ask yourself if you really need them or if you can survive without them. Instead of bringing home souvenirs, bring a journal to keep a record of what you did each day, where you went, who you met, how much you spent, what the weather was like. Take photographs or buy postcards.

A Federal Aviation Administration (FAA) rule implemented in 2001 limits passengers to one piece of carry-on baggage per person plus one additional personal item such as a purse, briefcase, or diaper bag. All other luggage must be checked. The size of the carry-on allowed varies by airline, but most allow a piece with dimensions adding up to no more than 45 inches (length plus width plus height). Check with your air carrier to confirm carry-on size restrictions.

Be prepared to open all carry-on bags for airport security inspection. Avoid overpacking so that they can be opened and closed easily. Pack small items together in a clear pouch or resealable plastic bag. Do not pack wrapped gifts in your carry-on bag as you may have to unwrap them. Pack any objects that might be perceived as weapons, such as knives, cutting instruments of any kind, manicure scissors, knitting needles, ice picks, or straight razors in your checked luggage, not your carry-on bag. Make sure that each piece of checked luggage has a name tag on the outside and your name, address, and telephone number inside. It's also a good idea to add your dates of travel and contact information at your destination.

Do not pack cameras and electronic equipment such as portable CD players and laptop computers in your checked luggage, which could get lost or stolen. In your carry-on, pack a complete change of clothes in case your checked luggage gets lost or arrives later than you do. Also keep with you any other items you will need in the next twenty-four hours, including vitamins and prescriptions, eyeglasses, contact lens supplies, makeup and toiletries. Important papers are also best packed

PLAY FIVE QUESTIONS

If you tend to pack too much when you go away, ask yourself these questions:

1. Where are you going? If you're traveling for business, find out what type of attire will be required. Some destinations such as Europe require dressier clothing even during the day. But if you're going to a low-key resort area, casual clothes may be all you need to bring.

2. When (in what season) will you be there? Research weather conditions at your destination using a weather forecasting service on the Internet or on television. Then choose attire accordingly.

3. What will you do while there? Review travel brochures and have a plan for places to go and things to do before your trip so you know what you will need to bring; for example, hiking boots, sun hat, or snorkeling equipment.

4. Why suffer with excess luggage? Pack what you want to bring, and then pare it down to what you really need. **KISS** — Keep It Simple, Sweetheart — by making a packing list.

5. How can I avoid packing too much? Color coordinate your attire with "mix and match" clothing. Plan to hand wash some items, use hotel laundry services, or go to a local laundry center.

—Donna D. McMillan, McMillan & Company Professional Organizing

in your carry-on bag. Everything else you pack in your carry-on is pretty much a matter of personal preference.

Consider organizing the contents of your suitcase with packing cubes — soft fabric and mesh squares — that let you keep like items such as socks and underwear together in your suitcase. Just put clothing into various-size cubes and put the cubes into your suitcase. You might also be able to keep smaller items together by placing them in large plastic zippered bags. Keeping categories of clothing separate helps keep you organized while you are away, especially if you will be moving around.

Many seasoned travelers swear by the *rolling method* for saving space and reducing wrinkles. If you roll two or three of the same item, such as pants, you may be able to save quite a bit of space. And rolling several items together around a soft core item such as a travel pouch or zippered bag filled with socks may help to minimize wrinkles even better.

Store anything that might leak in a resealable plastic, bag. Pack a tote bag or small backpack that you can use for shopping excursions or on day trips. When packing to come home, pack dirty clothes separately. Put all dirty laundry in one suitcase or use plastic bags to keep dirty clothes separate from clean clothes (if you have any clean clothes left!).

Traveling Abroad

Traveling to another country requires a little more planning and preparation than traveling within your country of residence. And there are some practical health and safety precautions that you should take as well.

• **Passports and visas.** The first thing you need to do is check your passport to make sure that it is valid. Some countries require that your passport be valid at least six months or longer beyond the dates of your trip. If your passport expires before the required validity, or you don't have a passport, you will have to apply for a new one. Allow two to three months before your departure to avoid having to pay expediting fees. Depending on where you are going and how long you are staying, you may also need to apply for a visa from the country you are going to and provide proof of required immunizations. (On page 284, you'll find contact information for visa services.)

When traveling abroad, do not carry your passport with your money or pack it in your checked luggage. Do fill in the emergency

LOOK MA, NO WRINKLES!

Wrinkles can't be avoided completely, but they can be minimized. Pack things tightly so they don't move around. Packing suits, dresses, shirts, and blouses individually in dry-cleaning bags helps. Placing a sheet of tissue paper between each layer of folded clothing is another way to minimize wrinkles. Consider packing a wrinkle-releasing spray product instead of a travel iron. Roll wrinkle-resistant clothes such as pajamas, T-shirts, and sweaters, and stuff them into small spaces, wherever they fit.

— *Diane Hatcher, Timesavers Services Professional Organizing* contact information page in your passport using pencil (so that it can be updated for your next trip). Leave copies of your itinerary, passport data page, and visas with family or friends at home, so that they can contact you in the event of an emergency.

- **Required reading.** Before you go, it's always a good idea to familiarize yourself with the culture, people, history, and geography of your destination. Guidebooks are great, but you can also get lots of free information from your travel agent or local library, or from the Internet. Be sure to pack a foreign language phrase book or dictionary — and use it whenever attempting to converse with someone in a foreign country. If you make the effort, you are more likely to get whatever assistance you need.

- **Laws and customs.** Be sure to obey and respect local laws and customs. Remember that when you are in another country, you are subject to its laws. Be aware that in some countries, it is unlawful to enter or exit with that country's currency. Ask your travel agent about currency restrictions at your destination. It is also illegal in some countries to exceed your credit card limit. On a more pleasant note, in many countries, it is customary to present small gifts in return for a home-cooked meal or other hospitality. These gifts might include a handmade item, postcards from your hometown, souvenir pins, or chocolate.

- **Money and purchases.** You can usually exchange money at the airport or at your hotel, but local banks generally give the most favorable rate. Deal only with authorized agents when you exchange money or you may end up

REPLACING A LOST PASSPORT

If your passport is lost or stolen while you are traveling, it will be much easier to get a replacement if you plan ahead for this possibility. Photocopy the data page at the front of your passport and write down the addresses and telephone numbers of the U.S. embassies and consulates in the countries you plan to visit. (See page 284 for contact information.) Pack this information along with two recent passport-size photographs in a place separate from your passport. Write down your passport number and the date and place it was issued, and give this information to a friend or relative at home as backup.

in jail. Using your credit card or ATM card will also give you the current rate of exchange with no markup or fee. Keep receipts for any items you purchase abroad, as you will need to declare them upon your return to the United States. Be aware that you are not allowed to bring some items back into the United States and that the number of allowable duty-free items is limited.

- **Safety and security.** For up-to-date travel information, obtain the U.S. Department of State's Consular Information Sheet on the country or countries you plan to visit. In addition to other valuable information, these sheets include the location of the U.S. embassy or consulate, unusual immigration practices, health conditions, and general crime and safety or security information. Information about travel warnings in effect, terrorist threats, and other conditions that might pose a risk to American travelers is also available. (Contact information for the U.S. Department of State is listed on page 283.) Schedule direct flights wherever possible, and avoid stops in high-risk areas.

- **Health precautions.** Ask your doctor about any health precautions you should take prior to leaving the United States. Some countries may require proof of immunization against such illnesses as typhoid, polio, and hepatitis. Contaminated food and drink are the major sources of intestinal illness while traveling, especially when traveling to developing countries, where sanitation practices leave much to be desired. Drink only bottled, canned, or boiled beverages. Do not even use the tap water to brush your teeth. Avoid raw vegetables and fruit (unless you peel them yourself), unpasteurized milk and milk products, raw meat, and shellfish. Remember this rule of thumb: If you can't peel it or cook it, don't eat it. This includes ice cubes.

- **Medical insurance.** It's very important to review your health insurance policy to make sure that it will cover medical and hospital expenses while you are abroad. If it does, be sure to bring your insurance card with you and a claim form. If not, buy a short-term health insurance policy. You can and should also buy an insurance policy that will cover the cost of medical evacuation in the event of an accident, serious illness, or death, as this could cost thousands of dollars. Health and emergency medical assistance insurance usually includes other valuable benefits such as emergency consultation by telephone and interpretation services. Ask your travel agent where you can buy this type of insurance. If you have a preexisting medical condition or are over age sixty-two, read the policy carefully and make amendments as necessary to make sure that you are covered.

- **Other medical precautions.** Pack an extra pair of eyeglasses and prescriptions in your carry-on luggage. If you are traveling abroad with a preexisting medical condition, bring a letter from your physician describing your condition and any prescription medications, including the generic name of prescribed

medical insurance

Should you buy it? If you answer "Yes" to any of the questions below, it may be wise to purchase extended medical and/or evacuation insurance.

- Are you traveling to a country with questionable medical facilities? **Yes / No**
- Are you in frail health or taking numerous required medications? **Yes / No**
- Do you have a chronic medical condition that could flare up during your trip? **Yes / No**
- Do you plan to participate in a risky sport or activity while abroad? **Yes / No**
- Are you traveling to a country where you may encounter a hazard to your health due to political unrest or terrorism? **Yes / No**
- Are you currently covered by the Social Security Medicare Program? **Yes / No**

drugs. To avoid problems when passing through customs, keep prescription drugs and vitamins in their original, labeled containers. Pills in any other containers may be seized.

• **Emergencies.** If you encounter serious legal, medical, or financial difficulties or other problems abroad, contact the nearest U.S. embassy or consulate for assistance.

• **Reconfirming flights.** Don't forget to call the airline seventy-two hours prior to traveling to reconfirm your flight. Without this "reservation" call, you could find yourself stranded. When you call, provide the following information: your passport number, your date of birth, and your citizenship. This will speed the process of going through customs, as they will simply need to verify the information in the computer and not actually enter it.

Traveling with Kids

Planning ahead can make the difference between a fun family trip and a family disaster, especially if you're traveling by air. Prepare kids for the trip by showing them on a map where you are and where you are going. When possible, book nonstop flights so that you won't have the added hassle of changing planes. For long trips, consider booking a late evening flight; the kids might just sleep through it. Don't forget to bring your children's birth certificates; you may be asked for them by the airline, especially if you are traveling out of the country without the other parent.

If you're traveling with a child under two, a front pack or sling will make it easier to keep your baby on your lap. Consider buying a seat

for your infant on a long flight (usually available for half price). If you do this, you will need to bring a car seat. You'll probably need one anyway at your destination unless your car rental company has guaranteed to have one available for you. Even then, you may prefer the safety features of your own car seat.

Utilize gate-check service for your stroller so that you'll have it right away when you deplane. This is especially helpful if you have to make your way from one end of a terminal to the other to change planes. If you're planning to rent a stroller at your destination, a backpack carrier may be an option. You can check that at the gate as well.

Packing Tips. When packing for your children, plan on needing two outfits per child per day. You may be able to double up on some items such as sweatshirts or cardigans or dress clothes that may be worn for only short periods of time. All of this can go in checked luggage along with the bulk of the diapers, favorite videos, and whatever else you might want at your destination. Consider packing children's clothing in bundles that make up a complete outfit so you can just hand it to them when needed. Or pack outfits in individual resealable plastic bags labeled with each child's name.

Pack what you will need before, during, and immediately after the flight in carry-on bags. Every air traveler is allowed one piece of carry-on luggage plus a personal item such as a diaper bag or backpack — that goes for kids, too. Preschoolers and older children may enjoy having their own rolling carry-on bags to carry a sweatshirt, two extra changes of clothes, snacks, small games and books, a stuffed animal or two, or a favorite blanket. Just make sure it isn't too heavy for them to manage, or you'll end up carrying it.

Traveling can be especially hard on children. Pack some surprises to prevent them from getting bored or cranky. An inflatable beach ball or a game of cards might help time pass more quickly when waiting at the gate. To help prevent in-flight boredom, bring several small gifts for each kid that you can present at regular intervals or as needed. Older children will appreciate having a portable device for listening to music or books on tape. You can also show them how to plug into the onboard radio. Also, be sure to bring plenty of snacks (purchase individually wrapped packages or wrap them yourself) and beverages, preferably in resealable containers.

Other in-flight essentials include enough diapers for the flight plus two more just in case. You won't have a changing table on the airplane so consider using pull-up-type diapers if you can. Pack a quantity of diaper wipes in a large resealable plastic bag. Use a smaller bag to carry wipes for cleaning faces and hands. Bring plenty of baby food and formula if needed, as these items are hard to find at the airport. A pacifier, chewy fruit snack, or chewing gum may help keep your kid's ears comfortable during takeoff and landing.

Vacation. While on vacation, help children create their own special memories of the trip. One way to do this is to buy postcards of the places you visit. Have children write on the postcard what they want to remember about that place. When you return home, punch a hole in the corner of the cards and put them on a key ring. Or give each child a journal. Each day, write the date at the top of a new page and encourage children to draw or write about what they did that day. They can also paste postcards or brochures into their journals or ask people they meet for their autograph. Don't forget to bring along craft supplies, including scissors, tape, glue, markers, and crayons, for this project. Another great idea is to give kids disposable cameras of their own so they can take photographs from their own unique perspectives and create a special photo album when they get home.

Try not to overschedule your family. Resist the urge to see and do everything. Ask each family member what he or she most wants to do while on vacation. (You may need to give younger children some choices.) Make a list of these "must-see/must-do" activities and schedule them into your itinerary. Leave the rest of your vacation schedule free for making spontaneous plans or pursuing simple pleasures such as looking for seashells on the beach or bike riding.

Plan a vacation that offers something for everyone. If you're traveling with young children or teenagers, or as a single parent, consider travel destinations that cater to all ages and interests such as cruises, Club Med, and family resorts. Do you want an adventure? Consider going on a hiking or biking tour or exploring a foreign city. Wherever you go, find out what amenities are included, so there are no surprises when you get there.

For Safety's Sake

Check with your hotel to see if your room is or can be childproofed. If not, bring along a package of outlet covers. You might want doorknob covers, too. If you are traveling with young children, request a first-floor room rather than one with a balcony. Once you get there, take a good look around for possible hazards. Get down on the floor and look for any small items such as buttons, paper clips, coins, or pills that could end up in your crawling baby's mouth. Remove matches. Also remove plastic bags from trash cans. Bring a roll of masking tape to secure washcloths over sharp table corners and to tape down exposed electrical cords. Move hotel samples of soap, shampoo, and other toiletries out of reach of young children.

Packing a Diaper Bag

Keep the diaper bag packed and ready to go by creating a packing checklist. Creating a checklist makes it easy to delegate this project to a spouse or child.

Changing Needs
❑ Changing pad
❑ Disposable diapers (or cloth diapers, plastic pants, and extra diaper pins)
❑ Baby wipes or damp washcloth with a squirt of soap stored in a resealable plastic bag
❑ Diaper ointment
❑ Baby powder
❑ Waterless antibacterial hand cleaner
❑ At least one extra set of baby clothes
❑ Small plastic garbage bags (with twist ties) for disposing of dirty diapers or bringing home dirty clothes

Feeding Needs
❑ Formula, bottles with protective nipple covers, and bottle bags (or nursing pads if breastfeeding)
❑ Small bottle of water for making formula
❑ Burp cloth
❑ One or two bibs
❑ Baby food and utensils
❑ Bottle of juice with protective nipple cover
❑ Finger foods and beverages for older children

Rest and Play Needs
❑ Lightweight blanket or sweater
❑ Heavier blanket for cold weather
❑ Pacifier or teething ring
❑ One or two toys and/or books

Other Needs
❑ Small first-aid kit
❑ Any current baby medications (plus dispenser if needed)
❑ Hypoallergenic sunscreen

CHAPTER 22

MANAGING YOUR HOUSEHOLD

Most everyone admires an efficient, well-organized household. But for many people, it seems impossible to attain, let alone maintain. That's where systems come into play. With simple systems for meal planning, grocery shopping, housekeeping, and other routine household tasks, anyone can enjoy the benefits of an organized household with a minimal investment of time and energy. Yes, even you!

Meal Planning

Planning meals may be easier than you think. Just follow these four simple steps.

1. Make a list of your favorite meals and ask your partner or children to list their favorite meals. If you get stuck for ideas, skim through a cookbook or two.
2. Choose seven meals from your list and start a grocery list with the ingredients you need. Be sure to include vegetables, side dishes, and desserts.
3. Add your favorite breakfast, lunch, snack, and beverage items to your grocery list.
4. Post your meal plan on the refrigerator, along with any recipes you need or references to where you can find recipes.

If you have a computer with access to the Internet, you can do your meal planning and list making on-line at Myrecipe.com. Browse through the on-line cookbook. Then add the recipes you want to try this week to your personal recipe box. If requested, Myrecipe.com will create a detailed shopping list of ingredients based on the recipes you select. You can then delete items you have on hand and add other items you might need for the week such as beverages and ready-to-eat foods.

When you plan your weekly meals, consider doubling one recipe and freezing half for a night when you will be too busy to cook or just want a break. Be sure to label and date the freezer package and use within one month of freezing for best taste.

If your weekday schedule is hectic or inconsistent, stick with quick and easy meals and save gourmet recipes for your days off. If your budget permits, take advantage of prepackaged items, such as bagged lettuce mixes, cooked chicken, and frozen stir-fry meals. If you have a slow cooker, include at least one meal in your weekly plan that can be made in the slow cooker. You can assemble the ingredients in the cooker the night before and put it in the refrigerator. Then, in the morning, all you have to do is put the crock into the pot. It's great to come home in the evening and have dinner ready!

Save your list of favorite meals for planning the next week's meals. After several weeks of planning, you will have a variety of meals to choose from, so you won't have to spend so much time thinking about what to have for dinner. You may also save money on your groceries because you won't overbuy perishables. Meal planning also helps ensure that you and your family eat more healthy, nutritious foods rather than convenience foods.

Smart Food Shopping

To reduce the number of last-minute trips to the supermarket, post a running grocery list on your refrigerator or inside a cabinet door. As

TIME-SAVER

Develop a grocery list form that includes the items you buy on a regular basis (for example, milk, cheese, bread, eggs, butter, and flour), plus blank lines for other items. Organize your shopping list by categories, such as dairy, produce, and frozen foods. Make ten copies of the form and hang on your refrigerator with a large magnetic clip. Reprint as needed. When you are running low on or use up an item, circle it on your list or fill in one of the blanks.

you use up an item or notice that you are running low, add it to the list. Do this for refrigerator, freezer, and pantry items. Get other household members in the habit of adding items to the list as they use them up. If you buy paper goods and toiletries at the grocery store along with your groceries, add these items to your list, too.

At the supermarket, stock up on items you use often, such as canned tomatoes or tuna fish, when they are on sale. On the other hand, if you notice that your vegetable oil tends to go rancid or the honey crystallizes before you use it up, buy a smaller size next time.

Before each trip to the supermarket, clean out your refrigerator. Toss anything that is past its expiration date, along with anything that is questionable. If you need to replace an item, add it to your grocery list. Take note of items that will spoil within the next few days and plan to use them in your next few meals.

At the store, shop for nonperishable items first and fruits and vegetables, meat, dairy, and frozen food items last so that these perishable items stay cold. If you pack your own groceries at the checkout, pack refrigerated and frozen foods together to keep them cold. In hot climates or warmer seasons, keep a large cooler in your trunk for these items and purchase a bag of ice, especially if you have a long drive home.

Unpack purchases as soon as you get home, sorting foods into groups. Work first with items that can go directly into the freezer. Then sort the rest of your groceries into groups: dairy, meats and poultry to go into the refrigerator or to be rewrapped for freezing, fruits and vegetables that need refrigeration and those that don't, canned and packaged goods, and nonfood items. Sorting will make it easier and faster to put everything away.

TRIPLE RECIPES

In the course of your normal cooking, triple your recipes. If you're preparing lasagna, make three: one for eating tonight and two for the freezer. Tomorrow night, do the same thing with a different recipe. After one week of tripling your regular meals and freezing two, you'll have two weeks of meals with almost no extra effort. It's not much harder to prepare three lasagnas than it is to prepare one.

—*Deborah Taylor-Hough,* Frozen Assets Lite & Easy *(Fox Point, Wisc.: Champion Press, Ltd., 2001)*

If you buy dry, canned, and paper goods in bulk, look around your home for potential storage spaces. You might be able to install some shelving in a coat or linen closet, at the bottom of your basement stairs, or along one wall of your garage. An old kitchen cabinet would also make a great storage place in your basement or on your back porch. Cover it with a tablecloth and use as an end table. Another option is to store the overflow in boxes under your bed or a guest bed.

The Recycling Center

Most communities require recycling as a way to reduce the amount of waste that goes into our landfills. That means keeping recyclables separate from regular trash, which requires a system. How you set up your system depends on local recycling guidelines. If your recyclables get picked up at the curb, you probably don't need to do much sorting other than keeping paper separate from other recyclables.

If you take your recyclables to the recycling center yourself, you probably need to sort them into categories. You could collect all recyclables in one large bag or bin and sort them at the recycling center. Or you can do some or all of your sorting at home.

If you prefer to sort at home, write down the categories of recyclables that are accepted by your local recycling center; these may include glass (separated into green, brown, and clear), plastic, tin, plain paper, newspaper, magazines, catalogs, and cardboard. This is how many recycling containers you will need to sort your recyclables. And depending on the amount of recyclable glass you generate, you may need to sort further by color (green, brown, clear).

For recycling containers, use heavy-duty clear plastic bags or bins that you label accordingly. If you prefer bags, consider hanging the bags on hooks along one wall so that the bottoms of the bags touch the ground and one side is left open for easy collection. If your recyclables are clean, you can reuse these bags over and over. If you prefer bins, line them with bags that you can remove for carrying the contents to the recycling center. Since recyclables are similar to garbage, it's best to set up your recycling system in the garage or wherever you store your trash cans.

Because most recyclable material originates from the kitchen, it makes sense to set up a primary collection device there that you will empty daily or weekly, depending on volume. You can use a second garbage  can labeled "Recyclables Only" to collect all glass, plastic, and tin cans. If you generate a lot of recyclable paper (plain paper, newspaper, magazines, and catalogs), keep a collection device in the place where most of the recyclable material is generated.

Organized Housekeeping

When you save up all your housecleaning for one day, it seems like a lot of work because it *is* a lot of work. The trick is to do a little cleaning every day. The payoff is that you will never

TIME-SAVER

Line recycling bins with plastic bags to make it easy to haul away paper, cans, and bottles.

again feel overwhelmed by housecleaning — and you'll have a house that you'll enjoy coming home to.

- **Start with a thorough cleaning.** This might take all day or all weekend if you're really behind on housework. Or you can commit to cleaning one room each day until all rooms are brought up to par. Either way, make the commitment and stick to it. Put on some music or listen to a book on tape to keep you motivated. Better yet, enlist the help of family members, or work out an exchange with a friend.

- **Pick up clutter from floors, coffee tables, and other horizontal surfaces.** It's easier to do this if you have something to put things into such as a basket or a tote bag. Next, put all the tools and cleaning supplies you'll need in a bucket with a handle that you can carry from room to room. This will eliminate having to "go fetch," which adds unnecessary steps, time, and frustration to your cleaning session. Include a trash bag for emptying wastepaper baskets and for dumping other garbage. You'll also need a second bucket and a mop if you plan to wash floors. Choose cleaning products that are designed to handle more than one job, so you won't have so many to carry around. For example, use the same disinfectant product for cleaning toilets and bathroom floors. An old apron with pockets is also a great way to carry some cleaning supplies and is handy for picking up small items before they get sucked up in the vacuum cleaner.

• **Develop a routine.** Tackle the toughest rooms first, generally the bathroom and kitchen. Work in one room at a time, and work from top to bottom so that floors are the last thing you clean. Let cleaning products do their job while you do yours. Spray your shower and

cleaning supplies

To clean well, you must be prepared. Keep these basic supplies on hand at all times.

- Powdered abrasive cleaner
- Tile cleaner
- Glass cleaner
- Multipurpose disinfectant cleaner
- Wood floor and cabinet cleaner
- Furniture polish and rags
- Feather or lambswool duster
- Large scrubbing brush for floors
- Large sponge for shower, tub
- Smaller sponge for countertops
- Toilet brush
- Paper towels
- Trash bags
- Wet mop
- Broom
- Vacuum cleaner
- Mini-vacuum cleaner

tub with a "scrub-free" cleaner, and pour a little cleaner in the toilet to let sit while you wipe countertops and clean the mirror. Or pretreat a rug stain while you dust the family room.

• **Do a little at a time, more often.** If you spend five minutes cleaning the bathroom three times a week, it takes only fifteen minutes total. But if you wait to do it once a week, it can take up to twice as long to cut through the build-up of clutter and dirt. Try cleaning the toilet, sink, and mirror while your children are taking a bath, and clean the shower stall while you're in it. Scrub the walls and floor, then scrub yourself.

• **If you're in cleaning mode, don't stop until you have finished what you set out to do.** If the telephone rings, don't answer it. You might not realize it, but when you really get into cleaning, you gain some momentum that works in your favor. Also save rearranging things and organizing for another time.

• **Enlist the help of family members, even if it means lowering your standards.** Two people can get the job done in half the time. Three people can accomplish even more in less time. The added bonus of getting family members involved in the cleanup effort is that they might be more inclined to keep things cleaner. See page 189 for ways to divide household chores.

Daily Speed Cleaning

There are lots of things you can do daily to make cleanup easier and reduce the total amount of time it takes to maintain a clean and uncluttered home.

• **In the kitchen.** When cooking or baking, fill a dishpan with hot, sudsy water and wash bowls and utensils as soon as used. Fill pots with water as soon as they are emptied and let them soak. If washing dishes by hand, do so immediately after each meal. Between meals, use a dishwashing wand to wash individual items. Wipe up spills and splatters on the surface of your stove at once before they dry. Wash burner trays with a sponge or cloth. Wipe up any spills in the refrigerator, in your oven, or on the floor as they occur. Get in the habit of sweeping the kitchen floor each night. Clean rings in jewelry cleaner while you wash dishes. Clean out your refrigerator while waiting for water to boil or empty the dishwasher while waiting for your coffee to brew.

• **In the bathroom.** Keep a roll of paper towels under the sink. Each time you use the sink, wet a paper towel and use it to wipe the sink and counter, or use a damp washcloth

TIME-SAVER

When making a bed, it's faster to spread the top sheet and blankets and then tuck in corners rather than walking around the bed three or four times to tuck in one layer at a time.

that is ready for the wash anyway. You can also buy antibacterial wipes to clean and disinfect countertops, the sink, and the toilet seat. After each shower, use a store-bought spray that promises to keep your shower clean. (It's best to start with a clean shower for this product to work effectively.) Hang towels after each use to keep them fresh longer between laundering.

• **In bedrooms.** Each morning, take a few minutes to make your bed, pick up and discard or recycle read newspapers and magazines, and return glassware, dishes, and foodstuffs to the kitchen. Before going to bed, hang up or put away clothes you will wear again and put everything else in the hamper or in a bag that you will take to the dry cleaner. When it's time to change sheets, take them off, wash them, and put them right back on the bed. It eliminates having to fold them, put them away, and get them out again later. For variety, switch to a different set when the seasons change.

• **Around the house.** Set aside some time each day for extra cleaning in one particular room. Then move on to another room the next day. Repeat until all of the rooms have been cleaned. Extra cleaning might include vacuuming, mopping, dusting, changing linens, cleaning the toilet bowl, or doing laundry. If you spend ten to thirty minutes a day on extra cleaning, you'll rarely have to spend any more time than that on housecleaning. And your house will always look presentable.

Doing Laundry

Laundry is a chore that seems endless, especially if you have a family. As soon as you finish folding all the clean clothes, it's time to wash another load of dirty clothes. But you can organize the whole process to save time and effort while ensuring that everyone has clean clothes to wear. For starters, don't wait until you run out of socks or underwear to do laundry. Do it every Monday night or Saturday morning or whenever — and let everyone know the schedule.

If you have to do laundry every day to keep up with demand, let everyone know that if they want something washed, it should be in the laundry room by a certain time and can be picked up after such-and-such a time.

- **Sorting dirty laundry.** Set up a color-coded system for sorting dirty laundry. Use three different-colored baskets: white for white clothes, pink for light colors, and dark blue for dark colors. Or invest in a triple clothes sorter with tubular steel frame and canvas bags that you can label "White," "Light," and "Dark." Make it the responsibility of each family member to bring dirty laundry to the laundry room and put it into the appropriate basket or bag. Consider marking each basket with the washing machine settings for that particular type of load.

- **Washing and drying.** Before putting dirty clothes into the washer, check pockets to make sure they are empty and zip zippers. Start a load of laundry in the morning and have the kids put it in the dryer when they get home from school. Or start the wash at night before going to bed and toss it in the dryer first thing in the morning. Never leave a dryer running when you leave the house, because lint buildup or a faulty dryer can be a fire hazard. Be sure to clean the dryer's lint filter after every load. To cut down on the number of towels you may be washing, assign a set of towels to each household member and have them use it for one week, hanging it up after they're done in the bath.

- **Ironing.** Remove clothes from the dryer as soon as possible to avoid wrinkles. Do the ironing right away, or hang up unironed clothes in your closet. Then, when you need to iron something, iron as many items as you have time to iron. An alternative to ironing that works well is to spray clothes with a wrinkle-releasing product. It's a little on the expensive side but works quite well and is worth the price if you don't like to iron.

- **Folding and sorting clean laundry.**
Color-code your children's clothing. Dot clothing tags and the toes of socks by using a different-colored laundry marker for each child. Post a key to the coding system on your dryer so that whoever is doing the folding knows which clothes belong to whom. Folding is easiest if you have a flat surface at about waist height. Kids might find it easier (and more enjoyable) to carry laundry out to the family room and do their folding on the sofa in front of their favorite after-school television programs.

- **Distributing clean laundry.** Have baskets handy to carry clean and sorted laundry back to where it belongs. Consider assigning a laundry basket to each household member. Write their names on a piece of masking tape and affix to the baskets. Make it the responsibility of each household member to bring their clothes to their rooms and return the basket (empty or full of more dirty laundry to be done).

- **Doing laundry at a self-service laundry.** Make it easy on yourself to get the job done. Sort dirty laundry before leaving your home. If you have a lot of dirty laundry, consider putting it in large fabric bags that you can sling over your shoulder rather than in separate baskets that would require multiple trips from your home to the car and from the car to the laundry center. But do bring a basket or two along for collecting and carrying folded and sorted laundry. Premeasure powdered detergent for each load into resealable plastic bags. Leave economy-size bottles of liquid detergent, bleach, and fabric softener at home. Transfer the amount you need into small,

For Simplicity's Sake

If you really dislike matching socks, train everyone in the household to pin socks together. Or put all the clean socks in a basket and have children sort them while you sort everything else. Not only does it teach the value of teamwork, it's also a way to spend some time together getting things done. For younger children, make a game out of sock matching. The winner is the one who has the most pairs of socks when there are no more socks left in the basket. To avoid losing baby socks, pin them to a larger article of clothing and then wash and dry.

unbreakable bottles, properly labeled with their contents. As for how best to carry quarters, up to twenty fit in an empty film canister. Or you can ask for a roll of quarters at a bank. Most laundry centers have change machines, but if you bring your own you won't be frustrated by machines that are out of order or that don't accept worn or wrinkled bills.

For tips on how to set up your laundry room, see chapter 12, "Storage and Utility Areas."

Entertaining

The key to organizing a successful party is to plan ahead. That way, you can focus your attention on your guests, which will make the party more enjoyable for them and you. Follow these five steps for a seemingly effortless party.

1. Plan your menu in advance. Keep it simple. Choose dishes that you have prepared successfully in the past. The best choices are dishes that can be cooked ahead of time and either frozen or refrigerated, or dishes that can be put in the oven as guests arrive. If more than one dish requires cooking, be sure that they can be cooked at the same oven temperature. Also be sure that you will have enough room in your refrigerator for foods that need to be kept cold before the party. Plan to serve appetizers and desserts that require little or no last-minute preparation. Make a list of all the foods and beverages you plan to serve, along with notations of where to find the recipes.

2. Develop a timetable for preparation. Start with the day and time of your party and work backward to make a timetable. Your timetable should begin with a trip to the supermarket at least one day in advance, if not several days or one week beforehand, to make sure that everything you need is available. If there are any items you need to buy on the day of your party, such as fresh seafood, include that trip on your timetable. Estimate how much time you'll need to prepare each dish, and then add 20 percent to allow for distractions and unforeseen incidents. Start with the dish that requires the most preparation and finish with the one that requires the least preparation. The beauty of making a timetable is that you will know beforehand if your menu plan is overly ambitious, and you can adjust accordingly with no waste of time, effort, or money.

3. Make a shopping list. With recipes in hand, go through your pantry to make sure that you have everything you need, including the condiments you plan to serve with various foods. Don't assume that because you have a particular item, you're all set. Check to see that you have the quantity you need. Add beverages, paper goods, and nonfood items, such as toothpicks, to your list. Don't forget cream and sugar for coffee and garnishes for drinks and food.

4. Do as much as possible in advance. Plan which china, stemware, silver, and serving pieces you will use and make sure that everything is clean. Save the last hours before the party for simple preparations, such as setting the table or buffet and lighting candles. Plan to have everything ready at least one hour before your guests are scheduled to arrive. That way you'll have plenty of time to get yourself ready without having to race around.

5. Accept all offers of help. If your partner or children ask if they can help, put them to work on specific tasks, such as putting ice in buckets or taking coats. If you will be serving mixed drinks, you will need someone to do that so you are free to greet and mingle with guests. If guests ask if they can help, do not hesitate to delegate simple tasks that won't take more than a few minutes, such as putting music in the CD player, carrying something from the kitchen to the dining room, or refilling a bowl with chips or nuts.

CHAPTER 23

ORGANIZING FOR SAFETY

When it comes to your family's safety, prevention is the best protection. Keeping clutter off floors and stairs helps prevent falls, and safely storing hazardous materials can prevent fire or accidental ingestion. There are many simple things you can do to help prepare your family in the event of an emergency. When every second counts, being organized could prevent injuries and save lives.

Home Safe Home

While your home is generally a safe haven, some conditions and practices can be potentially hazardous, especially for younger family members. Play it safe. Take steps to protect your family by checking every room for safety hazards and making sure that everyone is aware of unsafe practices. Following are some home safety guidelines.

• **Kitchen.** Keep knives and sharp objects out of reach of children. Don't store things over the stove; you could be burned in the process of reaching for them while cooking. Never leave anything cooking unattended, whether it's on top of the stove, in the oven or toaster, or in the microwave. Keep cooking areas clear of combustibles, such as dishtowels or paper, and wear clothes with short, rolled-up, or tight-fitting sleeves when you cook. Turn pot handles inward on the stove, where you can't bump them and children can't grab them. Enforce a kid-free zone three feet around your kitchen stove. If grease catches fire in a pan, slide a lid over the pan to smother the flames and turn off the heat. Leave the lid on until the pan is cool. Make sure your hands are dry before using an electrical appliance to keep from getting a shock.

• **Bathroom.** Store medicines, vitamins, cosmetics, and any potentially hazardous materials out of reach of children or in cabinets with child-safety latches. Use caution when disposing of these products. Flush pills and medicines down the toilet; put all other items into a plastic bag secured with a twist tie and dispose of in a lidded trash can that children and pets cannot get into. Use nonslip mats in bathtubs and showers. Consider having grab bars installed in bathrooms for elderly family members. Make sure that your hands are dry and you are not standing on a wet floor before using an electrical appliance. Unplug hair dryers when not in use so they can't get turned on accidentally. Never leave a baby or young child alone in the bathtub. To avoid scalding, adjust the temperature of your hot water heater down to 120°F.

- **Family and living rooms.** Allow air space around the television and stereo to prevent overheating. Use a sturdy, metal fireplace screen. Have the chimney checked and cleaned annually or more frequently if you use your fireplace or woodstove often. Do not store newspapers near the fireplace or woodstove where they could be ignited by a stray spark.

- **Bedrooms and kids' rooms.** Buy fire escape ladders for bedrooms on upper floors, if needed. Make it impossible for younger children to get at toys with small parts. Store these items way up high on shelves that only you can reach. Explain the danger of choking to older children so that they do not leave games or projects with small parts unattended.

- **Baby's room.** Position the crib well away from potential hazards: heaters, lamps, electrical cords, wall decorations, windows, and furniture that could be used to climb out. Replace drapes and blinds that have cords that could accidentally strangle a baby. Buy window guards or locks that allow windows to be opened just a crack. Use the restraining strap on the changing table. Keep all toiletries out of baby's reach at all times. Keep the drop side of the crib up and locked. Once your baby can pull up to a standing position, remove the crib bumpers and keep the mattress in its lowest position. Before your baby is old enough to climb out of the crib unassisted, secure the room with a good-quality door gate. Cover electrical outlets with child-safety caps. Enclose heaters to prevent burns.

- **Office.** Do not plug multioutlet power strips into other multioutlet power strips. Distribute weight in filing cabinets; opening a full top drawer with empty or partly filled bottom drawers can cause the cabinet to tip over. For this same reason, close one drawer before pulling out another. Close all file cabinet drawers when not in use so you won't trip over them.

- **Basement, garage, and storage rooms.** Store gasoline and other flammables in tight metal containers away from heat sources. Do not store anything near your furnace or heater. Store lighter-weight items on upper shelves and heavier items closer to ground level to avoid potential breakage or injury when retrieving them. Have heating equipment checked and cleaned yearly.

- **Workshop.** Keep flammable objects away from spark-producing tools. If you have young children, keep the door to your workshop locked to prevent access to hazardous materials and sharp tools. Equip your workshop with safety equipment such as safety glasses, dust mask, and fire extinguisher.

FIRE SAFETY AND PREVENTION TIPS

For your own protection and for that of your family, read and follow these tips.

- Install at least one smoke detector on every level of your home, and outside each sleeping area.

- Unless you heat and cook solely with electric, install one carbon-monoxide detector on each floor of your home to provide early warning of faulty ventilation.

- Do not warm up vehicles in an attached garage without opening the garage door or use gas or diesel-powered machines indoors without proper ventilation.

- Purchase only smoke and carbon-monoxide detectors approved by Underwriters Laboratories or Factory Mutual.

- Test smoke and carbon-monoxide detectors every month.

- Replace smoke detector batteries once a year with fresh batteries or immediately if a detector "chirps." Never "borrow" a smoke detector battery from another appliance.

- Replace smoke detectors every seven to ten years and in any new residence.

- Equip each floor of your home with fire extinguishers, especially the kitchen and near fireplaces and woodstoves. Choose models rated "2-A:10-B:C" for use on any type of fire. Instruct household members in their proper use.

- Use only child-resistant lighters and store all matches and lighters up high, where small children can't see or reach them, preferably in a locked cabinet. Teach your children that matches and lighters are tools, not toys, and should be used only by adults. Instruct them to bring any matches or lighters they find to an adult.

- Never leave burning candles unattended.

- Never smoke in bed or when you are sleepy. Cigarettes are a leading cause of fire-related deaths in the United States. Use heavy, nontipping ashtrays. Discard butts and ashes in metal, sealed containers or in the toilet.

- If an electrical appliance smokes or has an unusual smell, unplug it immediately and have it serviced before using it again. If an appliance gets wet, get it serviced immediately.

- Do not use electrical appliances with cords that are cracked or frayed. Don't overload extension cords or run them under rugs. Turn off your television, stereo, and other electrical appliances when not in use.

- If a fuse blows, find the cause. Replace the fuse with one of the correct size.

- Keep portable heaters at least three feet from anything that can burn. Keep children and pets away from heaters, and never leave heaters on when you leave home or go to bed. Do not dry wet mittens or other clothing on space heaters.

Keeping Kids Safe

Many injuries that occur in the home are the result of falls. To protect young children (and older persons who may get up in the middle of the night and take a wrong turn), install safety gates at the top and bottom of stairs. Remove tripping hazards, such as papers, books, and shoes, from floors and stairs. Remove throw rugs that may slip, secure them with double-sided tape, or put rug pads underneath. Make sure that your home is well lit and that staircases have handrails.

Err on the side of overcautiousness when storing household chemicals. Store open containers of bleach, laundry detergent, and cleaning supplies on high shelves out of the reach of children to prevent accidental ingestion. Keep the phone number for the Poison Control Center (800-222-1222) handy and call it if you suspect that your child has been poisoned. Keep ipecac syrup and activated granular charcoal on hand to use if directed to do so by the

For Simplicity's Sake

For current information about known product hazards and recalls, visit the Web site of the United States Consumer Product Safety Commission at www.cpsc.gov. Check out the "New This Week" section on the home and the "Popular/New/Calendar" section. You can also subscribe to receive all recall notices by e-mail on the same day they are issued.

poison control specialists or your physician. If your child is not breathing, call 911 immediately instead of the Poison Control Center.

Small children have a natural tendency to put things into their mouths, which may cause them to start choking or stop breathing. Do not leave plastic bags, deflated balloons, cords, or small objects, such as buttons, coins, and beads, unattended. Also do not leave out candies or nuts. Supervise infants and children when they are eating so that you can respond immediately to choking.

Emergency Response Plans

All family members should know what to do in the event of a fire, earthquake, flood, or other disaster. It's important to develop a home emergency response plan for your family. Have a family meeting to discuss your plan and then practice it on a regular basis.

Fire. Does every family member know at least two ways out of your home in the event of a fire? Prepare for a fire emergency by developing an escape plan. Be sure that everyone knows at least two exits — doors and windows — from their bedrooms and from your home in general. If you live in an apartment building, plan to use fire exits, not elevators. Decide on a place outside, perhaps at the end of the driveway or at a neighbor's house where you can call 911, where everyone will meet. Practice your escape plan at least twice a year.

It's important to note that most deaths from home fires occur between the hours of 11 P.M. and 6 A.M. Have at least one fire drill between these hours. Practice yelling "Fire!" to alert family members in the event of a fire. You may want to keep a whistle in each bedroom. Be sure that all family members can operate the locks, windows, and doors. And get in the habit of sleeping with doors closed; this will keep searing heat and smoke out of bedrooms and allow additional time to escape. Teach children the five most important rules to remember in the event of a fire emergency (see box at right).

Power Outage. Your emergency response plan should also include what to do in case of a power outage. Check the fuse box, then call the electric utility company to report the outage. Keep flashlights in every bedroom and near every entrance. That way, if you come home to a power outage, you won't have to go bumping around in the dark to find a flashlight. Keep candles, matches, a flashlight, and extra batteries together in one place. Handy items to have include one or more oil lamps (filled and ready to light), fondue pot and fuel for heating up canned foods, nonelectric can opener, gas grill, battery-powered radio or television, kerosene space heater, and several large containers of water.

what to do in case of fire

1. Feel all doors before opening them. If a door is hot, don't open it. Find another way out.

2. Crawl under smoke. Because smoke rises, the air will be cleaner closer to the floor. Cover your mouth and nose with your pajama top to keep from getting smoke in your lungs.

3. Just get out. Don't waste time getting dressed. Don't search for your pets or anything else. We can buy new things, but we can't replace you!

4. Stop, drop, and roll if your clothes catch fire. Cover your face with your hands and roll over and over.

5. If you can't get out, don't hide. Stand by an open window, yell "Help," and wave a lit flashlight so that the firemen can see you. (Keep a flashlight in each bedroom.)

Evacuation. Some situations, such as an extended power outage, flood, or hurricane, may necessitate evacuation. Make a list of things you would need to take with you if you had to evacuate your home. Think first of those things family members need every day, such as medications, eyeglasses, or diapers. Plan to take a one- to three-day supply with you. You'll need money wherever you go, so be sure to put your checkbook on your list, along with some emergency cash or traveler's checks. Stash the cash and your list with your power outage emergency supplies.

Just in Case

It's always better to be prepared for the worst, just in case. A little organizing now could save you and your family a lot of unnecessary stress, legwork, and expense later.

Keep important legal documents, such as titles and deeds, in a fireproof box or bank safe deposit box. You might also consider making copies of your driver's license, passport, and

---

For Safety's Sake

Evacuating your home. If you have to evacuate your home, post a note telling the date and time, where you are going, and with whom. Bring the following items with you:

- Money
- Food
- Water
- Plates, glasses, and flatware
- Battery-powered radio or television
- Flashlight
- First aid kit
- Medications and eyeglasses
- List of valuables
- Important documents
- Change of clothes and sturdy shoes
- Sleeping bag or blankets
- Keys
- Pet supplies

Source: *Natural Disasters* (Itasca, IL: National Safety Council, 2001). Permission to reprint granted by the National Safety Council, a membership organization dedicated to protecting life and promoting health.

Social Security card and storing these identification papers along with your legal documents. If you really want to play it safe, make copies of all legal documents and send them for safekeeping to a friend or relative who lives outside your geographic area. It's also a good idea to make a home inventory list and store that in your fireproof box or safe deposit box, along with appraisal documents and photographs or videotape of and receipts for big-ticket items.

The American Red Cross recommends that you keep a well-stocked first aid kit in your home and car and bring one with you when you go hiking, biking, camping, or boating. You can buy many types of ready-made first aid kits or make your own kit by filling a small duffel bag, tackle box, or plastic storage bin with the necessary supplies (see the checklist on page 225) and labeling it. In addition to the supplies recommended by the American Red Cross, it's also a good idea to include a working flashlight, first aid manual, emergency telephone numbers, and a list of allergies and medications for each family member. If you use anything from your kit, be sure to restock it. And be sure to keep your first aid kit out of reach of young children.

Although you probably don't like to think about it, you never know when you may be faced with a life-or-death situation. Would you know what to do if a family member started choking or stopped breathing? Consider getting certified in standard first aid and cardiopulmonary resuscitation. Make sure that your babysitter is certified as well. The American

Red Cross regularly offers programs teaching first aid and cardiopulmonary resuscitation to children and adults who want to learn valuable lifesaving skills.

Pet Safety and First Aid

Pets rely on us for protection. Remember that before you buy, use, or store household cleaners, pesticides, or other potentially hazardous substances. Read the labels. Even common household foods, plants, and other items can cause stomach upset and vomiting if a cat or dog eats them. Other substances, such as certain plants and antifreeze, can be deadly. If your pet is vomiting repeatedly, is having seizures, is losing consciousness, is unconscious, or is having difficulty breathing, contact your veterinarian immediately.

Never give human medicine to a dog or cat unless directed to do so by a veterinarian. Also do not give dog medicine to a cat; it could be fatal. Be careful when taking your medications that you don't accidentally drop a pill on the floor. And don't leave medications out on a counter or table, where your curious pet could find them. Store all medications, including ointments, out of reach of pets. Dispose of expired medicines by flushing them down the toilet or wrapping them in a plastic bag and carrying to an outside waste receptacle with a tightly fitting lid.

Pets get sick just like people. And sometimes, despite your best efforts, pets get injured. The American Red Cross recommends that you pay attention to what is normal for your pet so you can detect signs of something

For Safety's Sake

Suggested first-aid kit supplies. A well-stocked first aid kit might help to save your life or the life of someone you love. Include:

- Activated charcoal (use only if instructed by Poison Control Center)
- Adhesive bandage strips (assorted sizes)
- Adhesive tape
- Antiseptic ointment
- Blanket
- Cold pack
- Disposable gloves
- Gauze pads and roller gauze (assorted sizes)
- Hand cleaner
- Ipecac syrup (use only if instructed by Poison Control Center)
- Plastic bags
- Scissors and tweezers
- Small flashlight and extra batteries
- Triangular bandage

Courtesy of the American Red Cross. All Rights Reserved in all Countries.

wrong. If your pet is ill or has been injured, approach slowly and cautiously. Speak gently and quietly to calm your pet. Bear in mind that any sick or injured animal, even your own, can become aggressive when frightened or in pain. If your pet growls as you attempt to move him, protect your hands and arms with thick sleeves and gloves. You may be able to subdue a small animal by covering and wrapping him tightly in a towel or small blanket.

For Safety's Sake

Pet Hazards. Following is a list of substances that are hazardous to the health of cats and dogs.

- Onions and onion powder
- Chocolate (all forms)
- Alcoholic beverages
- Yeast dough
- Coffee (grounds and beans) and caffeinated tea
- Salt
- Macadamia nuts
- Hops (used in home beer brewing)
- Tomato and potato leaves and stems (green parts)
- Rhubarb leaves
- Moldy foods
- Many plants, including azalea, oleander, cyclamen, daffodils, bird of paradise, castor bean, rhododendrons, sago palm, Easter lily (cats only), and Japanese Yew
- Flea control products and other insecticides
- Mouse and rat poisons
- Household chemicals, including mothballs, potpourri oils, fabric softener sheets, dishwashing detergent, and batteries
- Antifreeze and windshield washer fluid
- Medications

Source: American Society for the Prevention of Cruelty to Animals (ASPCA) (www.aspca.org)

Keep the following telephone numbers with other emergency numbers:

- Your veterinarian
- Nearest after-hours veterinary clinic
- ASPCA Animal Poison Control Center (1-888-426-4435)

If you have an after-hours emergency, call the clinic first to let them know you are coming. It's also a good idea to keep the address and directions, and maybe even a map, handy in case an emergency occurs in the care of a pet sitter or another family member. The Animal Poison Control Center provides a fee-based service, so you will need to have your credit card number ready.

Don't Panic. According to the ASPCA Animal Poison Control Center, if you suspect that your pet has been exposed to a poison, it is important not to panic. Although rapid response is important, panicking generally interferes with the process of helping your animal. Take thirty to sixty seconds to safely collect and have at hand the material involved. This may be of great benefit to the center professionals so that they can determine exactly what poison or poisons are involved. In the event that you need to take your animal to your local veterinarian, be sure to take with you the container for the product your pet ingested. Also bring any material your pet may have vomited or chewed, collected in a plastic bag.

PART VI

Organizing Transitions

Staying organized through change is one of life's most difficult challenges. But there are some simple steps you can take to make transitions easier, whether you are getting ready for the next season, moving into a new home, adopting a pet, preparing to welcome a child into your life or send one to college, or arranging for the transfer of assets to your heirs.

Your normal routines and schedules are bound to be upset by change. Organizing can help get you back on track. Prepare as much as possible in advance. And try to retain the organizing systems that have worked for you in the past. But recognize that a new situation may require that you modify some of your former habits and methods. Remember that there is never one right way to get and stay organized. This is especially true when you are preparing for and going through life transitions. Look for the simplest solutions.

CHAPTER 24

ORGANIZING FOR THE SEASONS

How can you be better prepared to greet the changing seasons? When is the best time to plant bulbs or reseed the lawn? How often should you clean gutters or drain the hot water heater? In this chapter, you'll learn what tasks and activities should be performed throughout the year to maintain your personal property, keep everything in good working order, and enjoy a clutter-free home.

Make Way for Spring

Once snow showers change to rain showers, it's time to put away snow removal equipment and supplies. If you have a powered snow thrower, follow the manufacturer's instructions for winterizing. Perform spring maintenance on your lawnmower or tractor as recommended by the manufacturer. Check fluid levels and inspect drive belts and blades. Get gasoline for your mower, propane for your gas grill, or lighter fuel and charcoal briquettes for your charcoal grill.

Around the time you stop heating your home, remove and store any removable storm windows and doors. If this is the first time you have removed them, be sure to indicate which windows go where. Write with a wide-tip permanent marker directly on the edges of the storm windows or on pieces of masking tape affixed to the edges. Label each window with its appropriate location, such as "Kitchen — Above Sink" or "Living Room — West Wall." Also, indicate the top of each storm window. Wash windows inside and out before putting up window screens.

Get out your garden hoses and check for leaks. Replace worn or frayed clothesline. If line is in good condition, clean with detergent, water, and an old washcloth or rag.

Springtime Home Maintenance

Doing simple home maintenance in spring can help to prevent small problems from becoming big problems. Take some time to walk through and around your house. Make notes of any repairs or problems that require your attention.

- Open windows or vents in the basement and attic to ventilate.
- Check for leaks or signs of water damage, especially in the basement, attic, garage and around your dishwasher and washing machine areas.
- Check washing machine hoses for cracks or bulges; replace if needed.
- Make a note of any stains or bulges on ceilings and walls that you want to have an inspector look at.
- Inspect caulking around tubs, showers, and sinks; recaulk if necessary.
- Check the roof for any needed repairs; secure loose shingles.
- Check to be sure that your television antenna is secure.
- Check for termite and other insect damage.
- Check siding for wood decay or popped nails; secure loose nails or replace.
- Check your foundation, masonry, or stucco for cracks; reseal as needed.
- Decide if and when you need to do any painting inside or out.
- Plan to reseal wood or slate floors or sand and varnish wood floors as necessary. Strip wax from linoleum floors and rewax.
- Have your central air conditioning system inspected.

TIME-SAVER

To freshen and remove dust from curtains, put them in the dryer on the "fluff" cycle for twenty minutes with a fabric softener sheet.

Spring Cleaning

When you think of spring, what do you think of? Showers? Flowers? How about cleaning? The season of rebirth is the perfect time to clean and freshen up your home. Take advantage of the extra hours of daylight to tackle some of the big stuff. But don't expect to get everything done in one day. Look at what needs to be done and work it into your regular schedule. Make it a family affair: Get the kids to help, and enjoy the satisfaction that comes from working together as a team. When the work is done, plan to celebrate with popcorn and a movie or a trip to the park.

Get a start on your spring cleaning by washing windows inside and out so you can let the sunshine in. It's generally recommended to do this on a cool, cloudy day to prevent the glass cleaner from streaking. It's hard to see the streaks if it's sunny, and the cleaner sometimes dries too fast to wipe away when the windows are warm.

It's easier to keep track of your progress — and see the results of your labor — when you work in one room at a time. High-traffic areas, such as the kitchen and bathrooms, are a good place to start.

reminders for all seasons

Following are some of the routine and preventive maintenance tasks that should be performed every few months. The easiest way to remember these things is to get in the habit of doing them on the first day of every new season. Routine safety checks should be done twice a year. Do these when you turn the clocks ahead or back, or on April Fool's Day and Halloween.

When seasons change
- Clean and clear all household drains.
- Drain the hot water heater.
- Wash quilts and bedspreads, shower curtains, and throw rugs.
- Turn your mattresses.
- Add fresh mothballs or fresh cedar products in your storage area.

Twice yearly
- Replace the batteries in your smoke and carbon monoxide detectors.
- Clean smoke detectors. Remove and wipe cover with a damp cloth; vacuum interior.
- Inspect fire extinguisher; recharge if pressure is below operating range.
- Hold a family fire drill.
- Check refrigerator and freezer temperatures with an appliance thermometer. Refrigerated foods should be kept at 40°F, frozen foods at 0°F.
- Clean or change furnace or air conditioning filters.
- Clean ceiling fans and light fixtures; wipe bulbs and replace nonworking bulbs.
- Roll up large area rugs and vacuum underneath.

- Clean scuff marks, handprints, and other marks off walls and doors.
- Clean baseboards and polish woodwork.
- Wipe smudges and spills off cabinet doors.
- Vacuum your refrigerator coils to keep your refrigerator running at peak performance.
- Clean the top of the refrigerator and cabinets.

Nothing spruces up a home like the look and smell of clean carpets. In addition, some people like to redecorate for spring and summer by changing curtains and furniture slipcovers.

- Rent or hire a carpet cleaner, after the muddy season has passed.
- Clean curtains and rehang or put them away until fall.
- Replace flannel and dark-colored sheets with lighter-colored cotton sheets.
- Replace heavy bedspreads with lighter ones.
- Launder all winter quilts, bedspreads, and blankets and store. See page 76 for tips on off-season storage of linens.
- Clean and waterproof leather boots, outerwear, and accessories and store.

Unclutter your house, room by room (see chapters in Part II, "Organizing Room by Room"). Pack up unwanted items for a spring garage sale. Tag and price these items as you box them. See page 18 for tips on organizing a successful garage sale.

Super-clean the interior of your car. Vacuum and shampoo carpets, rugs, and seats. Wash windows. Clean and shine the dash. Wash doors, ceiling, and molding.

Early-Spring Yard Work

If you live in a cold, snowy region, you probably can't wait to get your hands dirty out in your yard once spring arrives. On the first nice day, get to it! Start by picking up branches and other debris. As you're walking around, make a note of any repairs you might need to make to outbuildings and fences.

You might be able to promote early greening of your lawn. After the snow melts, rake debris from your lawn. If your lawn is still soggy, move quickly to avoid compacting the soil. When the soil is dry and firm enough, adjust your mower blade height to its lowest setting and mow, then rake and remove clippings.

Although fall is the best time to reseed your lawn, you can do it in spring, too. Rake the area with a heavy-duty garden rake to dig up the soil for planting, then seed and water. Fertilize your lawn after one or two spring cuttings. Then fertilize every eight to ten weeks thereafter (for example, May 15, July 30, and October 15). Apply fertilizer to a dry lawn and water. If you fertilized your lawn late in the fall, it is not necessary to fertilize in the spring.

Are you planning to plant late spring or early summer bulbs? Residents of southern

For Simplicity's Sake

Once your bulbs start coming up, set wooden stakes into the bare spots so you know where to plant new bulbs in the fall. Attach a piece of masking tape to the stake and write with a permanent marker what you wish to plant there.

states can do this as early as late February or early March. Northern dwellers should wait until late April or early May. Follow planting instructions on the packaging. Everyone else should be able to plant in late March or early April. Lettuce, peas, spinach, broccoli, and other hardy vegetables can be planted as early as you can work the soil. You can plant seeds for some flowers, such as annual phlox, California poppies, and sweet peas now, too. Also look for seedling violas and pansies. Spring is also a good time to plant trees and shrubs.

Summer's Almost Here

After the busyness of spring, reward yourself by getting ready for outdoor fun.

- Get your pool ready. Remove the cover, fill with water, and superchlorinate according to manufacturer instructions.
- Inspect bicycles; lubricate chains and adjust seat heights as necessary. Check that your children's bicycle helmets still fit. Also inspect outdoor play equipment for loose bolts or broken parts.

- Bring your outdoor furniture, grill, and play equipment out of storage; clean it off and set it up. If you see some rust, sand and repaint as needed. Get new cushions for your lawn furniture if necessary.
- Check your gas grill before using it. Use a pipe cleaner to remove possible blockage by insects or grease buildup in the tubes that lead to the burner. Check hoses for cracking, brittleness, holes, and leaks; replace as necessary.

Summer Garden Chores

For most people, working out in the yard is a pleasure rather than a chore. Regardless, certain things need to be done at certain times, and you can organize chores to keep your lawn and garden looking their best.

Let's start in the garden. When the danger of frost has passed and nighttime temperatures are holding steady at 55°F or higher, it's safe to plant annual flowers and vegetables. You can move houseplants outdoors then, too, and plant flower boxes. Dig up any spring bulbs you wish to transplant, but wait until after the foliage has died back. Save only the larger bulbs; the smaller ones will not bloom. Replant immediately and water. Or place in a mesh bag and store in your garage or other cool (50°F to 65°F), dry place until fall. Be sure to label the bag.

Once the soil has warmed up sufficiently, mulch vegetable and flower gardens to conserve water and prevent weeds from sprouting. Use grass clippings, straw, mulched leaves, or partially broken down compost.

If you wish to extend your vegetable-growing season, plan to do this as soon as your first crop is gone. Remove all plant debris and weeds and fertilize soil. Plant cool-season vegetables, such as spinach, turnips, radishes, onions, or leaf lettuce from seeds. When seedlings emerge, apply a two- to three-inch layer of light mulch. Water thoroughly and regularly, preferably early in the day.

Delegate yard chores to family members. Rotate chores so that one person doesn't get stuck doing the same ones all summer. Regular chores may include cleaning the pool, watering the lawn, watering gardens, and mowing. If you remove no more than one third of the grass leaf at one time, it is not necessary to rake clippings.

PLANNING AHEAD

Order early spring flowering bulbs in August. If buying at a retail store, choose the biggest bulbs. Be sure to buy enough to plant in clusters. Store in original packaging in the "cool and dry" compartment of your refrigerator or another cool (40°F to 50°F), dry place.

Back to School

Don't wait until the last minute to get organized for the start of a new school year. As early as July, clothing stores start phasing out summer apparel and introducing fall items. Plan to shop on a rainy day or an exceptionally hot day, when it might feel good to spend time in an air-conditioned mall.

Before you go shopping, have your child try on last year's clothes to see what still fits. If you dislike shopping, try catalog or on-line shopping for everything from pencils to underwear to coats. There's a charge for delivery, but if you add up the time you spend getting to and from the store and waiting to check out, it may be worth the added cost. Try to do as much shopping as you can from one catalog to defray shipping costs and, if possible, choose catalogs that do not need to collect sales tax in your state.

Do whatever you can to make a smooth transition from vacation to school. If your child is new to a school, arrange to have your kids meet their teachers and some classmates before school starts. At the very least, spend time talking about school in a positive manner and give children an opportunity to express concerns. About one week before school starts, adjust bedtimes and wake-up times to coincide with school schedules. See page 186 for tips on managing morning madness.

A Season of Change

Take advantage of fall's bounty. Watch for end-of-season markdowns on summer items, such as suntan lotion, insect repellent, beach toys, lawn furniture, and summer clothing. Collect

ARE YOU READY FOR SCHOOL?

Take time at the beginning of the school year to update all of your medical records and emergency information in your planner. While completing the forms that come home in the first week, cross-check your records. Ask permission from the people you choose to list as emergency contacts before submitting the form back to the school. Not only is it courteous, it allows your contact to get prepared. If possible, choose only one person to list as the contact for your entire family. And remember to carry your cell phone with you whenever you aren't at home or at work, so you can be reached if an emergency occurs at school.

—Molly Gold, GO MOM! INC.

leaves, pine cones, seeds, sticks, and other natural goodies for winter craft projects. Shop for fall mums and other hardy annual plants to replace fading summer blooms.

Of course, there's work to be done, too, inside and out. Do outdoor jobs on one of those beautiful fall days when the air is crisp and the sun is warm. Save your fall cleaning and redecorating for a rainy day. Indoor things to do include vacuuming refrigerator coils and heat vents before turning on your furnace. Following is a list of some of the major things to do outdoors each fall.

- Take down awnings and wash and store them.
- Clean window sills and screens.

- On the first cold day, check for drafts around windows; reglaze and seal drafty windows.
- Check your door sweeps; replace if you feel cold air coming in.
- Repair ripped or broken screens and replace or store.
- Wash and put away summer clothes and blankets. Bring out the winter clothes and blankets.
- Have your chimney and furnace inspected.
- Scrub mildew from decks, porches, and siding.
- Clean, drain, and cover your pool; winterize according to manufacturer instructions.
- Remove the oil and spark plugs from your lawnmower; perform routine maintenance as recommended by the manufacturer.
- After most of the leaves have fallen, clean accumulated leaves and other debris out of gutters and downspouts to prevent clogging or collapse.
- Clean and sand the wood handles on your garden tools. Apply a coat of wood preservative to keep wood from drying and splitting.
- Get your snow thrower ready for winter use. Follow manufacturer instructions. Get gas if you need it.

Fall Gardening

Fall and late fall are the ideal times to fertilize your lawn. Fertilizing now results in a healthier lawn in spring and summer. Rake leaves periodically as they begin to fall; it's easier to keep up than to

TIME-SAVER

If you don't need to remove screens for the winter, use a handheld vacuum cleaner to remove cobwebs, leaf pieces, and other debris rather than removing them and hosing them down.

catch up. Put some leaves in your perennial gardens and around bushes and shrubs to provide winter protection. Reseed bare spots in your lawn, if needed. Use a heavy-duty garden rake to dig up the soil for planting, then seed and water. Keep pets and children off that area of the lawn until the grass is hardy enough.

In your garden, protect tender plants from early frost. Cover plants with large cardboard boxes. Once the average daily temperature falls below 65°F, pick tomatoes and let them finish ripening indoors out of direct sunlight. Keep an eye on the weather forecast. Bring houseplants indoors before the nights start turning cold.

Plant early spring flowering bulbs in fall. Inspect stored bulbs and throw out any that are mushy or decayed. Residents of southern states can plant in late September or early October. Those who live in northern states must wait until late November or early December or just before the ground freezes. If you live somewhere in between southern and northern states, you can plant in late October or early November. Dig holes that are two to three times deeper than the height of bulb. If you're not sure which end is up, plant it sideways. Cover with soil, fertilize with bonemeal, and water. Your local nursery or Cooperative Extension service can provide more exact planting information based on your USDA Plant Hardiness Zone.

Last but not least, put your gardens to bed for the winter. Cover perennial beds with two inches of mulch made of leaves or other mulching material. Turn vegetables under along with some compost material.

Welcoming Winter

In the cold, dark winter months, plants bring special joy and hints of good things to come. Throughout the winter, check your houseplants frequently. You may need to water more often than usual because heating dries out the soil. Occasionally washing leaves with lukewarm water and a few drops of mild dishwashing liquid will help to enhance absorption of low light. Vacuum heat vents and dust radiators every time you vacuum your floors and carpets.

If you live in a cold place with temperatures below freezing, winter is a good time to defrost your freezer. You can put all your frozen items outside your door with no worries about spoilage.

Take advantage of after-holiday sales. After the first of the year, you'll find dramatic markdowns on boxed holiday cards, ornaments, wrapping paper, ribbon, and bows. Shop now and have more time to enjoy next holiday season. You'll also find good sales on toys, furniture, carpets, linens, winter clothing, and more.

Year-End Checklist

The first of the year is a great time to get your home and office paperwork in order. Following is a checklist of very important, but often overlooked, year-end "To Dos."

❑ Clean out financial files (including tax returns and supporting tax documentation that is no longer needed) to make room for the new year's paperwork; shred or transfer older documents to archive storage as appropriate.

❑ Remove other outdated documents from your active files; discard, or put into archive storage as appropriate.

❑ Gather all of your tax paperwork and finalize records for the year.

❑ Update your household inventories to include photos, receipts, and appraisals (if necessary) for any new purchases made in that year and upgrade the replacement value of your homeowner's or renter's insurance to match.

❑ Update your will and powers of attorney to take into account any changes in the tax and estate laws or a life change such as a move, marriage, divorce, birth of a child, or death of a beneficiary.

❑ Update your list of account numbers (bank, credit card, investment, insurance policies, for example) and important contacts such as your attorney, investment broker, doctors, accountant, insurance agent, and executor of will to include any changes since this time last year.

— Ramona Creel, OnlineOrganizing.com

Begin preparing your taxes in January and file as early as possible if you expect a refund. If you expect to owe, prepare your taxes early anyway, but hold off on mailing until April.

PLANNING AHEAD

- **Order late spring/ summer flowering bulbs in January.**
- **Start planning in January if you wish to take the family on vacation during the summer holidays.**

For gardeners, winter is the season to dream *and* the season for perusing seed catalogs. As spring nears, start seeds indoors under grow lights. While you're waiting for an opportunity to plant outdoors, try forcing a few bulbs indoors, which will add spirited splashes of color and even fragrance to your interior landscape. Another good indoor project for gardeners that really shows of houseplants is positioning shelving under windows to ensure that plants get appropriate levels of light. Consider removing drapes you never close and using the drapery rod for hanging plants.

Though you may have to wait for warmer weather to plant, there are several ways to tend your garden in winter. Cut and place branches from your holiday tree over bulb beds and perennial gardens for added winter protection. Take advantage of a warm, sunny day to repair broken arbors and trellises before spring growth makes this difficult. During the dormant months, you may also be able to move rocks, prepare raised beds, or dig a compost trench. You could even build a new bird feeder.

Winter is also a great time to unclutter and organize your home, especially for people who live "up north" and prefer staying indoors to going out in the snow and cold. Plan a "first day of spring" party and use it as motivation to get your house in order over the winter months. Work in one room at a time using tips from previous chapters. Or skip the party, and focus instead on an organizing project you've been meaning to get to for a while, such as organizing your photographs, recipes, or closets. When you're finished, reward yourself for a job well done.

new year's resolutions

Making New Year's resolutions is a tradition that dates back to ancient Babylonian times. New Year dissolutions have an equally long history! We begin with the best intentions, but keeping New Year's resolutions is challenging. Following are three tips to help you set goals that you can keep.

1. Make resolutions early. Choose resolutions that you've been thinking about. You're more likely to follow through on these resolutions than on those made last minute at the midnight hour.

2. Stick with one or two resolutions. Make a list of all the things you want to do. Then choose the one or two things you would most like to accomplish this year and focus on those goals.

3. Set obtainable goals. When making resolutions, think about what you will need to do on a daily, weekly, and monthly basis to achieve your goal. If it doesn't seem realistic, scale back your expectations.

CHAPTER 25

MOVING

Whether you're moving across town or across the country, there's no such thing as an easy move. But a little planning and organization can minimize chaos before, during, and after moving day. The more prepared you are, the less stress you'll feel and the sooner you'll be able to settle in and start enjoying your new home and community. Need help? Call in a professional organizer.

Planning a Move

Like any big project, an organized move begins with a plan. Start by creating a simple checklist to help prepare for your upcoming move. If you have access to the Internet, go to www.MoversGuide.com, where you can create a personalized moving checklist and timeline. At this site, you can also get maps and directions, purchase packing supplies, rent a moving truck, and make arrangements to connect utilities. You can also generate a personalized moving checklist at www.Homestore.com/moving. A Web site with a good standard checklist can be found at www.ClubMom.com. If you don't have access to the Internet, make your own simple checklist and timeline using the one on page 241 as a guide.

How Will You Move? The first decision to make is how to get your belongings from point A to point B. Should you hire a moving company or do it yourself? The answer depends on how much time and money you are willing to spend. Generally, the least expensive option is to rent a moving truck, pack up your stuff, and enlist the help of friends to load and unload everything. But cost shouldn't be the only consideration. Also consider your ability to lift and carry heavy furniture without damaging it, the walls, or your back. Keep in mind that your moving expenses may be tax-deductible, which makes hiring a professional mover more affordable. If you have more money than time, get an estimate for having the mover pack and unpack your belongings as well as move them.

If you are considering hiring a moving company, the United States Department of Transportation recommends the following:

- Get estimates from at least three companies. Ask about the conditions of each estimate (for instance, is it guaranteed not to exceed a certain amount?).
- Ask for each company's motor carrier number and call the Department of Transportation at 202-358-7000 to find out if they are properly registered and insured.
- Ask your moving company for a copy of *Your Mover's Rights and Responsibilities,* a publication of the Department of Transportation.

Don't base your selection on price only. If possible, get referrals from friends, family members, and business colleagues. Get a written estimate from each moving company you contact. If you are putting things into storage, you might want to get an estimate for having the movers do that for you. Don't forget to ask about payment policies. Will the mover bill for services? If not, will the mover accept a check on the day of the move, or do they require a money order?

Utilities. About three weeks before your move, arrange to disconnect utilities at your current residence and reconnect them at your new residence. You will need to cancel trash collection, lawn and yard care services, and delivery services. Use the spreadsheet software on your computer to create a chart like the one below. Print and keep this document with you on moving day so that you can follow up if needed.

Utilities and Services Record

New address:_____

New phone number:_____ New fax number: _____ New e-mail address:_____

Utility/Service	Date to Cancel	Date to Restart	Confirmation #	New Provider	Phone Number	Notes
Electric						
Gas						
Local phone						
Long-distance carrier*						
Cable** or satellite TV						
Internet						
Water and sewer						
Delivery services						
Garbage removal						
Lawn and yard care						
Other services						

*You will need to get your new phone number first.
**Make arrangements to have your cable box picked up to avoid charges.

Moving Checklist and Timeline

Following is a sample four-week schedule for moving. If you have more or less time, adjust the schedule accordingly. To allow yourself enough time for each step, get started as soon as you know you are moving.

When to Do It	What to Do
As soon as possible	• Select a mover or reserve a truck rental
	• Create a checklist and timeline
4 weeks before	• Submit official change of address form to post office
	• Notify banks, creditors, and other businesses of your new address
	• Arrange for transferring children to a new school
	• Get packing supplies
	• Begin packing belongings
2–3 weeks before	• Make arrangements to disconnect and reconnect utilities and cancel services
1–2 weeks before	• Drop off donations at a local charity or arrange for pickup
	• Begin your final house cleaning
	• Start saying goodbyes
1–2 days before	• Finish packing boxes
	• Back up computer files
	• Get traveler's checks if needed
	• Pack your moving day survival kit
	• Pack or give away refrigerator and freezer items
	• Clean refrigerator and defrost freezer
Moving day	• Direct movers
	• Vacuum and mop floors room by room
After your move	• Send moving announcements to friends, family, and clients

Plan to have utilities switched off at your old home the day *after* your move and switched on at your new residence the day *before* you move. Utilities are often switched off in the early morning hours; ask about this when you call and plan accordingly so that you are not without necessary services on the day of your move, such as electricity for vacuuming or telephone for emergencies. You may want to have a cellular phone on hand as a backup, especially if you are moving on a Friday or the day before a holiday. If you don't own one, you can rent one. That way, if your telephone service doesn't get connected, you can still make and receive calls. It's a good idea not to announce your new telephone number to the world until your service is hooked up. Sometimes, the number you get is not the number that was assigned when you placed your service order.

Easing the Transition. Are you moving with children? Contact the board of education in your new community to arrange for transferring or enrolling your children in schools there. Also make a point to talk to your children to learn how they feel about moving. This will give you an opportunity to address any concerns up front. Keep in mind that children will pick up on your emotions. If you're anxious and stressed out about moving, your anxiety may display itself in your children's behavior. In the weeks leading up to your move, find out as much as you can about your new community. You might try the following:

- Take a walk or drive around the new neighborhood.
- Make arrangements to visit the new school or day care facility.
- Stop by the local Chamber of Commerce to find out about things to do.
- Visit the local library or bookstores to find books on the area.
- Look on-line for information about your new community.
- Line up some extracurricular activities for your children at your destination.

Your Pets. Call your veterinarian to find out whether your pet will require any vaccinations before moving to your new location. Make arrangements to get copies of your pet's veterinary records, including a record of rabies vaccination if you do not have one. Call local officials in your new location to find out about pet licensing requirements, leash laws, and other ordinances. To find a veterinarian in your new neighborhood, ask your current veterinarian for a referral, check the Yellow Pages, or contact The American Animal Hospital Association at 800-883-6301 or at www.healthypet.com.

TIME-SAVER

Order new address labels or an address stamp with your new address as soon as you know it. If you receive your order early enough, you can use your labels or stamp to fill out change of address notifications, which will be faster than writing each one by hand.

Announcing Your Move

Make sure your mail moves with you by filing a change of address form with the U.S. Postal Service at least one month or more of your scheduled move date. You can pick up this form at any post office, or fill one out on-line at www.MoversGuide.com. First-class mail and packages will be forwarded to your new address for one year. Magazines and newspapers will be forwarded for sixty days. Catalogs and advertising mail will not be forwarded.

You can speed up the forwarding process by notifying personal and professional contacts of your new address. The Movers Guide packet available at post offices includes postcards you can use for this purpose. Or you can send a fax or e-mail form letter, or call everyone who sends you mail, including:

- Credit card companies
- Banks and savings and lending institutions
- Insurance agents
- Investment agents or institutions
- Physicians, dentists, and veterinarian (when you contact your family physician and dentist, arrange to have your medical records mailed to your new address or sent to your new physician and dentist)
- Attorney and accountant
- Schools and colleges
- Club memberships, including frequent flyer programs
- Magazines and newspapers
- Social Security Administration, if you are currently receiving benefits (800-772-1213 or www.ssa.gov)

MOVING ON

If you're moving to a new home, chances are you'll be buying new stuff to fit that home's decor. Remember that before packing. Give to charity any overabundance of linens, decorative items, duplicate kitchen gadgets, old cookware, and other items you don't use now or won't use later.

—*Pat S. Moore, The Queen of Clutter*

- Department of Motor Vehicles
- Board of Elections (for voter registration)
- Internal Revenue Service (800-TAX-FORM or www.irs.gov)
- Employer and previous employer (if you are expecting a wage statement for this tax year and if you have a pension plan with any previous employer)
- Clients (if self-employed)
- Friends and family

At www.Homestore.com/moving, you can create and send a free on-line postcard to family and friends by using one of the available photographs or one of your own. Or do an on-line search using the keywords "virtual postcards," and adapt a standard greeting card to suit your purposes.

The easiest way to notify anyone who sends you bills is to make a note of your new address on the next bill you receive. If you are paying the bill before your move, be sure to include an effective date for your new address. If you call magazines with your change of address, ask whether they handle address changes for any other magazines to which you subscribe.

Packing and Organizing

Moving is a good time to lighten your load, especially if you are moving to a smaller home or plan to change your decor. Resolve to take only what you can use at your new home and leave everything else behind. Less stuff means less time spent packing and unpacking and less expense for moving. And best of all, it also means more space at your new place!

As you are packing, ask yourself the following questions:

- Is this item worth the time it will take to pack and unpack it?
- Is it worth the expense of moving it?
- Will it fit in with the decor of my new home?
- Does it still fit my lifestyle?
- Am I the rightful owner of this item?

If you answer "no" to any of these questions, don't pack it and don't take it with you. For more help in determining whether you should take an item or leave it behind, take the "Keep or Toss" quiz on page 13.

As you start packing, keep a trash bag or box handy for those things that can be thrown away. Label one box "Give Away" and use it to collect items that you can donate to charity. When that box is full, start another one. Keep all of your donation boxes together in one room, separate from moving boxes. If you want to have a garage sale, do it at your current location before you move. There's no sense in moving things you plan to get rid of.

Packing is a time-consuming job; get started sooner rather than later. If you're overwhelmed by the thought of packing up everything you own, take it one day at a time. Pack four boxes a day, and you'll have 112 boxes packed in four weeks. Enlist some help from family and friends, and it'll go even faster.

You're going to need lots of boxes, probably more than you think. You can purchase boxes from your mover or rental company, or if you are on a limited budget, ask at your local drug, liquor, or grocery store if they can set aside some boxes for you. Also look for lidded copy

Packing Supplies

❑ Packing boxes in assorted sizes
❑ Packing paper (plain newsprint is best)
❑ Bubble wrap for fragile items
❑ Wide-tip markers for labeling boxes
❑ Rolls of packing tape
❑ Packing tape dispensers

paper boxes that you can bring home from work. It's helpful to have an assortment of boxes for packing various items:

- Larger boxes for lighter but bulky items, such as pillows and lampshades
- Smaller boxes for heavier items, such as books and paper files
- Wine or liquor cartons for fragile items
- Dish-pack boxes for dishes
- Special boxes for artwork and mirrors
- Wardrobe boxes for clothes
- Banker storage boxes for hanging files and fragile items
- Lidded copy paper boxes for fragile items
- Large, clear plastic bags are convenient for transporting unbreakable, unwieldy items such as wicker baskets

You may be able to leave clothes in dresser drawers and files in file cabinet drawers. Just remove and carry each drawer into the moving

truck, then replace drawers once you load the dresser or file cabinet. If you hired a moving company, ask if they will do that for you. Also ask if you can borrow wardrobe boxes; if not, purchase them. On moving day, transfer hanging clothes from your closets to the wardrobe boxes. Once the boxes arrive at your destination, simply remove clothes from the boxes and hang them in your new closets. A wardrobe box is about two feet wide, so if you have a ten-foot closet rod, you will need approximately five boxes. You can use the bottom of each wardrobe box to transport shoes. Bag each pair individually so you don't have to match them up at the other end. Or pack sweaters and jeans in plastic bags and put them at the bottom of the wardrobe box.

Start in a room that does not get regular use, such as a guest room, attic, basement, or formal dining room. You may need to repack things like holiday decorations to reduce the possibility of damage during shipping. Also repack boxes that are ripped or missing flaps or lids. Stack boxes neatly along one wall so that you can still walk through the room.

Pack one room at a time, keeping similar items, such as pots and pans, together in boxes. In each room, pack things you don't use or won't be needing for the next few weeks first

For Simplicity's Sake

Keep all relocation information in one pocket folder. Use this folder to store your moving calendar, moving estimates, contact numbers for vendors (utility companies, carpet cleaners, etc.), directions for your mover, and all other paperwork related to your move. That way, you'll have everything in one place.

—*Sally Allen, A Place for Everything*

and leave more frequently used items to be packed last. In the family room, for example, you might start by taking down and packing wall hangings or books and pack audio and videotapes last. If you have tapes organized alphabetically or by category, use a rubber band to keep them together, especially if you have movers packing for you. Leave the kitchen for last. Plan to use plastic utensils and paper plates and cups for the last few meals before moving so you can pack all of your dishes. Or keep out just enough dishes for your family and include them with your moving day essentials.

Label each box with the room name on all four sides, at the top right of each panel. Use a wide-tip felt marker and print clearly, preferably in capital letters. Under the room name, add the word *Fragile* if contents are breakable, or "This Side Up" with an arrow if the box contains a lamp or other items that should not be tipped upside down. On one side of the box, list the general or specific contents of that box. Or label boxes with the room name and a number and then keep a master list of what is in each box.

Pack heavier items at the bottom of each box and lighter items at the top. Use blank newspaper sheets to wrap breakables. You can buy sheets from your moving company. If you're on a limited budget, ask your local newspaper publisher if you could have their "end rolls," which is the unusable paper at the end of each roll of newsprint. Do not use printed newspapers; the ink tends to rub off on things, which makes more work at the other end.

ABCs OF PACKING

Everything you pack does not have to be unpacked the first day in your new home. If it contains essential items, mark it A. If the contents are important, but not crucial, mark the box B. If the box contains out-of-season items, holiday items, and other things you won't need right away, mark the box C. Then unpack in A, B, C order.

—*Maria Gracia, Get Organized Now!*

When packing fragile items, crumple up newsprint to provide extra padding on the bottom of the box, between items, and on top of contents. To wrap and pad larger kitchen breakables, you can use dish towels. In the bathroom, use washcloths, hand and bath towels to wrap and pad breakable bathroom items. Use sofa and bed pillows or light blankets to pad boxes that contain larger fragile items, such as statues or jewelry boxes. Do not pack fragile items with heavy items.

Pack and fill each box tightly to prevent contents from shifting during transport. But don't overload boxes. Keep them to a manageable weight, especially if you are doing your own lifting and moving. If you have space at the top of a box, fill it tightly to the top with crumpled newspaper so that other boxes can be stacked on top without crushing it. Secure boxes by taping the flaps closed, and reinforce the bottom with a strip of packing tape that wraps around the edges of the box.

Some items require special care when packing to avoid mishaps and damage during shipping. There are also things you can do to help speed up the process of settling in. Following are some suggestions for both.

- Pack opened bottles, jars, tubes, and containers in resealable plastic bags in case they leak.
- Remove and wrap ceramic and glass lids separately from the main item.
- Pack small, fragile items in small boxes that can be packed together in a larger box.
- Wrap small items in colored tissue to help prevent them from getting lost in a carton.
- Wrap each piece of china and glassware individually.
- Pack albums and CDs vertically, not flat, with large hardcover books on either end and mark the box "Fragile."
- Pack same-size books together, either flat or upright.
- Use original packaging to pack computer and electronic equipment.
- Cover both sides of mattresses with fitted sheets to keep them clean (you can always wash the sheets).
- Use blankets to protect wood furniture from nicks and scratches.
- As you remove artwork and decorations from walls, tape hardware for hanging to the back of the item.
- Put hardware from disassembled items into a labeled bag; tape the bag to the item.
- Ask a nursery about the best way to transport your plants.
- Drain gas and oil from power equipment.

- Use clean and disinfected trash cans with lids to transport outdoor toys or gardening tools and supplies.

Keep in mind that moving companies cannot transport items that are flammable, corrosive, or explosive. This includes but is not limited to aerosol products, matches, paint thinner and paints, pesticides, cooking fuel, lamp oil, liquid bleach, ammonia, and other cleaning solvents. Dispose of these products before moving, or take them with you in your car. Moving companies

WHERE DOES THIS GO?

When packing up your stuff, think about where everything is going to go in your new home. Get a floor plan of your new house or apartment and spend a few minutes deciding where your furniture and other large items will go. Then assign a color to each room of the house. As you pack up a box of stuff, decide what room it will go in and mark the box in that color with a magic marker or sticker or piece of construction paper. Do the same thing with furniture: Pin a colored tag on each item to indicate what room it will go in. When you get ready to unload, tape the appropriately colored piece of construction paper on the door of each room and put your colored floor plan on the front door. That way, no one will have to ask you, "Where does this go?" and you know that everything will end up in the right spot.

—*Ramona Creel, OnlineOrganizing.com*

moving day essentials

Your moving day essentials might include the following:

- Maps and directions to your new home for you and mover (exchange cell-phone numbers, too, if available)
- Paperwork and payment for moving company
- Vital phone numbers
- Record of utility and service connections (page 240)
- Pen and notepad
- Medications for family and pets
- Aspirin or other pain reliever
- Basic tools and a flashlight
- Cleaning products and tools
- Trash bags
- Toilet paper
- Toothpaste, soap, shampoo, and shower curtain
- Snacks and drinks
- Disposable plates, cups and utensils
- Dish detergent, sponge, paper towels
- Telephone (not cordless)
- Knife for opening sealed boxes
- Alarm clock
- Night lights

also cannot transport food, plants, or living things that may die or spoil in transit. Decide beforehand where you will donate anything that you cannot take with you. You may be able to donate unopened foodstuffs to a food pantry; folks living in a nursing home might appreciate getting some houseplants. Items that are not recommended for shipping include items with sentimental or monetary value and furs.

Moving Day

The day before moving, have each family member pack an overnight bag that includes one complete change of clothes, night clothes, toothbrush, and other necessities for the next twenty-four hours. For children, necessities might also include diapers, a favorite stuffed animal, blanket, and toy or game. Pack these bags into your car, not the moving truck. That way, you won't have to go searching through boxes, and you'll have what you need if the moving truck gets delayed. If you are driving the moving truck yourself, load these bags into the truck last so that they are the first to be unloaded at your destination.

Pack a bag for your pets, too. Include enough food for the next twenty-four hours, food and water bowls, treats, toys, and leash. Be sure that your pets are wearing identification tags in case they get loose. It's a good idea to put your pets in kennels or carriers before the movers arrive. Or confine them to one room, close the door, and place a note on the door that says, "Do Not Enter — Pets Inside." As much as possible, try to maintain your pet's regular feeding and exercise schedule on moving day.

Other things to have in your possession on moving day include paperwork and payment for the mover, important documents or computer discs, medications, maps, jewelry, and other valuables. Pack these items in a briefcase or tote bag that you can keep at your side. If you have a fireproof lock box, put valuables inside and lock it in your trunk. Pack kitchen, bathroom, and bedroom necessities and other essentials in boxes labeled "Open First" and load

One Challenge . . .

I'm in the process of moving my eighty-year-old mother from the three-bedroom home where she's lived for thirty years into an efficiency apartment. How can I help her "downsize" without feeling like she has to give up everything?

Three Solutions

1 FROM HELEN VOLK, BEYOND CLUTTER: I find that it helps if you can get the elderly to concentrate on one thing, and that is, what they're going to take with them. With the smaller stuff, I suggest that they choose what *they* want first. Then make decisions about what to give to family members. Surrounding themselves with things they love will help them to feel more at home in their new surroundings.

2 FROM JAN LIMPACH, ORGANIZING PLUS: It's important that at least some items with sentimental value make the move to the new residence. I bring my clients catalogs so that they can choose bookcases and shelving to hold their most precious photos and mementos. For everything else, it's easier to let go if they know that someone will use and enjoy these things. Usually we start with "Who can this go to that I know?" Then we move on to "Who can this go to that I don't know?"

3 FROM PAT S. MOORE, THE QUEEN OF CLUTTER: It's helpful to measure the rooms in the new home and draw a simple floor plan. Many retirement homes provide such drawings. Many home improvement stores sell a simple kit with furniture templates that you can use to arrange the rooms on paper. This will help tremendously in deciding what goes with her and what just goes. Also, as you're trying to make the decision of what to keep, collect all of the same type of item together. When you see all forty lamps together, it's easier to choose the three you like or need.

these boxes on the truck last. Or, if you prefer to move them yourself, label them "This Stays Here" so that the movers do not take them.

Consider arranging for children to stay with a friend or relative on moving day. If the kids will be present, give them a job to do or direct them to a designated play area so that they do not interfere with the loading and unloading. Or you can put your children to work unpacking their own things. Older children may be able to help out and direct movers to the appropriate rooms or help you to make beds.

Unpacking and Settling In

Plan to set up one room completely as soon as possible so that you have a place to take refuge from all the boxes elsewhere in your house or apartment. If you can't set up a whole room on the first day, there are some things you can do to make the first night and day in your new home more comfortable and fun.

- Make up everyone's bed, or have the whole family camp out in the living room.
- Put beverages in the refrigerator and favorite snacks in a cupboard.
- Hook up your telephone and order takeout for dinner, or go out to eat.
- Hook up the television and VCR, find the nearest video rental store, and spend the evening watching a movie.
- Make sure there is toilet paper in every bathroom.
- Hang a shower curtain if needed and put out towels, soap, and shampoo.

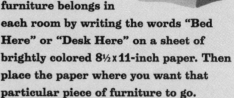

THE PAPERING TECHNIQUE

Show movers where furniture belongs in each room by writing the words "Bed Here" or "Desk Here" on a sheet of brightly colored 8½ x 11-inch paper. Then place the paper where you want that particular piece of furniture to go.

—*Donna D. McMillan, McMillan & Company Professional Organizing*

Unpack one room at a time. Put furniture where you want it and then start unpacking boxes. Don't put things just anywhere; find a place for everything. If you can't find a place for something, put it in a box labeled "Store Elsewhere." Bring that box with you to the next room. If, after unpacking and organizing all rooms, you still have things in the "Store Elsewhere" box, you'll need to decide what to do with those things. In addition to the "Store Elsewhere" box, you'll need large trash bags for collecting all the newsprint, which you can burn in your fireplace or recycle. Remove tape from empty boxes and flatten. Save them only if you know you will be moving again within the year or if you have enough space to store them. Recycle boxes you do not need. Pack small and medium flattened boxes into a large box for easy removal.

Professional organizers Lynn and Kevin Hall of Clutter No More, Inc., suggest using a ticking kitchen timer to get things done. Set the timer when you feel overwhelmed looking

For Simplicity's Sake

Before or after your move, put sticky notes on cabinets, drawers, and doors to indicate where you want things to go. This is especially helpful if others will be helping you to unpack.

—*Lynn and Kevin Hall, Clutter No More, Inc.*

at a stack of boxes to be emptied. The ticking timer keeps you going at a quick pace and helps you stay focused. Stop working on the project when the timer goes off. Reset the timer if you want to continue.

If you have pets, keep them confined for the first few days until they get adjusted to their new surroundings. If your pets go outside, keep them leashed to prevent them from running away in an attempt to get back to their old neighborhood.

It's natural to want to get settled in as soon as possible, but don't spend all your time unpacking. Take time to explore your new neighborhood and get familiar with your surroundings. Plan weekly outings with your family to explore cultural and recreational offerings.

Combining Households

One of the biggest moving challenges is trying to merge two fully furnished homes into one. Whatever you do, don't attempt to move everything from both homes and *then* decide what to do with it. It doesn't make sense to move things

twice, and the sheer volume of stuff will put unnecessary strain on your relationship.

Make an agreement to make a fresh start. Bring to your new home only the things you really love or use on a regular basis, and give the rest away. Sometimes it's easier to let go of things if you can find new homes for them. Think of family members or friends who may have admired a particular item in the past or could use something you no longer need. Or donate items to a charity with the knowledge that someone will appreciate your gift.

You may be able to help each other decide what goes and what stays with this exercise: The next time your loved one is in your home, have him or her make a list of those things he or she really likes. You do the same at his or her place. Use your lists to start a master list of things that you will definitely want to move into your combined household.

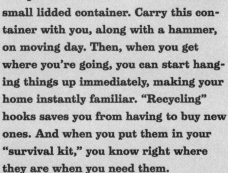

PICTURE THIS

Remove all picture hooks from the wall and put them into a small lidded container. Carry this container with you, along with a hammer, on moving day. Then, when you get where you're going, you can start hanging things up immediately, making your home instantly familiar. "Recycling" hooks saves you from having to buy new ones. And when you put them in your "survival kit," you know right where they are when you need them.

—*Sally Allen, A Place for Everything*

Give yourselves plenty of time — anywhere from six weeks to six months — so you can do a really thorough job of uncluttering. How long you need depends on several factors, including the size of your existing and prospective homes, how long you've lived at your existing addresses, how much stuff you've collected over the years, and how much time you are willing to devote to uncluttering.

Spend some time uncluttering your home every day. You'll find plenty of helpful ideas in chapter 2, "Uncluttering Your Home." On weekends, help each other tackle bigger projects, such as uncluttering basements, attics, and closets, and sorting through memorabilia. Don't be surprised if you learn more about each other in the process! Be prepared to accept the fact that both of you are going to keep things the other one thinks are crazy to save.

Selling Your Home

As soon as you decide to move, you should put your home on the market. Four out of five home sellers use a realtor to list and sell their homes. To find a good realtor, ask people who

have sold their homes recently if they would use their realtor again. The realtor you choose to list your home should work full time and have at least several years of experience in the business. It's a good idea to interview several realtors before signing with one. Ask where, when, and how often your property will be advertised. And don't get locked into a long-term listing contract without a reasonable cancellation clause so that you can change realtors if you are not satisfied with performance.

Selling your home directly to prospective buyers is the alternative to listing with an agent. The upside is that you might be able to sell your home without having to pay the agent's commission. The downside is that you may not be able to reach as many prospective buyers as you can when you list your home with a Multiple Listing Service (MLS), which is available through realtors. You'll also have to pay for your own brochures and advertising, field all telephone inquiries, be readily available to show your home to prospective buyers, and negotiate all offers on your own.

Regardless of how you decide to sell your home, you will need to locate the deed to your property, current tax bill, information pertaining to any liens, and Homeowners' Association documents if applicable. You'll also need to estimate the value of your property and set your price. A realtor can provide you with a comparative market analysis of recent home sale prices in your area. Or you can do a little research on your own by checking real estate listings for similar properties. Then consider how much you paid for your property, the condition of your property, how much you put into home improvements, and how much you want to make after all transaction fees are paid. Figure on 1 percent of the selling price for closing fees (attorney fees, title search, and recording fees) and another 1 percent if the seller pays the buyer's mortgage costs in your state. If you are using a realtor, you'll have the brokerage fee as well, which is typically 6 to 8 percent of the purchase price. But don't overprice your home in an effort to offset these fees, as overpriced homes are less likely to sell.

Real estate agents agree that a home shows best when it is clean, uncluttered, and nicely furnished. The next best way to show a house is completely empty. So if you need to move before you sell your home, plan to take everything with you and leave it spotless. If you can afford to make major repairs, you should, because some things, such as a leaky roof or rotting deck, could deter prospective buyers and make it harder to sell your home.

The Home Show

Don't underestimate the power of first impressions when it comes to showing your home. Here are some simple, inexpensive things you can do to increase the "curbside" appeal and marketability of your home.

Outdoors
❑ Take care of any minor repairs such as broken windows or gutters.
❑ Mow your lawn and weed your garden.
❑ Pick up any debris that may have fallen or blown into your yard.
❑ Put trash cans out of sight; keep the garage door closed.
❑ Plant a few annual flowers near the entrance or buy a few potted or hanging plants.
❑ Repaint the exterior of your home if needed.
❑ Wash windows.

Indoors
❑ Give your house a thorough cleaning, from top to bottom.
❑ Unclutter and organize every room including storage areas.
❑ Unclutter and organize closets and kitchen cabinets.
❑ Fix simple things like loose doorknobs, broken doorbells, and leaky faucets.
❑ Eliminate bad odors at the source.
❑ Make your home look, smell, and feel cozy for prospective buyers: put out vases of cut flowers, light scented candles or a fireplace, bake bread or cookies, or simmer something "homey" on the stovetop.
❑ Open blinds and curtains and turn on all lights to create a feeling of spaciousness and light.
❑ Turn off the television for "show time."

MAPPING YOUR MOVE

Get a detailed street map of your new neighborhood and study it before you move so you don't feel totally lost when you get there. Lessen relocation stress for your children by making a copy of the map for each child. Mark the location of your new home, their schools, community playgrounds, movie theaters, and other kid-oriented attractions. You can further relieve your children's stress by giving them photographs of your new home that they can show to friends.

CHAPTER 26

NEW BEGINNINGS

Life's big events come hand in hand with opportunities to test your organizational skills. Whatever your new adventure — adopting a pet, preparing to welcome a new baby into your home, or sending the kids off to college — you can be better prepared to handle the transition smoothly and efficiently with advance preparation. Grab a pen and start making a list!

Adopting a Pet

Now is not always the right time to get a pet. But when the time *is* right, the investment of time and energy pays off in years of companionship and love.

Are you ready for a pet? It's sad, but the main reason why so many dogs and cats end up in shelters is because their owners were unprepared for the realities of pet ownership. Cuddly kittens and puppies can be quite destructive and often require more work than expected. And, as they grow into full-sized pets, they demand loving care, training, and medical attention that can sometimes be costly.

Keep in mind, too, that having a pet means more housecleaning. Cats tend to track litter out of the litter box. Dogs come indoors with muddy paws. Both shed. Expect to do more vacuuming, especially if you choose a long-haired pet.

Would this be your first pet? Talk to pet owners about the pros and cons of pet ownership. If you don't have the time or energy required to care for and train a puppy or kitten, you might consider adopting an older animal from a humane shelter. They're more difficult to place in homes than are younger animals, even though they often are already trained and make the best pets.

Do some research to find out what breeds are best suited to your personality and lifestyle. For example, Greyhounds are more suited than other dogs to being home alone all day because they sleep 90 percent of the day.

Others, especially large breeds, need a fair amount of exercise each day. Some breeds of cats, such as the American Bobtail, make great traveling companions. Others, such as the Maine Coon, tend to get along very well with the family dog. If you have children, talk to a veterinarian about what breeds of dogs and cats are best with children.

If you would like to buy a purebred animal, be sure to buy from a reputable breeder. It's a good idea to see the mother and father if possible so that you can observe their temperaments as well as physical traits. A good breeder is generally very particular about placing puppies and kittens with new owners and may even have you sign a contract stating that you will feed your pet a particular brand of food or that you will send photos of him on a regular basis.

Whichever type of pet you choose, you'll need to budget for medical care in addition to food and toys. Unless you plan to breed your pet, get your cat or dog neutered or spayed so that you don't end up with an unexpected litter. Also plan to take your pet to the veterinarian at least once a year for a checkup and vaccinations.

Bringing Your Pet Home. Cats and dogs, especially kittens and puppies, are naturally curious. Before you bring your pet home, take a walk around your home and look for accidents waiting to happen. Look high and low. Do you see any dangling electrical cords? Is there anything that could topple and fall if bumped? Keep in mind that cats like high places. You may want to move breakables into a safer stor-age place, at least for a while. Cats and dogs sometimes learn to open cabinet doors, so be sure to store household cleaning products and other hazardous substances in upper cabinets or shelves. See page 225 for more information on pet safety.

Prepare as much as possible before bringing your new pet home. Where will he sleep? Who will be responsible for feeding or walking him?

What You Need

Pets need things, too. Here's a list of some essentials you'll want to have on hand.

❑ Water bowl
❑ Food dish
❑ Leash (for outdoor pets)
❑ Collar
❑ Identification tag
❑ Dry food
❑ Canned food (optional)
❑ Treats (especially good for puppy training)
❑ Litter, litter box, and plastic scooper (for cats)
❑ Scratching post (for cats)
❑ Safe chew toys (for dogs)
❑ Grooming brush
❑ Flea comb
❑ Nail clippers
❑ File folder for medical records
❑ Dog crate or cat carrier

What will you feed him? What will you do with him when you go to work each day? What will you do with him when you go on vacation or you are traveling? Will your new pet be allowed on the furniture? Have all the supplies you need before you bring your new pet home (see checklist on page 255). Make a list and bring it with you to your nearest pet supply store.

When you bring your new pet home, confine him to one room at first so that he can get familiar with his new surroundings. Then gradually, over the next few days, introduce him to the rest of the house. Right away, begin to establish sleeping, eating, and playing routines. Eventually, you'll want to expose your pet to other people and even other pets, but don't rush into it. Give your pet time to adjust to his new home. And play it safe. Confine your puppy or kitten to a room with a closed door when your attention is needed elsewhere or you need to go out. You may be able to use a baby gate to confine your puppy to one area of your home such as the kitchen.

Housebreaking Your Pet. Housebreaking a kitten is generally very easy. Just fill a box with litter and set your kitten in it after he drinks or eats. You might want to hold his front paws and make digging motions in the litter. If he doesn't use the litter box right then, don't worry. He'll be back. Place the litter box in a quiet, low-traffic area away from your kitten's food and water. If you adopt an older cat that is not using the litter box, call your veterinarian for advice.

Dogs present more of a housebreaking challenge. Paper training is best if you will be away all day. If you're home during the day or able to check in frequently, crate training is the preferred method for housebreaking.

Paper-Training 101. Paper training is a simple two-step method that helps puppies learn to use a specified area for elimination, then helps them make the transition to going outdoors.

1. Confine your puppy to a safe, enclosed area with a tile or linoleum floor. You may be able to use a baby gate as a doggy gate.
2. Cover the floor with newspaper. The puddles and piles may be random at first, but soon your puppy will choose one area far from his food and bed to make his "spot."
3. Layer several dirty papers on "the spot" to give it a strong scent so the puppy will be attracted there. Dogs prefer to eliminate where they have gone before.
4. Gradually shrink the paper-covered area until it is fairly small.
5. When you are home, help your puppy make the transition to eliminating outdoors by taking him out immediately after waking, playing, and eating; before going to bed; and any time your puppy heads for his indoor "spot" or the door.

Crate-Training 101. Dogs are clean animals and won't soil the place where they sleep. Crate training uses this natural instinct to help your puppy develop bladder and bowel control.

1. Introduce your puppy to his crate, which should be big enough for him to turn around and lie down comfortably. Or put a cardboard box at the back of an adult-size crate to make it puppy size.

2. Throw a treat or toy inside the crate and have your puppy go get it. Say a command like "In your crate!" or "Kennel!" Always praise him or give him a treat so that going into the crate is associated with pleasant experiences.

3. Crate your puppy at intervals throughout the day. Young puppies need lots of rest. Restrict your puppy to the safety of his crate whenever you cannot watch him closely, for naps, and at bedtime.

4. Take your puppy outdoors to eliminate. After waking, playing, or eating, ask your puppy, "Do you want to go out?" and then take him outdoors to the spot where you'd like him to go.

5. Praise your puppy for doing "it." Wait until your puppy starts eliminating and then say a command phrase, such as "Do it!" or "Go for it!" Lay on lots of praise.

6. Do not crate your puppy for any longer than 2 to 3 hours at a stretch. That's about as long as a 6- to 8-week old puppy can hold his bladder. For the first month or so, you'll need to get up a few times in the middle of the night to take your puppy out.

TIME-SAVER

To quickly clean pet hair from upholstery in your car and home, lightly wet your hand and run it across the fabric. Or don a latex glove and do the same thing — the hair will stick to the glove. A damp sponge or foam ball or masking tape also make quick picker-uppers.

Preparing for a Baby

A new baby brings so much joy — and so many organizational challenges. But getting ready is half the fun. Start your preparations early so you can savor the anticipation of your new arrival without feeling hurried or pressured.

Begin with the financial decisions surrounding your child's entrance into your world. The first thing your baby needs is adequate health insurance. Review your policy. Most health maintenance organizations cover maternity and well-baby care as well as hospitalization. More traditional plans do not always cover well-baby care visits. If you are pregnant now and don't have health insurance, you will need a plan that covers preexisting conditions. Your new baby (and other children) may be eligible for free or low-cost health insurance through the federal government's Insure Kids Now! Program, which is available in every state in the United States (see page 283).

Two other types of insurance to consider are disability and life insurance. Even if your employer provides disability insurance, you

baby basics

Following is a list of essentials for your baby's first month at home.

Coming home
- Newborn (rear-facing) car seat
- Outfit to wear home
- Six receiving blankets

Feeding and changing
- Baby bottles and formula (four to six 4-ounce bottles and six to eight 8-ounce bottles)
- Nursing supplies if you will be nursing (breast pump, two or more nursing bras, easy-access sleepwear)
- Six to eight bibs
- Up to a dozen burping cloths
- Five to eight diapers per day
- Diaper pail with locking lid (if using deodorizer cakes)
- Baby wipes
- Diaper rash ointment or petroleum jelly
- Three to four changing pad covers

Clothing
- Four to six nightgowns or sleeping sacks
- Four to eight one-piece coveralls with snaps
- Three to four short- or long-sleeved outfits (with feet for winter)
- Four to five undershirts
- One dress-up outfit
- One to two machine washable sweaters
- One to two hats
- Two pairs of booties
- Six pairs of stretchy socks
- Warm outerwear for cold weather

Bedding
- Crib bumper
- Three to four sets of crib sheets
- Two to three baby blankets
- Two to four waterproof mattress pads

Bathing
- Newborn tub
- Four to six washcloths
- Two to four hooded towels
- Baby shampoo and soap
- Baby lotion

Health care and grooming
- Cotton swabs and alcohol (for umbilical cord)
- Thermometer (rectal, tympanic, or axillary)
- Ear bulb or aspirator
- Saline nose drops
- Acetaminophen drops
- Baby nail clippers or scissors
- Brush and comb

Getting up and out
- Infant seat
- Cloth baby carrier
- Two or more pacifiers
- Diaper bag with portable changing mat
- Infant stroller or carriage

may wish to supplement it by buying additional coverage. Disability insurance pays benefits when you are unable to work. While life insurance is not necessary for single people or married couples without children, it's definitely something to consider when you have a young one counting on you for financial support. Both parents should be insured. See pages 117 and 118 for additional information about life and disability insurance.

With a child on the way, you need a simple will and trust that outlines how you wish to provide for your child in the event of your death. You'll need to name a guardian for your child and a trustee who will manage the inheritance. If you don't have a will, the state court will choose a guardian and trustee and split up your property in a way that might not be your first choice. Think about who you would want to watch over your child and your estate if you could not do so. Then make an appointment with an attorney to draw up a simple will and trust.

It may seem like a long way off, but your new arrival will be graduating from high school and heading off for college before you know it. The sooner you start saving, the more money you'll have to finance your child's education. See page 141 for tips on how to save painlessly. Then consult with your financial planner to determine the best plan for you.

Outfitting the Nursery

If you haven't started preparing your baby's room by your sixth or seventh month of pregnancy, now's the time. The first step is to furnish

and decorate the room where you will put your baby to sleep, change diapers, and store your baby's clothes and other necessities. Start by cleaning out the closet to make room for baby things. Consider adding shelving for easy access.

As you are decorating your child's room, keep in mind that nursery-themed wallpaper will become outdated as your little one grows. Look for wall decorations that can be peeled off later. Or paint the walls with washable latex paint and buy sheets, blankets, crib bumper, comforter, curtains, and other furnishings with your choice of decorative theme. When you want to update the look of the room, simply change the furnishings. Avoid throw rugs in the nursery that may cause you to slip or trip when carrying your baby.

Basic furniture for baby-to-be includes a crib, sturdy changing table, and dresser. The crib mattress should fit snugly in the crib with no more than two fingers' width between the crib and the mattress. Buy them together to make sure of a good fit. If you buy a used crib, check the labeling to make sure that it meets federal safety regulations and industry voluntary standards (those of the American Society

For Safety's Sake

If your home was built before 1978, the paint on your walls and woodwork may contain lead. If in doubt, call the National Lead Information Center at 800-LEAD-FYI (800-532-3394) and request a listing of certified lead professionals in your area.

for Testing and Materials). Consider getting a rocking chair or glider and ottoman if you don't have one. Babies love the comforting head-to-toe rocking motion. You might also consider getting a bassinet or cradle so you can keep your newborn in your bedroom. If your baby will be sleeping in the nursery, you might want to get a baby monitor.

You don't have to spend a fortune outfitting the nursery. Resist the urge to run out and buy stuff right away. Instead, set aside money each month while you are expecting. Look all you want, but do your buying in the last trimester.

Final Preparations. Tie up loose ends during your last trimester. Once your baby gets home, you'll want to be able to give him or her your full attention.

- Find a pediatrician.
- Set up interviews with child care professionals and choose one.
- Baby-proof your home.
- Learn baby cardiopulmonary resuscitation.

- Subscribe to a parenting magazine.
- Arrange for someone to care for pets and other children while you are in the hospital or picking up your adopted child.
- Create or shop for birth announcements and address the envelopes.
- Cook and freeze some meals.
- Do a thorough housecleaning before you bring your baby home.
- Set up the crib and changing table and organize baby things.
- Line up a friend or family member to help you during the first week or so.
- Make a list of people you want to notify right away by telephone. Prepare an e-mail message to send to a select group with or without scanned photos or photos uploaded to your computer from your digital camera. Or you can put photographs on your personal Web site, then send the address to friends and family.

As your due date approaches, memorize or keep your doctor's number with you at all times and don't hesitate to call if you have any questions or concerns. Pack an overnight bag with the things you want to bring to the hospital, including a comfortable, nonmaternity outfit to wear home. Make it a habit to keep enough gas in your gas tank to get you to the hospital; you won't want to stop on the way. Consider registering at the hospital in advance so that you don't have to fill out all the paperwork when you get there. It's also a good idea to map out and try more than one route to the hospital in case of road construction or closures.

Heading Off to College

Generally, colleges provide first-year students with a list of items to bring — and not to bring. Use these lists (or the one below) as a guideline for creating your own personalized list. Put a check in front of the items you already have. Estimate how much it will cost to buy what you don't have and establish a budget that will allow you to get everything you need before you leave for school.

If your list is long and you're short on cash, get "must-have" things first, such as bedding, books, and other school supplies. Then see whether you can borrow some of the "would-be-nice-to-have" things on your list. Or check out garage sales in your neighborhood.

One way to pare down your "to buy" list is to confer with your roommate about what he or she is bringing so that you can avoid cluttering your room with duplicate items, especially larger items, such as a television, stereo, and mini-fridge. For some things, such as area rugs, curtains, trashcans, and cleaning supplies, you can shop together and split the cost or divvy up what you need to buy.

Most likely, you won't be able to take all of your clothes with you. Choose to bring only the clothes you really love and wear on a regular basis and leave the rest at home. Also leave at home any seasonal clothing. You can always get these items when you come home on break. Bring a few week's worth of underwear

college basics

Following is a list of things you might need for your first year at college. If you are traveling by train or air or have a small car, consider buying some items when you get there.

- Two sets of sheets (most college dorm beds require extra-long twin sheets)
- Blankets, pillows, and bedspread
- Bedrest pillow (great for reading in bed)
- Two or three sets of towels
- Posters, wall hangings, area rug
- Television
- Stereo and music
- Mini-fridge
- Slippers, shower sandals
- Plastic shower caddy
- Personal hygiene items and cosmetics

- Multidrawer plastic storage unit for personal hygiene items and cosmetics
- Blow dryer
- Underbed storage containers
- Stackable crates or hanging bookshelves
- Large laundry bag and laundry supplies
- Backpack
- Portable umbrella
- School supplies (pencils, pens, highlighters, calculator, binders, notebooks, stapler, and paper clips)
- Clothing and accessories
- Major credit card with limit (for emergencies)
- Long-distance calling card
- First aid kit, sewing kit, small tool kit

and socks so you can spend more time studying and less time doing laundry. Good walking shoes are a must. Bring a bathing suit for the pool and some workout clothes, even if you think you won't do either. You might also want to bring one or two dressier outfits for special occasions. And don't forget your pajamas and robe.

You probably don't need as much stuff as you think you do. When deciding what to bring with you, look at what you use every day — things like your computer, television, stereo, sporting equipment, and telephone. If you forget something or realize that you need something, you can always go out and buy it or get it when you go home on break.

Organizing Your Dorm Room. Even if you don't bring a lot of stuff, it always seems like you brought too much. To avoid being overwhelmed by it all, make use of vertical storage space on walls and backs of doors. In closets, you may be able to install wire shelving to hold bulky sweaters or pegs to hold your laundry bag, pajamas and robe, book bag, or jacket. The more you can keep off the floor, the better. Stacking crates and hanging bookshelves also make good use of vertical space.

If available, use the space under your bed for storing extra sheets, shoes, and seldom-used items. A lidded plastic storage container does the trick. You might also be able to use a bookcase as a headboard, with storage for books and binders above and less frequently used items below your bed frame. A bed skirt will hide whatever you store underneath.

You'll also want to decorate your room. Bring things you can use to brighten up your room, express your personality, and help you feel more comfortable in your new surroundings. Hang your favorite posters, photographs, and artwork. Because space is limited, bring only the knick-knacks and mementos that are most meaningful to you. If an item is valuable, has deep sentimental value, or is desirable, such as an autographed baseball card or poster, it might be smart to leave it at home, to eliminate the possibility of its getting lost, stolen, or ruined.

great space-saving gadgets

Following are some organizational products that make efficient use of limited storage space in a dorm room.

- Under-the-bed storage containers
- Over-the-door towel rods
- Stacking, interlocking crates
- Rolling file cart or small filing cabinet
- Hanging book shelves
- Multitier shoe rack
- Stick-on plastic rods and hooks

CHAPTER 27

ORGANIZING YOUR ESTATE

No one likes to think about death and dying. But planning for the inevitable can alleviate a potentially huge emotional and financial burden on your family. Learn some simple things you can do to get your affairs in order today. In this chapter, you'll also learn what surviving family members need to do when a loved one dies — everything from obtaining the death certificate to settling the estate.

Estate Planning

Sooner or later, important decisions about your estate will need to be made. The best person to make these decisions is you. And the best time to make them is now.

An important part of estate organizing is estate planning. You may think that you don't need to do any estate planning because you haven't got "enough" in the way of assets. But estate planning isn't just for wealthy people. It's something that all of us should do for ourselves and our families.

Think of organizing your estate as a gift to your family — a gift that enables them to manage their grief without the added stress of trying to figure out what you would have wanted them to do. If you don't take the time to organize your estate, your heirs may lose part of it, whether it's to taxes, to probate fees, or simply because they are unaware of all of your assets.

Simply put, estate planning is doing *something* rather than *nothing* to prepare for the inevitability of death. Making a will, for example, ensures that what assets you do have are distributed as you wish — without controversy, wasted time, or unnecessary expense. It also establishes a plan for the physical and financial care of your dependents in the event of your death. And it can go a long way toward preventing the family upsets and bickering that often accompany the inheritance of property or its division when someone has not left a will specifying what should be done.

Another simple and smart thing you might want to do now is set up what's known as a *living revocable trust* for all of your titled property and assets. With a will alone, your estate must go through a court process before assets can be distributed. But by putting titled assets in the name of the trust ("The Jones Family Trust," for example) rather than leaving them in your name, you can pass these assets to your heirs quickly and easily — without federal estate tax, drawn-out estate proceedings, and unnecessary fees. A living revocable trust also protects your assets if you become incapacitated. For more information about the living revocable trust and other types of trusts, consult an attorney who specializes in setting up trusts.

Personal and Business Assets. The first step in organizing your estate is to identify and record all of your personal and business assets. This is important for three reasons:

1. In the event that you become incapacitated, the guardians of your estate will have to use your assets to take care of you.
2. All of your assets need to be found and accounted for before your estate can be settled.
3. Knowing what you have helps in planning to minimize or eliminate estate taxes.

Another good reason to do an inventory of your assets is that you may discover that your estate is worth more than you thought. Also, when you see an overview of your financial situation, you may decide to make some changes or decisions regarding your estate. For example, you may realize that you have more life insurance than you need or that you should get an appraisal on expensive jewelry, furs, or antiques. Your assets may include the following:

- Real property (home, rental, vacation, time-share, boats, etc.)
- Vehicles (automobile and recreational)
- Stocks, bonds, certificates
- Mutual funds, treasury bonds, notes, or bills
- IRAs and other retirement plans
- Annuities and royalties
- Life insurance benefits
- Money due you (bonus, alimony, child support, royalties, promissory notes)
- Prepaid assets (airline tickets not used, store credits, frequent flyer miles, etc.)
- Cash

Personal property is also an asset. But without a complete list of your personal property, it is difficult to put a dollar value on the possessions you've accumulated over time. Preparing a personal property inventory has the following benefits:

- It helps you to identify and record the location and value of your personal property.
- It helps you to decide what items you may want to bequeath to a particular heir.

SIMPLE HOME INVENTORY

One way to simplify the home inventory process is to take an arbitrary figure — say $500. Identify, locate, and record only those items valued at $500 or more. Document the smaller stuff, such as clothing and jewelry, with a "group" photo.

—*Norman Zalfa, Organize Your Estate, Inc.*

- It can be used to ensure that you have the appropriate amount of homeowner's or renter's insurance.
- It serves as a valuable record of your possessions should you ever have a loss due to theft, fire, or other disaster.

Insurance companies and professional organizers recommend that you document the contents of every room. Working in one room at a time, record each item along with the year purchased, manufacturer's name and model (if applicable), and cost. If you have multiples of certain items, such as end tables, list the item once and write the quantity in front of it. If possible, create your inventory on a diskette so that you can update it as you acquire new items or dispose of items.

Back up your written inventory with a photographic inventory. Using a video camera or standard camera loaded with film that is recommended for taking indoor photographs, photograph the contents of each room, including your attic, basement, garage, and porch or deck. Start by taking a photograph of each wall. Then take individual photographs of major pieces of furniture, appliances, electronic equipment, and other valuable or expensive items. Open cabinet and closet doors to photograph the contents. On the back of each print, write the date along with pertinent information such as general location shown or serial numbers. Store your personal property inventory, prints, negatives, and videotape along with receipts, appraisals, other important documents, and valuables. (See page 266 for safe, long-term storage options.)

Organizing Documents

One of the most helpful things you can do for surviving family members is to identify and organize your family's financial and legal documents and other important papers. Consider organizing documents into the following major categories of folders:

- Identification papers (birth certificate, citizenship papers, social security card, passport)
- Family papers (adoption, custody/guardianship, marriage, divorce)
- Military papers (DD214, discharge certificate)
- Estate documents and papers (will, trust, powers of attorney, letter of instruction, bank safe-deposit records)
- Deeds, titles, registrations (property, vehicles, cemetery plot)
- Personal property or home inventory (written and/or photographic with receipts and appraisals)

- Insurance papers (life, property and casualty, homeowner's, auto, health, disability, long-term care, plus supporting documentation for claims and awards)
- Statements for cash management accounts
- Statements for open bank accounts and related materials (canceled checks, checkbooks, passbooks, passwords)
- Debts (mortgage, outstanding loan records, credit card statements, promissory notes)
- Contracts and agreements (mortgage, lease agreements, IOUs, court orders)
- Investment certificates (CDs, stocks, bonds, and other investments)
- Retirement plan, survivor and annuity documents (IRA, military, other death benefits)
- Income tax returns, plus supporting documentation for last three or more years
- Business papers (incorporation, doing business as (d/b/a) certificates, computer backup disks, partner contracts or agreements)

Make a master list of all of your documents. Next to each item in your list, note where to find that particular document or related papers. Where appropriate, also note the name and telephone number for key contacts, such as your attorney, accountant, business partner, insurance agent, broker, and executor. If you have one or more bank safe-deposit boxes, record the number and location of the boxes. Also record the location of any assets, such as jewelry, that are hidden in your home or on loan to someone. If you keep this list on the hard drive of your computer, make a backup copy for your files.

Store originals of legal and financial documents in a bank safe-deposit box or a locking, Underwriters Laboratory (UL)–approved, fire-resistant file cabinet. Whichever storage method you choose, be sure to let someone else know where to find legal and financial documents and where you keep the key or combination. If you store documents in a bank safe-deposit box, be sure that the signature authorization card on file at the bank is up to date. Make copies for your home files of any original documents you choose to store in your safe-deposit box along with a list of any other contents.

IN CASE OF EMERGENCY

Take the time to record information that will be needed in the event of an emergency or your death, including but not limited to the following:

- **Key contacts**
- **Location of important legal and financial records**
- **Location of safe-deposit box key**
- **Lock combinations and passwords**
- **Memorial wishes**

Post your "key contacts" list near your telephone. Be sure that your contacts know where to find the information they will need to handle your legal and financial affairs. Do this now, while it is foremost in your mind, because later may be too late.

— *Donna D. McMillan, McMillan & Company Professional Organizing*

Be aware that a bank safe-deposit box registered in your name only will be sealed upon your death. If you store the original copy of your will here, your executor or trustee will, at minimum, need to present a copy of your death certificate plus a copy of your will in order to obtain access to your original will. In some states, opening the box may require a court order, which could take weeks.

Thy Will Be Done

A will is probably the most important legal document you will ever sign. And yet seventy percent of all Americans die without a will.

If you die without a will, someone will be appointed by the state to handle your affairs. That person could be someone in your family that you would never have chosen. If you have no children and no spouse, your assets may go to a remote family member instead of your closest friend. If you have children and you die without a will, a judge may decide who will raise your children. Dying without a will can also incur unnecessary taxes and expenses that may create a financial hardship for your heirs.

If you do nothing else in the way of estate planning, make a will. This will go a long way toward ensuring that your assets will go to the people and organizations you wish to receive them. It also lets you decide who should care for your minor children (if no other parent is living), who should manage any assets you leave to your minor children, and whom you want to carry out the terms of your will (your executor). In your will, you can also make provisions for your pets.

is a simple will enough?

If you answer "Yes" to the following questions, then a simple will is probably all you need.

1. Are you under age 50? **Yes** / **No**
2. Are you in good health? **Yes** / **No**
3. Is the total value of your estate less than one million dollars? **Yes** / **No**

Keep in mind that it is always a good idea to consult your attorney about current estate tax laws and how they apply to your particular situation. Generally, the older you are and the more assets you have, the more likely it is that you require *more* than a simple will.

Preparing a Will. A simple will can be prepared quickly and easily using inexpensive, standard legal forms or software (see page 287). Even if you hire an attorney to prepare a will for you, it's still relatively inexpensive.

Once you prepare your will, you may wish to discuss it with your family. Explain why you have decided to distribute your assets the way you did, especially if you are not dividing your assets equally among your heirs. Discussing the reasoning behind your decisions often makes it easier for everyone to understand and accept them.

Make a point to review your will periodically. If you get married or divorced, win the lottery, or want to change a beneficiary or any other terms, you will need to rewrite your will

ON GIFTING

Part of living is dying, and the more you can prepare in advance for this fact of life, the less stressful it will be for everyone involved. At a certain point in your life, you may wish to consider gifting some items to your eventual heirs. For example, if you're not using your good china or silverware, you could make a gift of it to ensure that it ends up where you want it to go. Gifting now also allows you to see the item being used and enjoyed by its inheritor. This can provide a great source of satisfaction and comfort.

— *Stephany Smith Gonser, Put Simply Consulting*

or update it with a codicil. If you move to another state, check to see if your current will is valid in that state.

Other Legal Wishes

It's important to make your wishes known — in life and in death. If you don't express your wishes, you put others in the uncomfortable and often stressful position of having to make decisions for you. This is particularly true of medical and financial decisions concerning the end of life. Taking time to make some critical decisions now can provide peace of mind for you and make things easier for your loved ones.

Just as preparing a will lets you make advance decisions about the handling of your estate, making a *living will* lets you decide in advance about critical end-of-life decisions that would otherwise need to be made by your family. If, for example, you suffered an illness or injury that caused your brain to stop functioning and your heart was beating only with the help of a life-support machine, would you want your body to be kept "alive" at all costs? Or would you want to spare your loved ones the overwhelming financial, emotional, and psychological costs of doing so? In a living will, you provide what's called an *advanced directive* to your physicians and family that guides them in deciding how aggressively to use medical treatments to delay death.

A *medical power of attorney,* or healthcare proxy, allows you to appoint someone you trust to act as your healthcare agent. With this legal document, the person you appoint is authorized to make medical decisions on your behalf if, at any time, you are unable to do so yourself. Ideally, this will be someone who is not afraid to ask questions of health-care professionals to get information needed to make decisions. It should be someone who knows your wishes about medical treatment, is willing to take responsibility, and is assertive enough to ensure that your instructions are followed.

A living will and medical power of attorney are legal documents that you prepare in accordance with the laws of the state in which you reside. (You'll find sources for preparing your own documents in the appendix.) Sign and keep the originals of these documents and give copies to your physician, immediate family members, and your appointed healthcare agent.

There is another legal document you will want to prepare in the process of organizing your estate. Have you ever considered what would happen to your financial affairs if you were suddenly incapacitated? Who would pay your personal bills or keep your business in business? A *durable power of attorney* is a legal document that gives one or more people authority to manage your finances. In this document, you specify what this person is

One Challenge . . .

When it comes to sorting through property and possessions left behind, many family members end up with irreconcilable differences. What can be done to make the whole process as fair and equitable as possible?

Three Solutions

❶ FROM JEANNE K. SMITH, EXIT, STAGE RIGHT: Together, go through all the items in each room, one by one. If only one person expresses interest in an item, move that item to that person's designated staging area or tag it. If two or more people express interest in an item, move it to a common room. If no one wants it, tag it for donation. Once you've been through every room, go back to the common area. Give the oldest family member first choice of items. Then allow younger siblings to make their first choice. Continue until all items are claimed.

❷ FROM NORMAN ZALFA, ORGANIZE YOUR ESTATE, INC.: Minimize the potential for animosity by deciding beforehand who will get what. One way to do this is to invite family members to your home, give them each different-colored sticky notes to put on the things they would like to inherit. If an item is wanted by more than one family member, they can negotiate for it. Another option is to give photographs of selected belongings to your family members and have them identify those items they wish to inherit by indicating a "yes" or "no" and initialing the backs of the photographs.

❸ FROM STEPHANY SMITH GONSER, PUT SIMPLY CONSULTING: You may want to call in a mediator to come up with a fair and partial distribution. It doesn't have to be a professional. It could be an impartial family member or friend of the deceased.

authorized to do on your behalf and for how long. You also specify how it should be determined that you are unable to manage your own affairs. This document should be prepared by an attorney.

If you wish to donate organs upon your death, tell your immediate family members because your body will need to be kept alive artificially for the surgical procedure. In many states, you can sign the back of your driver's license to indicate that you would like to be an organ donor. Or you can sign an organ donor card. Either way, it's important to get the signatures of the legally required number of witnesses. You may wish to bequeath or donate your entire body, in which case you should indicate that preference on your organ donor card or driver's license. Some medical schools and research institutions require that you make arrangements prior to your death and will not accept a body without that prior approval.

Last Wishes

It's not enough to verbalize your last wishes. What if your loved ones are not really listening to what you are saying to them because they don't want to talk about death? Or what if they forget what you said?

Make your last wishes known through a letter of instruction or "last wishes" form that provides instructions for what to do with your body after death, describes any arrangements you have made, and informs survivors of the location of important documents such as your will. This is not a legal document but rather a "love letter" to your family that can also include final words to loved ones and bequeathal of selected personal possessions.

Before you can write your letter of instruction, you will need to make some decisions. Remember that, as challenging as it may be to think about and make decisions about your death, it will be exponentially more difficult for others to make these decisions on your behalf.

Preplanning your death arrangements makes it so much easier for your family, especially if you die suddenly or unexpectedly. They won't have to try to figure out what you would have wanted; they'll know. And they won't overspend out of guilt or grief. Following are some questions to help you write your letter of instruction:

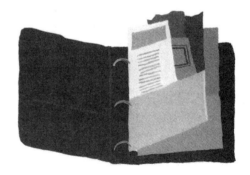

- **Do you want to be buried?** If so, what type of casket (wood or metal) do you prefer? What color do you want to be buried in? Would you like any personal possessions to be buried with you? Where would you like to be buried? What inscription do you want on your tombstone?
- **Do you prefer to be cremated?** Where and in what type of urn do you want your ashes kept? Or do you prefer them to be scattered? If so, where and by whom?

- **Do you want a wake so friends and family can pay their last respects?** If so, with open or closed casket?
- **Do you want a funeral service (with body) or memorial service (without body)?** Where would you like your service to be held? Do you want to have a particular type of flower or music at your service?
- **Is there anything else you would like survivors to do?** For instance, would you like them to send contributions to a particular charity or plant a tree in your memory?

You could meet with a local funeral director who can provide some of the choices available (as well as costs) to help you make decisions regarding your final arrangements. Find out what services are required in your state and which ones are optional. But don't feel obligated to prepay for any services. It may cost less to pay in advance for services or buy a cemetery plot for yourself and your spouse, but what if you move to another state or get divorced? It may make more sense for you to spell out your last wishes and let survivors make arrangements for you at the time of your death. Do make sure that you have a life insurance policy that will cover funeral costs so these do not create a hardship for your family.

If you have already made preplanning arrangements with a mortuary, crematory, or cemetery, include this information in your letter of instruction. List the company name, address, and telephone number to contact. Describe your arrangements. If you paid in advance or purchased insurance to cover the costs, list the contract or policy numbers.

With an average cost of $8,000 to $10,000, a funeral is one of the single largest expenses of a lifetime. Be aware that costs for goods and services vary widely. Call or visit at least three funeral homes and cemeteries to compare prices. One way to save on the cost of final arrangements is to join a memorial or funeral society. These are nonprofit, nonsectarian organizations that negotiate with local funeral homes to get special group prices on goods and services for their members. To become a member, you pay a lifetime fee of $20 to $45 and fill out a form to specify the goods and services you want. To find a memorial or funeral society, look in the yellow pages of

MISSING DOCUMENTS?

If you can't find important documents or papers, get new ones. It can take several months (or even longer) to obtain copies of some documents. (In the appendix, you will find contact information for government agencies through which you can obtain copies of vital records, military discharge papers, and tax returns.) This may not seem like much to you now, but a few months' delay in survivor benefits could spell hardship for others if you suddenly become totally incapacitated or die. This could even include loss of your home and/or business.

— *Norman Zalfa, Organize Your Estate, Inc.*

your telephone book under "Funeral Information and Advisory Services."

If you are a veteran, the U.S. Department of Veterans Affairs may pay a small allowance toward burial and funeral expenses. You may also be eligible for other benefits. Your survivors will need to present proof of your military service (DD214) for reimbursement, so be sure to let them know where to find that document. Determine the benefits available to you and note these benefits in your letter of instruction along with information on how to obtain the benefits.

Practical Matters for Those Left Behind

It's likely that you may be called upon someday to make final arrangements for someone who has died. If the deceased has left a letter of instruction or other form of last wishes, then you know exactly what kind of arrangements to make on his or her behalf. If not, you'll need to make these decisions on your own or with the help of a funeral director and family members. Notify relatives and friends as soon as possible so that they have the opportunity to grieve with you. Writing and placing an obituary in the newspaper is a good way to reach others who may have known the deceased. Another thing you should do is protect the residence of the deceased from unwanted visitors by making sure that all doors and windows are locked and perhaps placing a few lights on a timer to suggest that the house is still occupied.

The next step is to collect important papers. The first document you will need is the death certificate, which you can obtain from the funeral director or county health department. If the deceased died overseas, request a multilingual death certificate so that you don't have the extra step of getting it translated. You will need to present one certified copy for each insurance benefits claim; to access each bank account; and to transfer ownership of vehicles, stock certificates, and other titled property. If you don't know how many copies you need, get at least a dozen.

The next most important document to locate is the original will. Other papers you will need in the first few weeks following a death include copies of all insurance policies; veteran's discharge papers; marriage certificate (for spouse); birth certificates (to claim survivor benefits for children); and social security cards or numbers for the deceased, spouse, and dependent children.

DON'T DOS

Even though some beneficiaries may be anxious to snag a piece of the estate, don't make financial decisions for at least a month. Don't take any interest or dividends from the estate if you don't have to and keep good records if you do. If you need the services of an attorney or other professional, do not agree to pay a percentage of the estate. Pay them by the hour for a specific project or job.

— *Norman Zalfa, Organize Your Estate, Inc.*

Once you have collected the necessary documents, apply for any and all benefits from life insurance policies, retirement plans, social security, and Veterans Administration. When you notify the deceased's employer, ask about life insurance benefits as well as monies due from salary, bonuses, commissions, accrued vacation or sick time, and other employee benefits such as pension or company stock options, and the continuation of health insurance for a spouse or dependents.

Don't hesitate to apply for benefits to any organization, including social or fraternal groups. The worst that can happen is that the claim is denied. Check with any professional organizations or associations to find out if the deceased was covered by a group life insurance policy. Check for the same with financial and credit institutions. Also find out if any loans, mortgages, or credit card accounts are covered by credit life insurance that would pay off the account balance.

Other less urgent but critical things to do in the days and weeks following a death include the following:

- Cancel medical, disability, and long-term-care insurance.
- Cancel credit cards and charge accounts in writing.
- Cancel magazine and newspaper subscriptions and any ongoing memberships (health club, book club); request reimbursement of the unused portion of prepaid fees.
- Cancel cable or satellite television and other nonessential utilities.

Immediate To Dos

Following is a checklist of the things that need to be done in the first few days and weeks following the death of a loved one:

- ❏ Protect the residence of the deceased so that it is not burglarized.
- ❏ Make funeral arrangements.
- ❏ Write an obituary and arrange for it to be published in the local newspaper.
- ❏ Contact all close friends and family of the deceased.
- ❏ Contact executor or attorney.
- ❏ Notify the deceased's employer.
- ❏ Get multiple certified copies of the death certificate.
- ❏ Locate the original will and give it to the executor or attorney.
- ❏ Locate or obtain a copy of all insurance policies.
- ❏ Notify insurance companies (in writing) of the death.
- ❏ Contact the Social Security Administration to apply for burial benefits (and spouse benefits if the deceased was already receiving benefits).
- ❏ Contact the Veterans Administration office to apply for benefits (if deceased was an honorably discharged veteran).

Consider waiting a month or so before canceling telephone and Internet provider services. In keeping these services "live," you may discover other friends and acquaintances of the deceased who would want to know the news.

Final Business

If you have been appointed as the executor of the will, your role is to find, secure, and manage

PRESERVING FAMILY HISTORY

One simple way to safeguard family memorabilia such as a wedding album is to put it all in a trunk that can travel from family to family at any time. Have copies made of other photographs for every family; this cost can be paid for out of the estate. The estate could also pay to make copies of family recipes or to purchase a second (or third) copy of a favorite old cookbook, which you may be able to find at a used or antique bookstore. You can flip a coin to see who gets to keep the original.

—Jeanne K. Smith, Exit, Stage Right

assets until such time as they are transferred to the heirs. This includes such business details as identifying pension and insurance benefits, notifying banks, distributing personal effects, and paying debts and taxes for the deceased.

When a person dies without a written will, however, state law determines how the deceased's assets and property will be distributed. The court appoints a personal representative, usually a senior member of the family, to manage the deceased's final business.

If you have been appointed to settle the estate, establish a new bank account to be used to handle all financial matters involved in closing out the deceased's estate. Keep a detailed, dated diary of all activities done on behalf of the deceased. This will protect you in the event of future disputes or claims.

Locate and make a complete list of what the deceased owned, including real estate, stocks, bonds, bank accounts, deeds, and personal property. Keep all of this information together with associated documents and paperwork. In the process of looking for assets, search the house for hidden cash, jewelry, or other things of value. It is not uncommon for valuables to be hidden in the freezer, in medicine cabinets or pantries, in coat pockets, or sewn into drapes.

All assets have to be found before you can determine if the estate has to go to probate. Probate is the court-supervised process of paying the deceased's debts and distributing the estate to the rightful beneficiaries. Jointly owned property, property in trust, and assets with a designated beneficiary, such as life insurance policies and retirement plans, do not have to go through the probate process. Settling the estate also involves receiving claims against the estate (outstanding loans, for example), paying taxes and claims, and distributing assets.

Be aware that the probate process can take a full year or more. If probate is not necessary, the estate can be settled in a matter of weeks. (Avoiding probate is something that can be planned for in advance by putting assets into a trust or arranging for direct transfer to beneficiaries upon your death.) If you have any questions about the probate process or about settling the estate, you should consult an attorney. You may also wish to contact an accountant to help you file final income tax returns for the deceased.

One of the most time-consuming aspects of settling an estate is sorting through personal and household effects, deciding what to do with everything, removing items from a home, and preparing for sale of the home. (See chapter 25 for helpful advice on selling a home.)

Go through one room at a time, sorting items into four categories: give away, throw away, sell, and keep. Use labeled boxes or bags to help you sort and collect each category of items. Tape a note to larger items to indicate the appropriate action. If you're planning to have a yard or garage sale, it's easier to put a price tag on items as you are sorting through them. This keeps you from having to rehandle every item.

Take the time you need to sort through your feelings as well as through the material things. It's all part of the grieving process. Don't keep things out of guilt; keep only what you really want and let go of the rest. You may be able to disburse some belongings among friends and family members. If family members are scattered or there are bills owing, you may want to keep a few precious memory items for yourself and sell everything else.

Once you decide what you want to keep, you might want to contact an estate company to sell off the contents of the house in an estate sale. Or you can sell everything (including the junk) to an auction house or liquidator. This is often the quickest way to empty a house. Estate-sale professionals generally collect a percentage of the sale revenue so there is no out-of-pocket expense for you, the person selling the items. Be sure to get an appraisal on antiques, artwork, and collections from a third party before selling to an auction house or liquidator.

Another option is to hire a professional organizer who can assist with the details of a home closure, especially if you live far away or don't have the time. You can deduct the cost of these services from the estate, and you may be able to deduct this expense on the deceased's final federal income tax returns. A professional organizer can do the following:

- Help you decide what to keep, sell, give away, or throw away
- Suggest places to donate items
- Obtain appraisals for valuables
- Pack household effects
- Arrange for storage or shipping

Many professional organizers are beginning to specialize in estate organizing in response to growing need. Every one of them advises clients to do themselves, their family members, and their heirs one last big favor: Organize your estate now.

ONE LAST DONATION

If your loved one had a favorite charity, have an estate sale and plan to donate the proceeds to that organization. Keep in mind that it would have made that person happy to help a worthwhile cause — and everyone will benefit more in the end than if you packed everything into a storage unit to mildew and rot.

— Ramona Creel, OnlineOrganizing.com

One Challenge . . .

One of the most difficult challenges for those left behind is letting go of a loved one's personal possessions. We often feel guilty, even disloyal about selling or giving away someone else's things, especially when every item is a reminder of that person. But it is simply not practical or possible to keep everything. What are some ways we can feel better about letting go of these things while keeping the memories?

Three Solutions

1 FROM RAMONA CREEL, ONLINEORGANIZING.COM: Allow yourself to reminisce and grieve as you go through cleaning out the deceased's house. Don't be in such a rush to "be done with it" that you miss out on the opportunity to really say good-bye. Take photos of those treasured items you really want to remember. You might put together an album of your mother's favorite Sunday dresses or your grandfather's pipe collection or the furniture you grew up with. That way, you can look back fondly and reminisce, without needing an extra storage unit to keep it all.

2 FROM JEANNE K. SMITH, EXIT, STAGE RIGHT: If you decide to hold an estate sale, don't be there. It's too emotionally draining. Hire a professional and pay the fee. But do it after you've had a chance to relive memories by holding items, taking photographs, or simply sharing your remembrances with others.

3 FROM STEPHANY SMITH GONSER, PUT SIMPLY CONSULTING: Ask yourself this: If you could keep only one thing, what would it be? Focusing on what's really important helps to let go of the less important things. Keep only the best of the best. And keep only what you really like. If your space is limited, keep things that don't take up a lot of space. You may also need to put a limit on the number of items you will keep from collections of things like books, recipes, letters, or postcards.

Appendixes

RESOURCES

Professional Organizer Services

National Association of Professional Organizers

35 Technology Parkway, Suite 150
Norcross, GA 30092
www.napo.net
Information about professional organizers and referral to professional organizers in your area. Order forms for "Golden Tips for Getting Organized" booklet from Golden Circle Members also available.

OnlineOrganizing.com

www.onlineorganizing.com
Free home and office organizing tips; products to help you regain control over your time, space, and paper; and free referral to a professional organizer near you.

Professional Organizers Web Ring

www.organizerswebring.com
Post an organizing question or join the discussion forum for advice from professional organizers. Search by state to find a professional organizer near you.

Day Planners

Day-Timer

800-225-5005
www.daytimer.com
On-line store plus information resource for time-management articles, productivity tips, and other time-related information.

Franklin Covey

800-654-1776
www.franklincovey.com
Productivity solutions — from paper and electronic organizing products to leadership training — for home, family, and business.

GO MOM! Planner

26037 Talamore Drive
South Riding, VA 20152
703-327-7722
www.gomominc.com
The ultimate daily planner system for busy moms who want to manage time more effectively, plan ahead, and keep track of their family's busy schedules. System includes an undated weekly scheduler and 18-month flip calendar, plus pages for planning menus, grocery and bulk shopping lists, and for writing to call, to do, and to buy lists and other important notes and reminders.

Planner Pads

800-410-6654

www.plannerpads.com

A unique, two-page-per-week format lets you organize all your business and personal activities in one place. Each page works like a funnel to find priorities, organize workflow, and plan your day. It also funnels events from idea stage to point of action, which helps to establish a productive workflow.

Yahoo!

www.yahoo.com

Offers a free calendar tool that lets you share your schedules with other people, find free times, and send appointment reminders.

Virtual Office Assistants

Pat Voyajopoulos, Oasis

51 Valley Road

Dedham, MA 02026

781-329-2236

pat@oasisadmin.com

Oasis provides administrative support to small and home-based business owners. With an MBA (concentration in Marketing and Computer Systems) and more than twenty years of professional experience, Pat Voyajopoulos can help you complete tasks that you don't have the time or desire to do.

Type4U Business Support Services

950 Herrington Road, Suite C

PMB 218

Lawrenceville, GA 30044

770-682-8636

www.type4u.com

A fully staffed and equipped office for your administrative support on an as-needed basis. Hire the services of an on-staff secretary, administrative assistant, or bookkeeper without the cost of a full-time employee. Staff includes experts on office support services, transcription, contact management, and desktop publishing.

Filing Systems

FileSolutions Filing Systems

800-336-2046

www.filesolutions.com

Custom-designed filing systems for home, business, doctors, educators, and students. Each complete system includes a set of preprinted and blank adhesive labels, guidebook for selecting file names, and alphabetical FileIndex to help you find documents. Available at The Container Store, Stacks and Stacks stores, Organized Living stores, and Storables stores; through distributors and professional organizers; and direct from the makers.

Kiplinger's Taming the Paper Tiger

The Monticello Corporation

4060 Peachtree Road, Suite D-339

Atlanta, GA 30319-3006

800-430-0794

freetrial@thepapertiger.com

www.thepapertiger.com

A revolutionary software product that combines an easy-to-use computer indexing system with proven paper-management methods. The complete kit includes Windows-based software, multimedia tutorial, preprinted labels, and a user's guide. "Find any document in your office within five seconds or your money back."

"Office-on-the-Go" System

www.onlineorganizing.com

Designed to fit in the trunk of your car, this traveling office puts the tools you need at your fingertips. Comes with color-coded and prelabeled files, organized into either standard business or personal categories. Includes storage for business cards, letterhead, and forms; ten hanging folders and eighteen interior folders; and side pockets for pens, stapler, and other supplies. The bottom is edged with hook-and-loop fastener to keep it from flipping over in your trunk.

Tax Tabs

www.onlineorganizing.com

Provides a mechanism for storing receipts gathered throughout the year, making them easy to retrieve in order to prepare your personal or business income tax returns quickly and conveniently. Includes preprinted filing labels, instructions for integrating Tax Tabs into your current system, and more. Available in home and sole proprietor versions.

On-line Office Supplies

www.OfficeDepot.com

On-line business solutions center and products.

www.OfficeMax.com

One-stop shopping for home and office organization products and business services.

www.Staples.com

Home organization products, office supplies, electronic organizers, and business services, with weekly specials and a business-reward program.

Electronic Reminder Systems

www.My-Home-Maintenance.com

Lets you set up free preventive maintenance reminders for your home, appliances, automobile, and more.

www.NeverForget.com

Download a free trial of NeverForget Personal Reminder Software to set up and send e-mail reminders on a one-time, weekly, monthly, or annual basis.

www.RememberIt.com

Allows you to set up e-mail reminders for important dates and events.

Clutter Support Groups and Services

Clutterless Recovery Groups, Inc.

800-321-5605

www.clutterless.org

A nonprofit self-help organization for clutterers by clutterers, Clutterless Recovery Groups sponsors workshops in cities across the United States. At the Web site, you'll find helpful information about hoarding.

Messies Anonymous

5025 S.W. 114th Avenue

Miami, FL 33165

800-MESS-AWAY (637-7292)

www.messies.com

Contact Messies Anonymous for support group information or a free introductory newsletter. (Send a self-addressed, stamped envelope to receive the newsletter.)

National Study Group on Chronic Disorganization

1142 Chatsworth Drive

Avondale Estates, GA 30002

404-231-6172

www.nsgcd.org

Call or go to Web site to get a referral to a professional organizer in your area or to order a reading list of books for chronically disorganized people.

Organizing Products

Contact the following companies to request a catalog, shop on-line, or for more information about retail stores and distributors in your area.

California Closets

888-336-9709
www.calclosets.com
California Closets specializes in restructuring traditional pole-and-shelf closets into more efficient, less cluttered storage areas. Call or visit the Web site for the location of stores worldwide.

The Container Store

888-CONTAIN (266-8246)
www.thecontainerstore.com
A store devoted to helping streamline and simplify lives by offering an exceptional mix of storage and organization products.

Hold Everything

800-421-2264
www.holdeverything.com
Well-designed, attractive storage solutions for the home, from closet and shelving systems to furnishings for the home office.

Ikea

www.ikea.com (www.ikea.ca in Canada)
Through retail stores around the world, Ikea offers functional, beautifully designed storage solutions for every room in the house — at affordable prices. Visit the Web site to find the store nearest you or to browse the on-line catalog.

Kitchen Accessories Unlimited

800-667-8721
www.kitchensource.com
Designer kitchen accessories and storage solutions, including simple, do-it-yourself cabinets and pantries.

Organization, etc.

877-ORGANIZE (674-2649)
www.org-etc.com
Quality home organizing products and ideas for simplifying daily routines, making better use of space, and increasing productivity.

Stacks & Stacks

877-278-2257
www.stacksandstacks.com
Thousands of storage and organization products to organize your home and office and simplify your life, including hard-to-find but useful items.

Lillian Vernon

800-285-5555
www.lillianvernon.com
Call to request a catalog, browse catalogs on-line, or search the Web site for a specific organizing product or category.

Recipes and Meal Planning Tools

www.Allrecipes.com

A twenty-three-chapter on-line cookbook. You can search for recipes by ingredient or category, create a personal recipe box, and make a shopping list for your weekly meal plan.

www.Cooking.com

Recipes, menus, cooking tips and techniques, and entertaining ideas from award-winning chefs on-line and through free e-mail newsletter.

www.FabulousFoods.com

Dedicated to teaching and inspiring people "to cook, entertain, to interact, and most importantly to create lasting memories between themselves and the important people in their lives.

www.Myrecipe.com

Browse through an on-line cookbook with thousands of recipes. Add the recipes you want to try this week to your personal recipe box. If requested, Myrecipe.com will create a detailed shopping list of ingredients based on the recipes you select.

www.30DayGourmet.com

Make-ahead-and-freeze menus and recipes to save you time and money. Free e-mail newsletter.

Financial Planner Referrals

Certified Financial Planner Board of Standards

888-237-6275
www.cfp-board.org
A professional regulatory organization that fosters professional standards in personal financial planning so that the public values, has access to, and benefits from competent financial planning.

Financial Products and Services

Bankrate.com

www.bankrate.com
Bankrate.com provides objective financial data and research and editorial information to help consumers make informed decisions about loans and credit cards, savings, and investments.

Upromise

www.upromise.com
A free program designed to help families reach their college savings goals. Contributing companies, such as AT&T, General Motors, and McDonald's, give you back part of your spending as college savings. They also allow you to invest your savings in a tax-deferred college investing account managed by some of the world's leading financial services firms.

Credit Counseling Services

American Consumer Credit Counseling, Inc.

130 Rumford Avenue, Suite 202
Newton, MA 02466-1316
800-769-3571
www.consumercredit.com
A nationally recognized consumer credit 501(3c) nonprofit organization helping people regain financial control through debt consolidation and credit counseling.

AmeriDebt

12800 Middlebrook Road, Suite 300
Germantown, MD 20874
800-408-0044
www.ameridebt.com
A nonprofit organization dedicated to assisting consumers who are having difficulties with their personal finances.

National Foundation for Credit Counseling

801 Roeder Road, Suite 900
Silver Spring, MD 20910
800-388-2227
www.nfcc.org
A national nonprofit network of more than 1,300 locations designed to provide assistance to people dealing with stressful financial situations.

Money-Saving Tips

The Dollar Stretcher

P.O. Box 23785
Fort Lauderdale, FL 33307
954-772-1696
www.stretcher.com
Search for and read articles and tips on such topics as home organization, space management, and time management. Or send $2 (U.S.) to the address above for a sample issue.

ValuPage

www.valupage.com

On-line resource that provides simple, money-saving alternatives to paper coupons.

Yearning for Balance Action Kit

The Center for a New American Dream
6930 Carroll Avenue, Suite 900
Takoma Park, MD 20912
301-891-ENUF (3683)
www.newdream.org

Tips and resources for people who subscribe to the belief that "more" is not necessarily better.

Government Services

Insure Kids Now!

877-543-7669

www.insurekidsnow.gov

A program of the U.S. Health Resources and Services Administration, Insure Kids Now! provides free or low-cost health insurance program for infants, children, and teens. Eligibility rules vary from state to state, but in most states, uninsured children 18 years of age or younger whose families earn up to $34,100 a year (for a family of four) are eligible.

Internal Revenue Service

800-TAX-FORM (829-3676)

www.irs.gov

Request IRS Form 4506 if you cannot locate a copy of the most recent income tax return for yourself or on behalf of a deceased individual. Use the forms and publication finder on the Web site to search for "Recordkeeping for Individuals," which contains complete and current guidelines for keeping tax-related papers.

National Center for Health Statistics

Division of Data Services
6525 Belcrest Road
Hyattsville, MD 20782-2003
301-458-4636
www.cdc.gov/nchs

Provides information on how to obtain vital records (birth, death, marriage, divorce certificates) in every state.

National Personnel Records

9700 Page Boulevard
St. Louis, MO 63132-5200

Write in care of the branch of the military in which you served for a copy of your discharge papers.

Social Security Administration

800-772-1213

www.ssa.gov

Information about social security benefits and payments, including on-line forms for address changes and how to apply for benefits, including survivor and death benefits.

U.S. Department of State (Consular Services)

Office of Overseas Citizens Services
Bureau of Consular Affairs, Room 4811
U.S. Department of State
Washington, DC 20520-4818
888-407-4747 (317-472-2328 from outside U.S.)
www.travel.state.gov

Go to the Web site or call the hotline for up-to-date Consular Information Sheets, Travel Warnings, and Public Announcements for any country. Or send a self-addressed, stamped envelope and request for information about a particular country or countries. Information is also available at any of the thirteen regional passport agencies, field offices of the Department of Commerce, and U.S. embassies and consulates abroad.

U.S. Department of State (Passport Services)

Office of Overseas Citizens Services
Bureau of Consular Affairs Passport Services,
Room 6811
U.S. Department of State
Washington, DC 20520-4818
900-225-5674
www.travel.state.gov
Go to the Web site for information about passport services and to download a passport application. Information is also available 24 hours a day via an automated 900 number for a cost of thirty-five cents per minute. Information is also available at any of the thirteen regional passport agencies, field offices of the Department of Commerce, and U.S. embassies and consulates abroad.

U.S. Department of State (Visa Services)

Office of Overseas Citizens Services
Bureau of Consular Affairs Visa Services
U.S. Department of State
Washington, DC 20522-1225
202-663-1225
usvisa@state.gov
www.travel.state.gov
Call, send e-mail, write, or go to the Web site to obtain visa requirements and contact information for countries worldwide.

U.S. Department of Veteran Affairs

National Cemetery Administration
800-827-1000
www.cem.va.gov
Information about eligibility and application for burial and memorial benefits for veterans.

Family Resources

Disney On-line Family Fun

www.familyfun.com
Ideas for indoor or outdoor activities, arts and crafts ideas, and fun learning activities, as well as money-saving tips.

Learning Network

www.familyeducation.com
Features learning activities by age group. Select an age group and then click on an activity topic. You also can sign up for a free e-mail newsletter.

ParentSoup

www.parentsoup.com
An iVillage Web site with ideas for parties and crafts as well as a variety of parenting information.

Travel Services and Products (also see Government Services)

AAA Map 'n' Go

DeLorme
2 DeLorme Drive
Yarmouth, ME 04096
800-561-5104
www.delorme.com
Mapping and trip planning software for your computer that includes the latest AAA information and ratings on lodgings, restaurants, campgrounds, museums, parks, fairs, and family events.

Magellan's

800-962-4943
www.magellans.com
An award-winning mail-order catalog featuring a wide selection of state-of-the-art, high-quality travel organizing products from adaptor plugs to wrinkle-free clothing.

Rand McNally

www.randmcnally.com
Detailed electronic road maps include turn-by-turn directions, road construction updates, and estimated travel times from the makers of "indispensable guides to where things are and how to get there."

Travelex Worldwide Money

877-394-2247

customerservice@travelex.com

www.travelex.com

Order foreign currency online, track currency rates, and be notified when you want to buy. The Web site also features a currency converter to see how much your dollars will buy. Travelex is also a global source for Visa TravelMoney.

The Weather Channel

www.weather.com

Detailed weather reports and forecasts for anywhere in the world including airport weather forecasts, travel advisories, and flight on-time status.

Home Safety

National Lead Information Center

800-LEAD-FYI (532-3394)

For answers to questions about lead poisoning, free publications, and referral to a listing of lead-service professionals in your area.

United States Consumer Product Safety Commission

www.cpsc.gov

Provides current information about product hazards and recalls. You can also subscribe to receive all recall notices by e-mail on the same day they are issued.

Trash and Recycling Information

Computers & Education Computer Recycling Center

3249 Santa Rosa Avenue

Santa Rosa, CA 95407

www.crc.org

The mission of the Computer Recycling Center is "to promote the highest and best reuse of computer and electronic equipment, and recycle unusable items to keep them out of landfills." This nonprofit organization provides refurbished computers to public schools and community nonprofits. Check the Web site for recycling center locations, then drop off your old equipment and receive a charitable receipt.

Computers for Schools Program

3350 N. Kedzie Avenue

Chicago, IL 60618

800-939-6000

www.pcsforschools.org

This nonprofit organization welcomes contributions of color monitors, computers with high-speed microprocessors, and quality peripherals. Equipment is refurbished at various sites (correctional facilities, vocational centers, community colleges, etc.) and then placed in schools according to local program parameters and/or the preference of the donor. A donation receipt is provided.

Dress for Success

www.dressforsuccess.org

A nonprofit organization that helps low-income women make tailored transitions into the workforce, Dress for Success affiliates accept donations of interview suits. Check the Web site to find a donation location near you.

Earth 911

800-CLEANUP (800-253-2687)

www.earth911.org

Information about environmentally friendly recycling and disposal.

Got Junk

800-GOT-JUNK (468-5865)

www.1800gotjunk.com

Fee-based service that hauls away old furniture and appliances, construction debris, yard refuse, and other household junk for disposal or recycling.

Moving Resources

American School Directory

www.asd.com
Facts about local schools, including district phone numbers and statistics on class sizes.

Current Address Labels

www.currentlabels.com
On-line resource for address labels and stamps, stationery, and pet tags.

ForSaleByOwner.com

www.forsalebyowner.com
The official Web site for buying and selling real estate without brokers or commissions.

Homestore.com

www.homestore.com/moving
Research cities, find local services, get tips for packing and unpacking, make arrangements to hook up utilities, and more.

United States Postal Service

www.moversguide.com
Lets you create a personalized moving checklist and timeline, get maps and directions, purchase packing supplies, rent a moving truck, and make arrangements to connect utilities.

Pet Care and Safety

The American Animal Hospital Association

800-883-6301
www.healthypet.com
To find a veterinarian in a new neighborhood.

ASPCA Animal Poison Control Center

424 E. 92nd Street
New York, NY 10128
888-4ANI-HELP (426-4435)
www.aspca.org
The only animal poison control center in the United States. Staffed by veterinarians and veterinary toxicologists 24 hours a day, 7 days a week. The center receives no state, federal, or hospital funding; therefore, they charge a $45 case fee to maintain their expert veterinary staff around the clock. The center's hotline veterinarians can quickly answer questions about toxic substances found in our everyday surroundings that can be dangerous to animals. The Center will do as many follow-up calls as necessary in critical cases and, at the owner's request, will contact his or her veterinarian. The Center also provides specific treatment protocols by fax. They accept VISA, Master Card, Discover, and American Express.

American Kennel Club

260 Madison Avenue
New York, NY 10016
www.akc.org
Information about selecting and buying a puppy, health care, nutrition, AKC events and registration.

The Cat Fanciers' Association, Inc.

P.O. Box 1005
Manasquan, NJ 08736-0805
732-528-9797
www.cfainc.org
Information on cat shows, cat breeds, and cat care from the world's largest registry of pedigreed cats.

Pet First Aid: Cats and Dogs

(St. Louis: StayWell, 1997) by Bobbie Mammato, DMV, MPH
Information to help you learn more about caring for your pet in an emergency. This book can be purchased through your local branch of the Red Cross or a bookstore.

Estate Organizing Products

Estate Organization Portfolio

Exit, Stage Right
P.O. Box 60794
Palo Alto, CA 94306
650-493-3948
www.exitstageright.com
A 70-page guide that includes all the information you and your family will need to handle the practical and administrative issues surrounding loss — be it from disaster, incapacity, or death. Deluxe binder includes data sheet pages to record personal choices and information as well as legal and financial data.

Personal Assets Inventory Workbook

McMillan & Company Professional Organizing
12021 Wilshire Blvd., Suite 670
West Los Angeles, CA 90025
310-391-7392
www.organizer4me.com
A safe-deposit–size workbook for recording locations of important documents and records, a room-by-room inventory of household possessions, and key people to contact in an emergency.

Estate Planning Documents

Nolo

www.nolopress.com
Software and forms you can use to prepare your own will; manuals included.

LegalZoom

www.legalzoom.com
LegalZoom uses Internet technology to help you prepare wills, living wills, powers of attorney, and other legal documents on-line. Once you complete a simple questionnaire, your documents will be prepared within 48 hours for significantly less than you would pay an attorney to prepare similar documents.

Legaldocs

www.legaldocs.com
At this site, you can prepare customized legal documents on-line, including a free living will that is written in accordance with the laws of the state where you reside. All documents can be previewed free of charge. Fees vary according to type and complexity of document.

PLAN4ever

888-845-9040
www.plan4ever.com
At this site, you'll find an easy-to-use Last Wishes form that will help walk you through the many end-of-life issues you may want to consider. After completing the form, you can print it out to file with your personal records and to distribute as necessary. Free.

Aging with Dignity

888-5-WISHES
www.agingwithdignity.org
This nonprofit organization offers Five Wishes, a legal document that helps you plan for such end-of-life issues as whom you want to make health-care decisions for you if you can't make them, the kind of medical treatment you want or don't want, and what you want your loved ones to know.

Other

Direct Marketing Association

Mail Preference Service
P.O. Box 9008
Farmington, NY 11735-9008
Send a postcard or letter to request that your name be removed from mailing lists.

Direct Marketing Association

Telephone Preference Service
P.O. Box 9014
Farmingdale, NY 11735-9014
Send a postcard or letter to request that your name be removed from telephone marketing lists.

CONTRIBUTING EXPERTS

Following is a list of experts whose organizing tips, strategies, and solutions appear in this book. *Note:* Some contact information has been omitted at the request of the organizers.

Professional Organizers

Sally Allen • A Place for Everything, LLC(SM)
23735 Bluestem Drive
Golden, CO 80401
303-526-5357
sa@sallyallenorganizer.com
www.sallyallenorganizer.com

Treva Berends • The Organizing Specialists
3430 Shady Place N.E.
Grand Rapids, MI 49525
616-363-3377
104240.464@compuserve.com
www.theorganizingspecialists.com

Nancy Black • Organization Plus
14 Palmer Road
Beverly, MA 01915-2710
978-922-6136
nancy@organizationplus.com
www.organizationplus.com

Lorraine Chalicki • YouNeedMe.com Personal Systems
Box 31503
Seattle, WA 98103-1503
lorraine@youneedme.com
www.youneedme.com

Kim Cosentino • The De-Clutter Box, Inc.
228 Robinson Lane
Westmont, IL 60559
630-968-7557
DeClutter2@aol.com
www.declutterbox.com

Donna Cowan • Cowan & Company Professional Organizing
P.O. Box 500728
San Diego, CA 92150-0728
858-451-2344
donna_cowan@compuserve.com

Ramona Creel • OnlineOrganizing.com
ramona@onlineorganizing.com
www.onlineorganizing.com

Lynne Crew • Affairs in Order
Sarasota, FL
941-907-6064
aioorganize@aol.com

Sheila Delson • FREEDomain Concepts
5 Oak Bend Road
Poughkeepsie, NY 12603
845-463-4140
freedomain@aol.com

Stephanie Denton • Denton & Company
1220 Paxton Avenue
Cincinnati, OH 45208
513-871-8800
sdenton@organizingsolutions.com

Ronni Eisenberg • Ronni Eisenberg & Assoc.
29 Darbrook Road
Westport, CT 06880
203-227-1222
ronni@reisenberg.com
www.reisenberg.com

Paulette Ensign • Tips Products International
12675 Camino Mira Del Mar, #179
San Diego, CA 92130
858-481-0890
paulette@tipsbooklets.com
www.tipsbooklets.com

Barbara Fields • PAPERCHASERS
180 West End Avenue
New York, NY 10023
212-721-4991
organize@paperchasers.com
www.paperchasers.com

LaNita Filer • LFJ Organizing Concepts Plus
6140 S. Hwy. 6 , #176
Missouri City, TX 77459
281-431-2527
orgconplus@aol.com
www.lanitafiler.com

Stephany Smith Gonser • Put Simply Consulting
P.O. Box 1195
San Leandro, CA 94577-7719
510-569-8833
stephany@putsimply.com
www.putsimply.com

Maria Gracia • Get Organized Now!
P.O. Box 240398
Milwaukee, WI 53223-9015
414-354-5891
getorgnow@wi.rr.com
www.getorganizednow.com

Lynn & Kevin Hall • Clutter No More, Inc.
11808 Rancho Bernardo Road, Suite 123#27
San Diego, CA 92128
858-485-0410
clutternomore@compuserve.com
www.clutternomore.com

Diane Hatcher • Timesavers Services Professional Organizing
5249 SW 117 Terrace
Cooper City, FL 33330
954-252-7511
diane@timesaversusa.com
www.timesaversusa.com

Do'reen A. Hein • Artistic Designs
2124 Broadway, Suite 167
New York, NY 10023
212-592-3745 or 203-855-9363
103275.734@compuserve.com

Barbara Hemphill • Hemphill Productivity Institute
1464 Garner Station Boulevard, #330
Raleigh, NC 27603-3634
800-427-0237
barbara@productiveenvironment.com
www.productiveenvironment.com

Barbara Landsman • Dial-a-Decorator
54 Riverside Drive, Suite 11-AA
New York, NY 10024
800-486-REDO (7336)
dialadec@aol.com

Jan Limpach • Organizing Plus
6909 Pratt Street
Omaha, NE 68104-2528
402-571-4397
organizing_plus@compuserve.com
www.organizingplus.com

Melinda Louise • Organize It
402 W. Ojai Avenue, Suite 101–217
Ojai, CA 93023
805-339-1745
organizeitusa.com

Dorothy Madden • ORGANIZE IT!
10 Park Place
Rochester, NY 14625-2165
585-381-5511
dmadden@organizeit.biz

Bette Martin • Necessary Indulgence Professional Organizing
11684 Ventura Boulevard #656
Studio City, CA 91604
818-753-2927
www.necessaryorganizing.com
necindorg@aol.com

Donna D. McMillan • McMillan & Company Professional Organizing
12021 Wilshire Boulevard, #670
West Los Angeles, CA 90025
310-391-7392
donna@organizer4me.com
www.organizer4me.com

Pat S. Moore • The Queen of Clutter
10321 Doyle Boulevard
McKenney, VA 23872
804-478-5537
patsmoore@aol.com
www.queenofclutter.com

Gloria Ritter • Paper Matters and more, inc.
202-441-0079
gloriakritter@cs.com

Linda Samuels • Oh, So Organized!
202 Cleveland Drive
Croton on Hudson, NY 10520
914-271-5673
linda@ohsoorganized.com
www.ohsoorganized.com

Harriet Schechter • The Miracle Worker Organizing Service
1324 State Street, Suite J-168
Santa Barbara, CA 93101
858-581-1241
miracle@cts.com
www.miracleorganizing.com

Cyndi Seidler • HandyGirl Professional Organizing
3727 W. Magnolia Boulevard #134
Burbank, CA 91510
818-508-1555
info@organized-living.com
www.organized-living.com

Julie Signore • The PHOENIX Organizational Consulting Services/1,2,3 SORT IT
P.O. Box 1112
Kula, HI 96790
808-878-2617
71042.2107@compuserve.com
www.123sortit.com

Jeanne K. Smith • Exit, Stage Right
P.O. Box 60794
Palo Alto, CA 94306
650-493-3948
jeanne@exitstageright.com
www.exitstageright.com

Judy Stern • Organize NOW
244 Schenck Avenue
Great Neck, NY 11021
516-829-0862
organizenow4@cs.com

Jackie Tiani • Organizing Systems, Inc.
P.O. Box 5085
Glendale Heights, IL 60139-5085
630-681-9080
jtiani@compuserve.com
www.organizingsystems.com

Allison Van Norman • Organizing Solutions
1048 Kains Avenue
Albany, CA 94706-2208
510-525-4542
avn@organizing-solutions.net
www.organizing-solutions.net

Helen Volk • Beyond Clutter
P.O. Box 12293
Albany, NY 12212-2293
518-456-4265
helen@beyondclutter.com
www.beyondclutter.com

Debbie Williams • Let's Get It Together
P.O. Box 590860
Houston, TX 77259
281-286-9512
debbie@organizedtimes.com
www.organizedtimes.com

Norman Zalfa • Organize Your Estate, Inc.
4645 4th Road North
Arlington, VA 22203-2348
703-522-5813
nzalfa@comcast.net
www.organizeyourestate.com

Business and Personal Coaches

Rose Hill, Certified Business and Professional Coach
President, The Academy for Business Success
503-629-4804
rose@coachrose.com
www.coachrose.com

Kathy Paauw, Productivity Consultant and Life Coach
Paauwerfully Organized
Redmond, WA 98052-5922
425-881-6627
orgcoach@gte.net
www.orgcoach.net

Computer Organization Experts

Debbie Gilster • Organize & Computerize
25002 Hollyberry Lane
Laguna Niguel, CA 92677
949-389-0440
debbie@organizeandcomputerize.com
www.organizeandcomputerize.com

Karen Simon • PC Tech Associates
2118 Wilshire Boulevard, #257
Santa Monica, CA 90403
310-390-3370
karen@yourpctech.com
www.yourpctech.com

Time Management Experts

Jan Jasper, Productivity Trainer and Speaker
Author, *Take Back Your Time: How to Regain Control of Work, Information, and Technology*
(New York: St. Martin's Press, 1999)
New York, NY
212-465-7472
jan@janjasper.com
www.janjasper.com

Judy Warmington • Woman Time Management
6089 Ganton Court
Hudsonville, MI 49426
616-669-4855
j.warmington@attbi.com
www.womantimemanagement.com

Mitzi Weinman • TimeFinder
268 Melrose Street
Newton, MA 02466
800-410-3220
mitzi@timefinder.net
www.timefinder.net

Feng Shui Consultant

Lorraine M. Duvall, Ph.D.
Styles Brook Road
Keene, NY 12942
518-576-9109
lduvall@kvvi.net

Financial Advisor

Bob Colley, CFP, CEBS
Cornerstone Financial Advisors
P.O. Box 788
Clifton Park, NY 12065
518-877-8800

Home Organization Experts

Deborah Taylor-Hough, Author
*Frozen Assets Lite & Easy: How to Cook for a Day
and Eat for a Month* (Fox Point, Wisc.:
Champion Press, 2001)
Champion Press, Ltd.
500 West Bradley Road, A129
Fox Point, WI 53217
414-540-9873
info@championpress.com
www.championpress.com

Molly Gold, Founder • GO MOM !NC.
26037 Talamore Drive
South Riding, VA 20152
703-327-7722
mgold@gomominc.com
www.gomominc.com

Productivity Consultants

**Paula Royalty • WorkSmart Productivity
Consulting**
P.O. Box 5791
Bellevue, WA 98006-0291
425-562-3147
smartpro@worksmartpro.com
www.worksmartpro.com

Virtual Office Assistant

Pat Voyajopoulos • Oasis
781-329-2236
51 Valley Road
Dedham, MA 02026
pat@oasisadmin.com

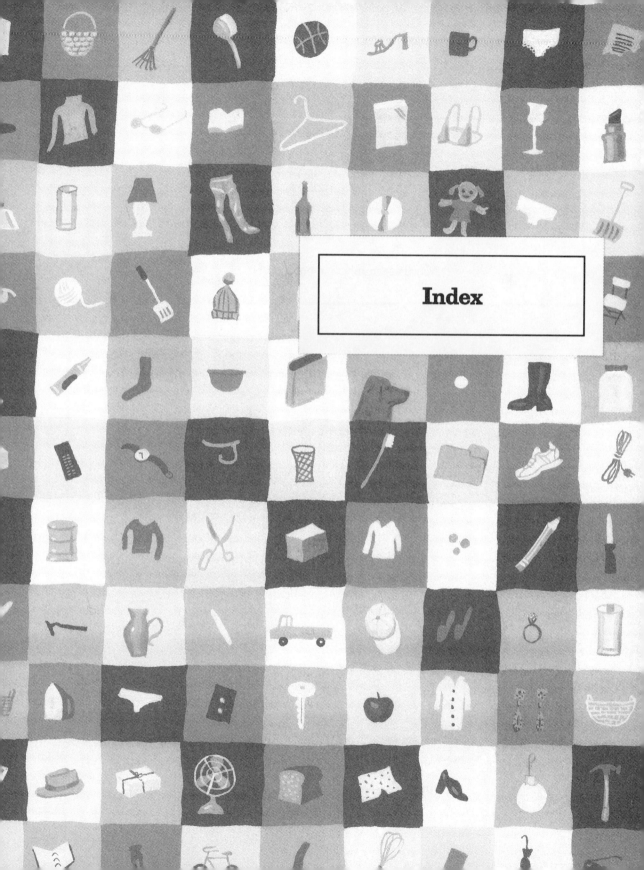

Index

INDEX

Note: Page numbers in **boldface** refer to charts.

B

Babies, 257–60

Babies' rooms, 220, 259–60

Baby-wipe containers, as organizers, 26

Backpacks, 43

Back-to-school chores, 235

Balance, of home and work

    defining priorities, 173–74

    friends and family, 179–80

    juggling priorities, 174–76

    saying no, 176–77

    self-care, 177–79

Balance sheets, 116–17

Bankruptcy, 137

Bank statements, 124, 125

Barter, 146–47

Basements, 103–4, 220

Bathrooms

    cleaning, 214, 215

    cleaning supplies, 90

    feminine hygiene products, 90

    medicine cabinets, 87–88

    safety, 219–20

    toilet paper, 90

    toiletries, 88–89

    towel racks, 89

    towels, 90

    uncluttering, 86–87

Bath toys, 87

Bedrooms. *See also* Kids' rooms

    cleaning, 215

    closets, 68–72

    drawers, 73–74

    jewelry, 74–75

    linens, 77–78

    off-season storage, 75–77

    safety, 220

Beds

    making, 215

    storage under, 75, 78, 83, 84, 85, 262

Bedspreads, 78

Bedtime routines, 186

Beliefs, 7, 176

Belts, 72

Beneficiary designations, 117, 118, 274

Benefits, of organization, 4–5

Bicycles, 233

Bills

    paying, 14, 33, 123–24

    reducing, 133–34

Birthdays, remembering, 37–38

Blankets, 76, 78

Block sales, 21

Bonds, 142–43

Book bags, 43

Books

    donating or selling, **15,** 59–60

    kids', 84

    returning to library, 25, 31, 59

    storing, 59–60

Bookstores, entertainment in, 151, 152

Boots, 43, 76

Boredom, and kids, 152

Borrowed items

    returning, 11–12

    as money saver, 146

Boxes

    discarding, 33

    as organizers, 26–27

Herbs, storing, 52

Holiday decorations, 111–12

Home-based workers. *See also* Offices
office set-up, 92–93
time management, 169–70

Home inventory, 224, 237, 265

Home maintenance
fall, 235–36
spring, 231

Homeowner's insurance, 118

Homes, selling, 252–53

"Homes" for items, finding
clutter control, 22–23, 24
entryways, 43–45
family rooms, 58–59

Hotels
booking, 194–95
childproofing, 209

Hot files, 167

Hot water heaters, 134

Housebreaking pets, 256

Household chemicals, 222

Houseplants, 237

House rules, 31

Humidity, in basements, 103

Hydration, 163

I

Immunizations, for travel abroad, 206

Income taxes. *See* Taxes

Index, for filing system, 100–101

Individual retirement accounts (IRAs), 143–44

Inkjet printer cartridges, 21

Insects, storage and, 64, 75, 78

Insurance. *See also specific types*
money management and, 126, 134

types, 117–19

Insure Kids Now! program, 258

Interior decor, simplifying, 58, 60

Internet
coupons, 149
moving resources, 239, 243
organization resources, 29
recipe resources, 57, 210, 281
selling on, 17

Investment clubs, 144

Investments
making, 143–44
records, 127

IRAs, 143–44

Ironing, 216

J

Jewelry
organizing, 74–75
travel and, 202

Job jars, 189, 191

Juggling priorities, 174–76

Junk drawer, 54

Junk haulers, 103

Junk mail, 32, 33–34, 287

K

Keep or Toss quiz, 12, 13

Keogh plans, 143

Keys, 44

Kids. *See also* Family organization
clothing, 147
clutter, 35–37, 79
entertaining, 151–52
morning organization, 185, 186–88
moving with, 242, 248, 250

M

OTHER STOREY TITLES
YOU MIGHT ENJOY

50 Simple Ways to Pamper Yourself by Stephanie Tourles. Recipes, tips, and techniques for relieving stress, promoting relaxation, and beautifying your body. 144 pages. Paperback. ISBN 1-58017-210-5.

50 Simple Ways to Pamper Your Baby by Karyn Siegel-Maier. A perfect book for new moms or anyone who cares for children. Includes hundreds of tips on nurturing and caring for babies. 144 pages. Paperback. ISBN 1-58017-257-1.

How to Feel Fabulous Today! by Stephanie Tourles. A balanced life is the key to health and longevity. Learn how to eat for health and vitality, make exercise fun, and raise your spirits. 208 pages. Paperback. ISBN 1-58017-313-6.

How to Sleep Soundly Tonight by Barbara L. Heller. Say goodnight to sleeplessness! Alternative therapies, exercises, lifestyle and nutritional changes, and recipes for sleep-inducing foods, herbal baths, sleep pillows, room sprays, and more. 192 pages. Paperback. ISBN 1-58017-314-4.

Keeping Life Simple by Karen Levine. Live a simpler, more satisfying life. Find out what's really important to you, and learn to create a more rewarding lifestyle. 160 pages. Paperback. ISBN 0-88266-943-5.

Mindful Moments for Stressful Days by Tzivia Gover. Tips and exercises focusing on simple ways to make even mundane tasks meaningful. Create a harmonious, conscious life with simple breathing exercises and meditation techniques. 192 pages. Paperback. ISBN 1-58017-428-0.

7 Steps to Unclutter Your Life by Donna Smallin. Hundreds of quick tips for enhancing physical, emotional, and spiritual well-being while creating a simpler, more rewarding lifestyle. Practical and inspirational advice on managing time, money, work, health, and relationships. 176 pages. Paperback. ISBN 1-58017-237-7.

The Stain and Spot Remover Handbook by Jean Cooper. An invaluable reference that explains how to treat stains caused by different sources and how to avoid making a problem worse. 160 pages. Paperback. ISBN 0-88266-811-0.

Too Busy to Clean? by Patti Barrett. Shortcuts and tricks for making cleaning more tolerable and efficient. 160 pages. Paperback. ISBN 1-58017-029-3.

Unclutter Your Home by Donna Smallin. Hundreds of practical ideas for sorting, evaluating, and getting rid of material items that get in the way. Learn how to eliminate unnecessary belongings without guilt or regret; contain clutter with simple storage techniques; reclaim closets, cabinets, basements, and attics; and simplify daily routines to keep homes clutter-free. 192 pages. Paperback. ISBN 1-58017-108-7.

Welcome Home by Elizabeth Knight. Simple tips and inspiring ideas help you create a warm, peaceful, and welcoming home environment. Includes modern-day and age-old traditions for transforming a house into a home from cultures around the world. 160 pages. Paperback. ISBN 1-58017-187-7.

Working at Home by Meredith Gould. More than five hundred tips for making the work-at-home experience pleasant and productive. A complete guide to enjoying the "one-minute commute." 176 pages. Paperback. ISBN 1-58017-238-5.

These books and other Storey Books are available at your bookstore, farm store, garden center, or directly from Storey Books, 210 MASS MoCA Way, North Adams, MA 01247, or by calling 1-800-441-5700. Or visit our Web site at www.storey.com